100 Documents
that Changed the World

First published in the United States of America in 2015 by
Universe Publishing
A Division of Rizzoli International Publications, Inc.
300 Park Avenue South
New York, NY 10010
www.rizzoliusa.com

Originally published in the United Kingdom in 2015 by
Pavilion Books
1 Gower Street
London, WC1E 6HD

Produced by Salamander Books, an imprint of Pavilion Books Group Limited.

2015 2016 2017 2018 / 10 9 8 7 6 5 4 3 2 1

ISBN: 978-0-7893-2936-3

Library of Congress Control Number: 2015940312

Printed in China

Previous page: The Magna Carta (see page 34).

100 Documents

that Changed the World

From the Magna Carta to WikiLeaks

Scott Christianson

UNIVERSE

For Eve, Michael, Adam, Joel, and Julia

Contents

ABOVE: The Declaration of Independence—the birth of a nation and one of the most significant landmarks in the history of democracy (see page 82).

doc·u·ment

noun \ **dä-ky** -mənt, -kyü-\
an official paper that gives information about something or
   that is used as proof of something
a computer file that contains written text

1. a: an original or official paper relied on as the basis,
       proof, or support of something
   b: something (as a photograph or a recording) that
       serves as evidence or proof
2. a: a writing conveying information
   b: a material substance (as a coin or stone) having on
       it a representation of thoughts by means of some
       conventional mark or symbol
3. a: a computer file containing information input by a
       computer user

ORIGIN Middle English, precept, teaching, from Anglo-French,
from Late Latin & Latin; Late Latin *documentum* official paper,
from Latin, lesson, proof, from *docere* to teach.

FIRST KNOWN USE fifteenth century

Introduction

We live in the Age of Documents. They are the signposts of our history and the currency of twenty-first-century life. In the digital era, as computer files, documents have become even more ubiquitous as they are infinitely viewed, produced, reproduced, and archived. We are flooded by them in our everyday existence; they both enrich and clutter our lives. Documents have become integral to the way people think; we use them to navigate through our current world and connect to the past.

O f course not all documents are in themselves important or worth saving. Yet we rely on certain documents to tell us what is new and important, just as we consult others to learn about history. Without authentic documentation, recorded and preserved, there would be no inscribed remembered history and we would have no knowledge of the distant past.

Although the definition of "document" has continued to evolve and expand, as evident from the dictionary meanings shown opposite, it seems reasonable to expect that documents will continue to be even more important in the digital future and beyond. How could they not?

By viewing documents in historical perspective, as this book does, we gain a window onto the vast artifactual record of knowledge, civilization, power, and society. *100 Documents that Changed the World* presents a variety of notable examples in all forms, from the last 5,000 years of human existence. The documents are time capsules that take us into the minds of their creators and the historical situations that impelled their creation.

The chronological listing reflects the changing material form of documents, as the historical record shows the earliest documents recorded in bamboo, silk slips, carved stones, and papyri, to finely printed manuscripts, paper documents in hand-print and type, and computerized files that collect and synthesize big data.

The different types or genres of documents presented include decrees and proclamations, holy books, legal codes, treaties and secret agreements, official warrants and certificates, patents, literary classics, philosophical treatises, diaries and letters, business contracts and commercial records, memoranda and electronic messages, and data maps, all of which made a significant mark in history.

There are government documents, church records and private communications, some of which appear as works of art but most of them simply impart important information—plain documents that nevertheless started

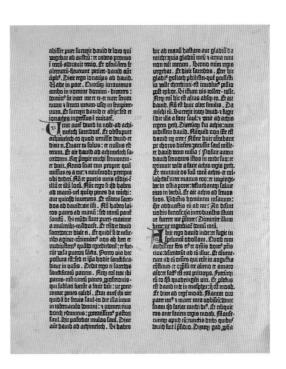

ABOVE: The Gutenberg Bible—the first book to be printed with metal movable type—changed the nature of document production (see page 42).

ABOVE: Jean-François Champollion's code for deciphering the Rosetta Stone held the key to two forgotten languages (see page 98).

or ended wars, inspired religious worship for millions, or advanced the cause of science or human rights to new heights.

Several of the authors of these documents are among the great figures in history: Christopher Columbus, Leonardo da Vinci, Martin Luther, Isaac Newton, Charles Darwin, Abraham Lincoln, Sigmund Freud, Thomas Edison, and Martin Luther King, Jr. Others are lesser known players: Shakespeare's appreciative fellow actors; the guilt-ridden conquistador Bartolomé de las Casas; the eccentric lexicographer Samuel Johnson; the meticulous polymath Peter Mark Roget who always sought to use the right word; and the eighteenth-century French feminist Olympe de Gouges, who was beheaded for her courageous women's rights manifesto. There are also kings and queens, generals, popes, presidents, bureaucrats, and computer hackers.

While we generally need not consult the original handwritten manuscript of the Declaration of Independence in order to grasp the meaning of such a document, the artifact itself has enormous symbolic importance and the act of looking at it takes on the quality of ritual. Important original documents possess an "aura" that transcends their content and purpose, and renders them enormously valuable—even priceless— in need of state protection and conservation. Such documents embody and encode such large-scale, historic concepts as national identity, human rights, world-changing wars, massive transfers of wealth and population, and seminal scholarship in the arts and sciences. Thus readers of this book who cannot travel to the institutions in which the documents are housed, get to glimpse the oldest known versions as well as images of some of their makers and learn something of their background and context.

Some of the documents described here clearly altered the course of history—legal documents such as the Code of Hammurabi, Magna Carta, or United States Constitution; rulers' decrees such as the Alhambra Decree, Edict of Worms, or Emancipation Proclamation; famous treaties and secret pacts such as the Sykes-Picot Agreement and Treaty of Versailles; religious tracts such as the Dead Sea Scrolls or the Quran; and assorted other accounts.

There are also a few iconic documents that have influenced popular culture and modern media—the Beatles' EMI recording contract, the first TV listings, the documents that founded the Apple Computer Company, as well as the first website and the first tweet.

Each carries a story, and many of these are woven with the others to form a documentary history.

Human beings have sought to preserve important documents for as long as civilizations have existed. Archaeologists have discovered archives of records made of clay tablets, papyrus, and other materials, going back to the ancient Mesopotamians, Chinese, Persians, Greeks, and Romans (who called them *tabularia*) in the third and second millennia BC. Such accumulated historical records were important in their day for helping to maintain order and continuity in legal, military, administrative, commercial, and social affairs, keeping track of taxes, crimes, victories and other vital statistics. Long kept by governments, churches, corporations, and other private entities, archives have also provided a key building block of historiography, communicating to posterity historical information about previous regimes, cultures, and events. Archivists have always been selective, however, saving only those records deemed worthy of retention and special care.

In the beginning, each document was unique, like a work of handmade art. But as its stature grew, copies or replicas were made, and as those copies deteriorated more copies of copies were made by scribes so as to preserve the sacred work. Unfortunately, many of these manuscripts perished over time. But some ancient works survived—the *I Ching,* Dead Sea Scrolls, *Mahabharata,* and Plato's *Republic* being a few examples.

Later there were also translations and copies made that had been mechanically reproduced by printing and other means. In some instances the printing of an authorized version, such as the King James Bible or Mao Tse-tung's "Little Red Book," took on enormous political significance.

Today, there is yet another new twist to some of the copying. Governments and corporations have been relentlessly and intrusively compiling secret documents and dossiers on a scale that is mind boggling. But lately, as evidenced by such phenomena as WikiLeaks and Edward Snowden's whistleblowing, a small but effective movement of computer hackers has turned the tables on the document keepers to make them the document leakers. Huge batches of hitherto secret, private, or classified files are now being released en masse to the public, to expose wrongdoing.

The term document used to simply mean an official written proof used as evidence. However the Dutch documentalist Frits Donker Duyvis (1894–1961), who was a pioneer in information science, nevertheless contended that since a document is the "repository of an expressed thought," its contents have a "spiritual character."

Many of the documents included in this book do seem to possess an aura that can still be felt, decades or even centuries after their creation and following countless reproductions. Maybe this unique human quality shining through is one of the attributes contributing to their power. In some instances that power was used as an instrument of the king, the pope, the state, or the corporation, or as a "prop" in the theater of ruling and policing. The document may have embodied the governmental power to command a specific action, the sacred or artistic power to reach the reader in a profound way, the messianic power to convey a vital message at the right moment, or the power of an inventor to conceive a revolutionary new idea in its simplest form.

All evinced some power to make things happen either now or in the future. To make it so, and in some cases to change the world. Here are one hundred of those documents.

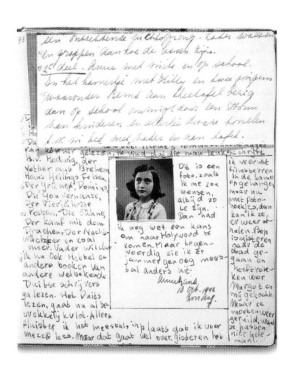

ABOVE: *Anne Frank's diary has become the most famous account of life during the Holocaust, read by tens of millions of people (see page 162).*

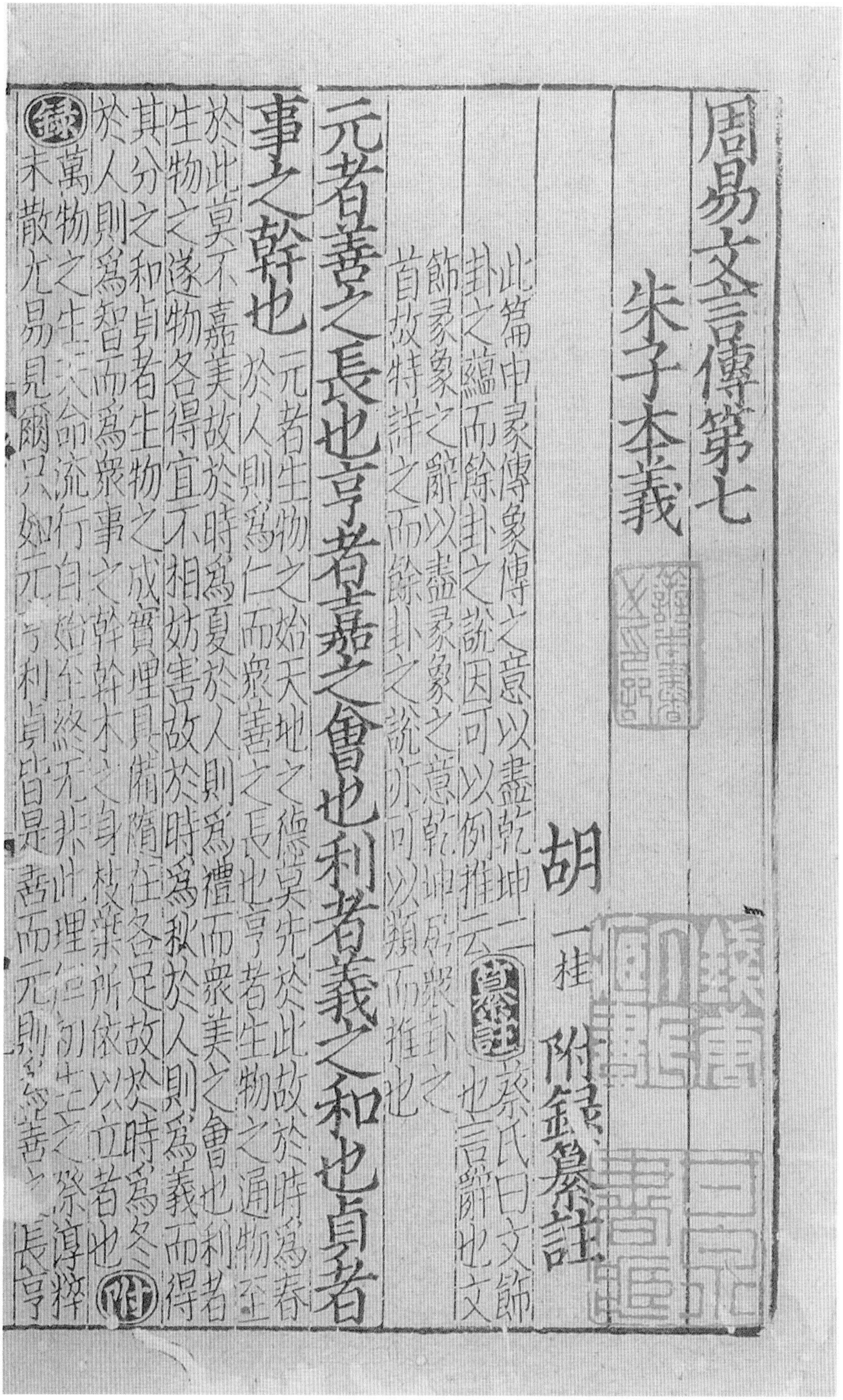

周易文言傳第七

朱子本義

胡 一桂 附錄纂註

此篇申彖傳象傳之意以盡乾坤二
卦之蘊而餘卦之說因可以例推云
節彖象之辭以盡彖象之意乾坤殽
首故特詳之而餘卦之說所可以類而推也

元者善之長也亨者嘉之會也利者義之和也貞者
事之幹也

元者生物之始天地之德莫先於此故於時為春
於人則為仁而眾善之長也亨者生物之通物至
於此莫不嘉美故於時為夏於人則為禮而眾美之會也利者
生物之遂物各得宜不相妨害故於時為秋於人則為義而得
其分之和貞者生物之成實理具備隨往各足故於時為冬而得
於人則為智而為眾事之幹也○枝棄所依以立者也○亨者

萬物之生天命流行自有終
木散尤易見顧只如元
於人則為智而為眾事之幹而元則元善也
方利貞皆是善而元則之總善也
長亨

I Ching

(2800 BC)

An ancient Chinese manual of divination employs patterns of trigrams and hexagrams, interpreted according to the principles of Yin and Yang, to offer sage guidance about an individual's present situation and future. Scholars consider it the epitome of Chinese philosophy.

No philosophical work has exerted more influence in Chinese culture over the millennia than the ancient *I Ching*, the "Book of Changes."

While its origins remain shrouded in legend, some historians trace its evolution back more than 5,000 years to a mythical emperor, Fu-Hsi, followed by other holy men, including King Wên who lived in the Shang dynasty of 1766–1121 BC and his son the Duke of Chou, and later Confucius (Kung Fu-Tze) who lived from 551 to 479 BC. It appears to be the oldest document still in continuous use.

The oldest extant version, consisting of bamboo strips found in Guodian, has been dated to about 300 BC; it is held in the Shanghai Museum. Westerners did not begin to learn of the *I Ching*'s existence until the eighteenth century and the first complete publication (in Latin) occurred in Germany in the 1830s. Scholars agree it is a composite work that was frequently copied and revised over the course of many centuries.

The ancient Chinese practice of cleromancy entailed casting lots (usually sticks or stones) to determine divine intent, and the *I Ching* remains its

LEFT: A page from a Song Dynasty (AD 960–1279) version of the I Ching, *complete with scholarly commentary.*

RIGHT: These bamboo sticks date to around 300 BC and are the oldest extant examples of the I Ching.

most sophisticated example. In this case, the divining is done by tossing yarrow stalks or coins, which is called "casting the *I Ching*." After posing a question and casting, the order they form can be looked up to reveal its cosmological significance. The document offers sixty-four readings, and each chapter consists of a different six-line hexagram made up of long or short stalks.

The Hsü hexagram, for example, reveals: "Hsü intimates that, with the sincerity which is declared in it, there will be brilliant success. With firmness there will be good fortune; and it will be advantageous to cross the great stream." This answer is then open to interpretation.

Transformation is the central idea behind the *I Ching*. All living things change through time and *I Ching* defines change in terms of Yin and Yang. Yin is negative, dark and feminine; Yang is positive, bright, and masculine.

The *I Ching* professes that all change can be understood in terms of the relationship between the two. When they are in balance, there is harmony.

The *I Ching* indicates whether a given action will bring good fortune or misfortune, but it is not a fortune-telling book. It provides many basic precepts about life's vicissitudes such as the following: "Before the beginning of great brilliance, there must be chaos. Before a brilliant person begins something great, they must look foolish in the crowd."

The ancient work also has much to offer in the study of Chinese civilization.

Code of Hammurabi

(1754 BC)

A French archaeologist in the former Babylon kingdom unearths an artifact that documents the world's most ancient yet surprisingly advanced legal code. Many of its provisions reflect a deep commitment to justice under the rule of law.

Atwo-and-a-quarter-meter-high stele of black basalt in the shape of a large index finger once stood in Babylon for all to see. At the top of the volcanic rock was an engraved depiction of the state's ruling king, Hammurabi, sitting on his throne, receiving the Mesopotamian god of law, justice, and salvation, Shamash. And beneath them, the carvers had inscribed long columns of text on both sides of the stone.

In 1901 a French archaeologist discovered the object in what is now Khuzestan Province, Iran. Conquerors had apparently removed it from Sippar (in present-day Iraq) on the eastern bank of the Euphrates sometime in the twelfth century BC. Translation from its ancient Akkadian language revealed that the stone proclaims a comprehensive legal code—the code of Hammurabi—consisting of a lengthy prologue invoking the power of the gods and the king, a long list of laws, and an epilogue. "LAWS of justice which Hammurabi, the wise king, established," the epilogue states. "A righteous law, and pious statute did he teach the land. Hammurabi, the protecting king am I."

Hammurabi, the sixth Babylonian king, was an able administrator who ruled a multi-tribal and multi-ethnic Mesopotamian empire of walled cities, fertile fields and irrigation canals from about 1792 to 1750 BC. His sophisticated code has been dated to about 1754 BC.

Nearly half of these 282 laws deal with issues of liability and other business matters; another third address a range of domestic relations such as paternity, inheritance, adultery, and incest. But commercial interests often govern domestic affairs. Marriages, for example, are treated as a business arrangement.

Modern legal scholars are especially interested in the code's elaborate punishment provisions as its inclusion of the principle of *lex talionis* (an eye for an eye) predates Mosaic Law, the Law of Moses, by two centuries or more. The code's system of scaled punishments adjusts penalties according to grades of slave versus free and other marks of social status.

The penalties are harsh: a total of twenty-eight crimes, ranging from adultery and witchcraft to robbery and murder, warrant the death penalty. Yet King Hammurabi also claims to seek to protect the weak and to foster justice for all his people. Thus one statute establishes that a judge who has handed down an incorrect decision shall be fined and removed from the bench. Others display the earliest known example of the principle of presumption of innocence—a protection that wouldn't appear in Western legal codes until much later.

The original stele found in 1901 is on display at the Louvre in Paris. Additional stones bearing the code are in other museums as well.

RIGHT: The stele is 2.25 meters tall and depicts a seated King Hammurabi directing Shamash, the Mesopotamian god of law. Beneath this relief are the king's 282 laws (see detail), which cover twenty-eight crimes that warrant the death penalty, including adultery, witchcraft, robbery, and murder.

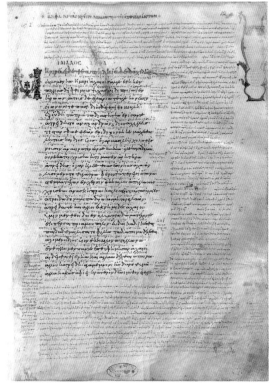

ABOVE: *A page from the oldest complete manuscript of* The Iliad. *Known as Venetus A, this AD 900 version is handwritten on vellum and contains five levels of scholarly annotation.*

LEFT: *This 285–250 BC papyrus is the oldest known fragment of* The Odyssey. *It contains lines from Book Twenty that do not appear in standard versions. Other third-century BC examples show that Homer's texts contained local variations that were subsequently standardized by Alexandrian scholars.*

Homer's The Iliad and The Odyssey

(c. 750 BC)

Preserved for 3,000 years by memory, writing, and print, the two greatest epic poems from ancient Greek culture have served for millennia as a pillar of Western literature, leaving scholars to speculate about the genius or geniuses who created these timeless classics.

Plato, writing in 400 BC or so, called Homer "the teacher of [all] Greece." Five hundred years later, the Roman rhetorician Quintilian called him "the river from which all literature flows," and 1,400 years after that the French novelist and stylist Raymond Queneau commented: "Every great work of literature is either *The Iliad* or *The Odyssey*." Yet little is known about the ascribed author, Homer, including his true ancestry and biography, whether he was really blind as ancient historians later claimed, and even when and whether he lived.

What is known is that Homer is credited with having written the two great epic poems, *The Iliad* and *The Odyssey*, in about 750 BC, although some modern historians have dated their origins to more than 1,000 years before that and others have suggested different time frames.

The Iliad depicts the siege of Ilion or Troy during the Trojan War, and while the account takes up twenty-four books, it covers only a few weeks of a long war, offering passages such as, "Like cicadas, which sit upon a tree in the forest and pour out their piping voices, so the leaders of Trojans were sitting on the tower."

The Odyssey focuses on the character Odysseus and his ten-year perilous journey from Troy to Ithaca after the end of the war, also telling what has befallen his family when he was away. "Tell me, muse, of the man of many resources who wandered far and wide after he sacked the holy citadel of Troy, and he saw the cities and learned the thoughts of many men, and on the sea he suffered in his heart many woes." Composed in 12,110 lines of dactylic hexameter, the poem also features a modern plot.

Most historians believe the works were orally transmitted and performed over a long period, perhaps for centuries, before they were eventually written down, and certainly no first manuscript has survived from 3,000 years ago or more. The oldest known fragments of *The Odyssey*, written on papyri and discovered in the sarcophagi of mummified Greek Egyptians dated to 285–250 BC, are displayed at the Metropolitan Museum of Art. The oldest complete manuscript version of *The Iliad*, handwritten on vellum and dated to about AD 900, is known as Venetus A, and it has been preserved at the Marciana Library in Venice since the fifteenth century. Each page contains twenty-five lines of Homeric text, accompanied by scholia (marginal notations and annotations) which were inscribed by editors in Alexandria sometime between the first century BC and the first century AD. A fine photographic facsimile edition was made in 1901 and scholars have recently completed a greatly improved version using the latest digital imaging technology.

The Art of War

(512 BC)

An ancient Chinese military treatise ranks as the greatest primer ever written on warfare strategy and tactics, providing a timeless and savvy guide for many field generals over the ages; it is also consulted by corporate executives, trial lawyers, and other serious competitors.

"The art of war is of vital importance to the state. It is a matter of life and death, a road either to safety or to ruin. Hence it is a subject of inquiry which can on no account be neglected." So begins history's greatest published meditation on warfare, the literary origins of which remain in dispute. Some authorities wonder whether it was authored by a fabled Chinese military leader named Sun Tzu or Sunzi, if indeed he really existed; others suggest that the ideas may have been compiled and modified by many hands over a long period. Everyone, however, agrees that the work is very ancient: an archaeological discovery in Shandong in 1972 unearthed a nearly complete bamboo scroll copy, known as the Yinqueshan Han Slips (206 BC–AD 220), which is nearly identical to modern editions of *The Art of War*.

Considered the greatest of China's Seven Military Classics, the work was first translated into French in 1772 and partially put into English in 1905, and its readers have long marveled that the document's guidance never seems to have become outmoded. Commanders from Napoléon Bonaparte to Generals Võ Nguyên Giáp and Norman Schwarzkopf have credited its teachings for some of their successful military strategies and tactics. In a 2001 TV episode of *The Sopranos*, the mobster Tony Soprano tells his psychiatrist, "Here's this guy—a Chinese general, wrote this thing 2,400 years ago and most of it still applies today."

The Art of War consists of thirteen chapters. Each grouping offers wise and time-tested instruction on a key aspect of warfare. Written in plain but lucid terms, the text presents basic principles and strategies on when and how to fight, providing cardinal rules such as "He will win who knows how to handle both superior and inferior forces" and "He will win whose army is animated by the same spirit throughout all its ranks."

Sun Tzu considers war a necessary evil to be avoided whenever possible. All wars should be waged swiftly or the army will lose the will to fight and "the resources of the State will not be equal to the strain." "There is no instance of a country having benefited from prolonged warfare." "All warfare," he writes, "is based on deception. Hence, when we are able to attack, we must seem unable; when using our forces, we must appear inactive; when we are near, we must make the enemy believe we are far away; when far away, we must make him believe we are near."

The text identifies the six main "calamities" that a general might expose his army to: 1. flight; 2. insubordination; 3. collapse; 4. ruin; 5. disorganization; and 6. rout. Conversely, a great general will have the "power of estimating the adversary, of controlling the forces of victory, and of shrewdly calculating difficulties, dangers and distances."

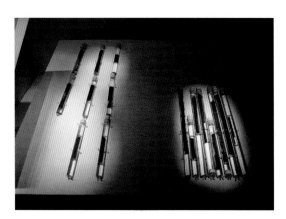

LEFT: These bamboo strips, known as the Yinqueshan Han Slips, date from 206 BC–AD 220 and are the oldest extant example of the sixth-century BC Art of War *text.*

ABOVE: An eighteenth-century bamboo edition of The Art of War *commissioned by the Qianlong Emperor (1711–99), the sixth Qing Emperor of China.*

ABOVE: This fragment from the Dead Sea Scrolls is taken from The
Book of War. *Written in Hebrew, it dates to AD 20–30 and tells the
story of a forty-year battle between the forces of good and evil.*

Dead Sea Scrolls

(408 BC–AD 318)

Discoveries in caves of the Judean Desert yield caches of ancient manuscripts containing some of the earliest known pieces of the Old Testament and other writings from early Hebrew culture. Their ownership and meaning can prove controversial.

In November 1946 a young Bedouin shepherd was searching for a stray amid the limestone cliffs that line the northwestern rim of the Dead Sea, around Qumran in the West Bank, when he came upon a cave in the rocky hillside. Upon casting a stone into the dark entrance, he heard clay pottery breaking, so he ventured inside to investigate. He found several large earthen jars with sealed lids. In them were long objects wrapped in linen—old scrolls covered with writing he couldn't decipher.

Over the next three months the Arab youth and three companions retrieved and sold seven of the mysterious objects to antiques dealers in Bethlehem without knowing their true value.

When Professor Eliezer Lipa Sukenik of Hebrew University glimpsed what was written on one of the scrolls, he shook with excitement. "I looked and looked," he later recalled, "and I suddenly had the feeling that I was privileged by destiny to gaze upon a Hebrew scroll which had not been read for more than 2,000 years."

Over the next nine years the number of discoveries in the region grew to more than 900 scrolls and fragments. The writers had scrawled their accounts on animal hide or papyrus, using reed pens and varied brightly colored inks. Most of the texts are written in Hebrew, with some in Aramaic, Greek, Latin, and Arabic.

The collected documents became known as the Dead Sea Scrolls. And they created an international sensation, for several reasons. Because scholars placed their origin at between 408 BC and AD 318—a crucial moment in the development of monotheistic Judeo-Christian religions—the manuscripts hold great historical, religious, and linguistic significance on issues that are often fiercely disputed.

As new technologies have developed, samples of the scrolls have been carbon-14 dated and analyzed using DNA testing, X-ray, and Particle Induced X-ray emission testing and other techniques. This indicates that some of the scrolls were created in the third century BC, but most seem to be originals or copies from the first century BC. A large number relate to a particular sectarian community.

The scrolls represent what are probably the earliest known copies of biblical texts, including most of the books of the Old Testament, as well as many additional writings. Together they shed light on the Old Testament's textual evolution. Findings from the scrolls have leaked out over several decades, yet even today the contents of certain documents have not been publicly revealed and analyzed, which has generated even more controversy.

Some of the scrolls are currently on display at the Israel Museum in Jerusalem, where their ownership and meaning remains hotly contested.

LEFT: One of the pottery jars found in the caves of Qumran. These lidded clay containers were used for storing the Dead Sea Scrolls.

Mahabharata

(c. 400 BC)

The world's longest epic poem, which includes Hinduism's most widely read sacred scripture, the *Bhagavad Gita*, as one of its seven principal *parvas* (sections), ranks as one of the greatest literary achievements in history—one of the high points of Indian culture for more than 2,000 years.

Along with the *Ramayana*, the *Mahabharata* is one of ancient India's greatest Sanskrit epics—a saga of such staggering size it takes close to two full weeks to recite, with over 100,000 *shloka* (couplets) and long prose passages that combine to form a total length of 1.8 million words.

With a title that has been translated as "The Great Tale of the Bharata Dynasty," the core story follows the struggle for the throne of Hastinapur, the kingdom ruled by the Kuru clan, which is waged by the Pandavas and the Kauravas. It includes innumerable episodes about the role of kings, princes, sages, demons, and gods. The deeply philosophical work embodies the ethos of Hinduism and Vedic tradition, recounting much of Indian culture's sacred history, and is told with a scope and grandeur that dwarf all other epic works.

Some of the events described in the *Mahabharata* are supposed to have occurred as far back at 1000 BC, while the oldest extant text has been dated to the eighth or ninth century AD, according to Professor Rajeswari Sunder Rajan of Oxford University, writing in 2000. Teams of scholars have labored for decades in an effort to ascertain how the document may have evolved to reach its final form between the third and fifth centuries. One research team has gathered and compared many manuscripts of the huge epic to compile a master reference series of twenty-eight volumes.

The *Mahabharata* is usually attributed to Rishi Vyasa, a revered mythical figure in Hindu traditions who is both an author and a main character in the story. Vyasa says one of his aims is to explain the four *purusarthas* (goals of life) that lead to happiness, and this deep didactic aspect has made the work the foundational guide to Indian moral philosophy and law.

Some scholars suspect that roots of the epic may lie in actual events that happened several centuries before the Common Era; others accept the work as a compendium of swirling and crisscrossed legends, religious beliefs and semi-historical accounts that nevertheless provide a rich picture of Hindu life and philosophy in ancient India.

All agree it is impossible to prove if or when Vyasa really lived, or to disentangle facts from fiction in the labyrinthine epic, in part because much of Vyasa's storytelling is recited by his sage disciple, Vaisampayana, and the rich narrative employs an exceedingly complex "tale-within-a-tale" structure which is common to many traditional Indian religious and secular works. A short excerpt conveys its highly embellished style:

> Sauti said, Having heard the diverse sacred and wonderful stories which were composed in his *Mahabharata* by Krishna-Dwaipayana, and which were recited in full by Vaisampayana at the Snake-sacrifice of the high-souled royal sage Janamejaya and in the presence also of that chief of Princes, the son of Parikshit, and having wandered about, visiting many sacred waters and holy shrines, I journeyed to the country venerated by the Dwijas twice-born and called Samantapanchaka where formerly was fought the battle between the children of Kuru and Pandu, and all the chiefs of the land ranged on either side.

RIGHT: These richly illustrated plates from an early nineteenth-century edition of the Mahabharata *capture the cyclical nature of this literary epic. There are no complete copies of the original text, which is thought to have reached its final form by the fifth-century BC.*

Kama Sutra

(400 BC–AD 200)

Although widely known today as a manual of ingeniously contorted coital positions, the original (and unillustrated) ancient Sanskrit text provides a comprehensive and surprisingly modern guide to living a sensually fulfilling life, in which sexual intercourse is simply one ingredient.

The Sanskrit term *kama sutra* signifies a guide to sexual pleasure. The ancient literary work of that title is generally attributed to the sage Vatsyayana of northern India, who claims to be a celibate monk, and has compiled all of the accumulated sexual knowledge of the ages through deep meditation and contemplation of the deity; however, its origins are unclear. Written in an archaic form of Sanskrit, the *Kama Sutra* is the only known philosophical text from that period of ancient Indian history.

Organized into thirty-six chapters containing 1,250 verses, the work presents itself as a guide to a pleasurable life. Although the central character is a worldly but virtuous male, its guidance about courtship and romance also applies to women, more or less. "A man," it says,

> should fix his affections upon a girl who is of good family, whose parents are alive, and who is three years or more younger than himself. She should be born of a highly respectable family, possessed of wealth, well connected, and with many relations and friends. She should also be beautiful, of a good disposition, with lucky marks on her body, and with good hair, nails, teeth, ears, eyes and breasts, neither more nor less than they ought to be, and no one of them entirely wanting, and not troubled with a sickly body. The man should, of course, also possess these qualities himself.

A basic tenet is that a happy marriage requires both parties to be well-versed in pleasure in many different ways. The text gives instruction on extramarital and same-sex relationships, including recipes for spices that will help attract lovers. It also presents charts explaining which male or female body types are most compatible, and demonstrates an assortment of love techniques from embracing and kissing to oral sex and intercourse. But sexual topics actually comprise only one of the work's seven parts.

Indeed, the *Kama Sutra* values the pursuit of each *purusartha*, or Hindu aim in life, as worthwhile, but stresses that each four *purusarthas*—*dharma, artha, kama* and *moksha*—should be kept in balance. Thus the work catalogs the holistic lifestyles of refined Hindu culture, teaching a range of social skills that constitute elegant living. The graces covered include music, cooking, literature, sports, and lively conversation.

Copied and passed down for centuries, it was rediscovered by a noted British linguist, Sir Richard Burton, in the late nineteenth century. Burton labored with his Indian and British collaborators to recompile the original text from scattered manuscript collections, which the team used to produce an English translation.

Since the nineteenth century, the document has been widely circulated outside of India, giving the work a unique place in world literature as it serves as a practical guide for human relations across many cultures and times—the forerunner of today's how-to books.

LEFT: This brightly colored eighteenth-century painting of one of the techniques described in the Kama Sutra *is from the Rajput school, which flourished in the royal courts of Rajputana. There are no surviving copies of the original Sanskrit text, which is thought to have been compiled some time between the fifth century BC and the third century AD.*

Plato's Republic

(c. 380 BC)

The Athenian thinker Plato—a student of Socrates and mentor of Aristotle—is credited with one of the most influential works of philosophy and moral/political theory ever written. Presented as a dialogue, it examines such core issues as the meaning of justice and the immortality of the soul.

Of the thirty-five dialogues and thirteen letters that are traditionally attributed to the ancient Greek philosopher Plato (428/427 or 424/423 BC–348/347 BC), the best-known is the *Republic*, in which Plato's teacher Socrates interrogates fellow Athenians and foreigners about an ideal state.

Kallipolis is described as the most beautiful city-state in part because it is ruled by philosopher-kings. "Until philosophers are kings," he writes,

> or the kings and princes of this world have the spirit and power of philosophy, and political greatness and wisdom meet in one, and those commoner natures who pursue either to the exclusion of the other side are compelled to stand aside, critics will never have rest from their evils— no, nor the human race, as I believe—and then only will this our State have a possibility of life and behold the light of day.

Plato asserts that Kallipolis's form of government—*politeia* (rule by the aristocracy)—is superior to other approaches such as *timocracy* (rule by the honorable), *oligarchy* (rule by the wealthy few), *democracy* (rule by the people), or *tyranny* (rule by one). Plato analyzes the nature of each type of state and its corresponding rulers.

Plato describes the democratic state (Athens) as "a charming form of government, full of variety and disorder, and dispensing a sort of equality to equals and unequals alike." But he views democracy as an undisciplined society that devolves into chaos and conflicts between rich and poor that ultimately leads to the rise of a popular champion who increases oppression and becomes a tyrant. "The people have always some champion whom they set over them and nurse into greatness… This and no other is the root from which a tyrant springs, when he first appears he is a protector."

One of the *Republic*'s central ideas is that "justice and happiness stand and fall together. Not because good consequences… follow from being just, but because justice itself is so great that nothing gained by injustice could be greater."

Today Plato's work is valued as much for its Socratic methods of analysis and accounts of ancient Greek history as it is for the ideas. Its place in the canon of Western thought would not have occurred were it not for the discovery of hundreds of manuscript fragments attributed to him and other ancient commentators who had referenced him with Socrates and Aristotle.

The *Republic* documents were copies made from earlier copies of the original ancient text; some of those made by Arab copyists were later found in medieval times. The oldest surviving versions are written in Attic Greek, which was the main Greek dialect spoken in ancient Attica of which Athens was a part. Following the fall of Constantinople in the mid-fifteenth century, handwritten copies of Plato's *Republic* and other works eventually found their way into Italy where they helped to fuel the Renaissance.

ABOVE: Fragments from the Gandharan scrolls, acquired by the British Library in 1994. Written in ink on birch bark, these first-century AD scriptures are the oldest surviving Buddhist texts.

Gandharan Buddhist Texts

(AD 50)

Buddhist monks' sutras, inscribed on birch bark scrolls and buried in the desert of eastern Afghanistan 2,000 years ago, are the earliest known Buddhist texts and the oldest documents extant from South Asia. They are the Indian Buddhist equivalent of the Dead Sea Scrolls.

From the sixth century BC to the eleventh century AD, Gandhara was a vibrant multi-ethnic kingdom of Ancient India in what is now northern Pakistan, Kashmir, and eastern Afghanistan—a crossroads of Indian, Iranian, and Central Asian cultures. At the peak of its influence, from about 100 BC to AD 200, it was the gateway through which Buddhist religion was transmitted from India to China and elsewhere. From the time of its conquest by Alexander the Great, Gandhara was also a principal point of contact between India and the Western world, producing much exchange in philosophy, art, and commerce.

Two thousand years ago, Buddhist monks rolled up *sutras* written on birch bark, stuffed them into round earthen pots, and buried them in a desert mound—possibly because they had already made new copies of the text and were using the discarded ones as part of the consecration of a *stupa* or meditation shrine. In keeping with their Buddhist principles of vegetarianism and *ahimsa*, the monks employed inner bark from the *bhurja* or birch tree instead of animal hide. They flattened and glued the bark together into scrolls that could be written upon using a stylus and ink.

Acquired by the British Library in 1994, the Kharosthi manuscript collection of thirteen unique scrolls written in the Kharosthi script and the Gandhara language dates from the middle of the first century. Although the original provenance of the scrolls is uncertain, they

appear to have come from the ancient Greco-Buddhist center of Hadda near the city of Jalalabad in eastern Afghanistan. The scrolls were most likely written during the reign of the Saka rulers, in the mid-first century AD, making them the oldest Buddhist texts ever found as well as the earliest surviving manuscripts in any Indic language.

Additional archaeological discoveries have increased the number of ancient birch-bark scrolls under study to seventy-six, some of which along with other fragments are held by the University of Washington Libraries, the Library of Congress, the Schøyen Collection, the Hirayama Collection, the Hayashidera Collection and the Bibliothèque nationale de France.

Many of the texts are still partly readable and cover a range of Buddhist teachings. Thus far some

of the translated works include philosophical and technical teachings as well as popular didactic verse, such as the "Rhinoceros Horn Sutra" and the "Song of Lake Anavatapta."

They have revealed many new insights about early Indian Buddhism, which is believed to have originated in the same period when Siddhartha Gautama ("the Buddha") achieved enlightenment through meditation under a fig tree. As many as 500 million persons in the world today consider themselves Buddhist.

LEFT: This late first-century AD Gandharan sculpture is one of the earliest representations of Buddha.

The Quran

(AD 609–632)

Over a period of twenty-three years, the word of Allah is revealed to the Prophet Muhammad through the angel Gabriel, in the form of sacred verses, and Muhammad later recites every word to his followers. Believers in the sacred religious text of Islam today comprise one-sixth of the world's population.

Islamic tradition holds that on December 23, AD 609, an Arab from Mecca named Muhammad, who was forty years old, was taking a solitary retreat into the mountains when he was visited by an angel in a cave at Mount Hira. The angel Gabriel (Jibril) revealed the very word of Allah (God), accompanied by visions, in what would be the first of many revelations Muhammad would receive up until his death in 632.

Being illiterate (*ummi*), he was unable to read earlier scriptures or to write his own accounts, but the Prophet Muhammad faithfully recounted Allah's words to others, directing his followers to memorize and recite them in prayers. Eventually some listeners began recording the words on clay tablets, bones, and date palm fronds.

Upon Muhammad's death, his closest friend, the first caliph Abu Bakr (d. 634), wanted the words collected into a single authorized volume so that they would be preserved for all time. He selected Zayd ibn Thabit (d. 655) for the task. Zayd worked with a group of scribes to gather the sacred verses into the first handwritten manuscript, recorded in Arabic. A few years later a standard copy was commissioned.

Entitled the Quran, the sacred work consists of 114 brief *suras* (chapters) comprised of *ayats* (verses), totaling about 77,000 words. The verses are designed to be memorized for prayer. The work describes itself as "the discernment or the criterion between truth and falsehood," "the guide," "the wisdom," and "the revelation," offering detailed accounts of historical events with commentary about their moral significance. Its core tenets include belief in one almighty God, and the resurrection. "Wherever ye be, God will bring you all back to the resurrection." About one-third of the verses deal with the afterlife and the final judgment day. The verses also call for its followers to "Fight for the religion of God."

The work's language has been described as "rhymed prose," and its structure is without a beginning, middle, or end. Some critics say this unusual nonlinear approach can act to both intensify the power of its prophetic messages and impart different levels of meaning.

First translated into Latin in 1143 and English in 1649, the Quran now appears in more than 100 languages.

In 1972, manuscripts of the sacred verses were discovered in a mosque in Sana'a, Yemen which have been dated to 671, making them possibly the oldest known copy of the document.

LEFT: The Sana'a palimpsest (AD 671) is one of the oldest surviving Quranic manuscripts.

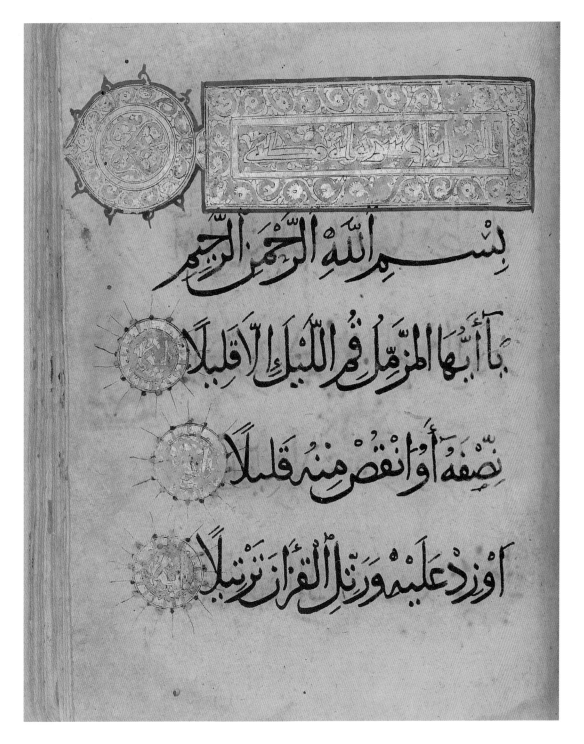

The Magna Carta

(1215)

Agreed between King John and his barons at Runnymede, as the first document to limit the power of the monarchy and assert the certain liberties granted to free men, the medieval Great Charter of 1215 is considered the foundation of English common law.

Magna Carta (Latin for Great Charter), also called Magna Carta Libertatum or The Great Charter of the Liberties of England, was originally issued in Latin in June 1215. It was sealed under oath by King John at Runnymede, on the banks of the River Thames near Windsor, on June 15, 1215. At the time he issued it, the charter was intended to promote peace between the king and his powerful barons, yet it provoked war instead. In fact, it was legally valid for barely three months and its terms were never fully executed; yet it was issued several times in different forms during the thirteenth century.

Nevertheless, the Magna Carta was the first document forced onto a king of England by a group of his subjects, in an attempt to limit royal powers by law and protect the subjects' feudal rights. By putting royal power under secular law, the charter initiated the protracted historical process that led to the rule of constitutional law in England and beyond, giving rise to such basic protections as representative government, common law, *habeas corpus* and other trial rights.

The charter has over sixty clauses, covering many areas of the nation's life, including the right to a fair trial. For example:

> No freeman is to be taken or imprisoned or disseised of his free tenement or of his liberties or free customs, or outlawed or exiled or in any way ruined, nor will we go against such a man or send against him save by lawful judgment of his peers or by the law of the land. To no-one will we sell or deny or delay right or justice.

Several copies of the charter were written immediately after King John agreed to peace terms with his barons at Runnymede. They were sent around the country as evidence of the king's decision. It was written in Latin by hand, by an expert scribe, on vellum.

The document's importance has endured to make it a cornerstone of the rule of law. As the first codification of English civil liberties, the Magna Carta has come to symbolize justice, fairness, and human rights. Its laws were important in the colonization of America, as England's legal system was used as a model for many of the colonies as they were developing their own legal systems. Three clauses still remain part of the law of England and Wales, and it is still considered to be one of the most important constitutional documents of all time.

The four surviving original copies of the Magna Carta (two held at the British Library in London, one at Salisbury Cathedral, and one at Lincoln Cathedral) were displayed together for the first time in 2015, marking the document's 800th anniversary.

ABOVE: An original 1215 Magna Carta. Only four survive: one in Lincoln, one in Salisbury, and two in the British Library in London.

LEFT: This version of the Magna Carta, issued under Edward I in 1297, was confirmed in parliament and became law. A copy of it was sold in 2007 for $21.3 million.

Ad Extirpanda

(1252)

Pope Innocent IV didn't start the medieval Inquisition, but he is the first to explicitly authorize its tribunals' use of torture for obtaining confessions from heretics. Guilt, it seems, is never to be doubted. And everyone must confess to something.

The medieval Inquisition began in 1231 when Pope Gregory IX instituted a system of special courts to root out heresy, which was considered the most serious crime confronting church and state. Such a court was known as the Holy Office. At first much of the prosecution involved members of dissident religious sects such as the Cathars, who were based in southern France.

After Cathars were alleged to have murdered a papal legate in Lombardy, Pope Innocent IV (born Sinibaldo Fieschi, 1195–1254) issued a papal bull (decree) in 1252 which set forth the ways and means by which heretics were to be judged, tried, and punished under the Inquisition. Innocent wanted them treated no better than thieves and murderers, but proving their crimes under law required evidence of their guilt. He also stated, "Necessity overrides every law."

His bull, Ad extirpanda, defined the circumstances and methods for torturing heretics to obtain the confessions that would furnish such evidence. The approach assumed that the guilty suspect always had to admit his or her own guilt and implicate others.

Pope Innocent IV directed that his bull be entered into every city's municipal statutes. The inquisitors themselves were not permitted to apply the torture, but they were expected to direct it, and the courts were vested with the full power of the Church. In exchange for carrying out the punishment, the state was entitled to a portion of the proceeds of the property that had been seized from the heretics. Defendants could be imprisoned for long periods as evidence against them was gathered, and every sort of painful punishment could be employed to extract the confessions, provided it did not cause loss of life or limb, was used only once, and the inquisitor considered the evidence virtually certain. For example, Number twenty-six of the thirty-nine laws proclaimed:

The head of state or ruler must force all the heretics whom he has in custody, provided he does so without killing them or breaking their arms or legs, as actual robbers and murderers of souls and thieves of the sacraments of God and Christian faith, to confess their errors and accuse other heretics whom they know, and specify their motives, and those whom they have seduced, and those who have lodged them and defended them, as thieves and robbers of material goods are made to accuse their accomplices and confess the crimes they have committed.

Pope Innocent IV's "Proclamation of the Laws and Regulations to be followed by Magistrates and Secular Officials against Heretics and their Accomplices and Protectors" was issued on May 15, 1252, paving the way for several centuries of suffering.

ABOVE: An illustration from a 1330s manuscript showing Pope Innocent IV sending a mission of Dominicans and Franciscans out to the Tartars.

ABOVE: Pope Innocent IV's papal bull gave him the authority to use torture to extract confessions from suspects. It granted state rulers the right to arrest and execute non-Catholic Christians. The bull made torture legal in the punishment of heretics for five-and-a-half centuries, until it was finally abolished by Pope Pius VII in 1816.

ABOVE: A 1471 edition of Thomas Aquinas's Summa Theologica,
complete with fifteenth-century handwritten annotations.

Summa Theologica

(1265–74)

Thomas Aquinas is the greatest Catholic philosopher and theologian of the high Middle Ages and his masterpiece, *Summa Theologica*, offers what is perhaps the finest explanation of Christian faith, although he dies before completing it. The work is considered one of the most influential works of Western literature.

Thomas Aquinas (1225–74) was born in Roccasecca, near Rome, and grew up in the great Benedictine abbey of Monte Cassino. While studying at the University of Naples, he joined the controversial new Dominican order over the objections of his parents, who held him prisoner for a year in the family castle in a futile effort to dissuade him from becoming a Dominican priest. His brothers even hired a prostitute to seduce him, but that didn't work either.

After many years studying and teaching theology in Paris, Cologne, Rome, and other learning centers, the seasoned Dominican scholar in 1265 undertook the writing of the *Summa Theologica*. Originally intended as an instructional guide for moderate young theologians, Thomas's collection of the main teachings of the Catholic Church turned into the definitive examination of Christian reasoning on all of the major matters confronting persons of faith.

What is the proof for God's existence and what is his nature? How was the world created? What is the way to God? And many other questions.

Thomas's judgment was sound and sober and his use of the Scriptures masterful. Thomas also educated his readers about more than the sacred doctrines of the Catholic Church. In the tradition of scholasticism, he drew from Muslim, Hebrew, and pagan sources as well, citing works by Aristotle, Boethius, Plato, Maimonides, the Roman jurist Ulpian, and other great thinkers, offering a universal interpretation of their ideas. "Law,"

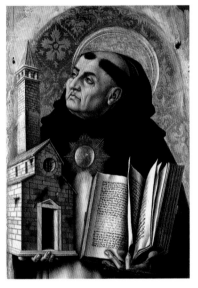

LEFT: This detail from The Demidoff Altarpiece (1476) shows Thomas Aquinas surrounded by symbols of his sacred learning.

he writes, is "an ordinance of reason for the common good, made by him who has care of the community ... The human mind may perceive truth only through thinking, as is clear from Augustine."

The *Summa* is both a compendium and a manual of theology, the study of which he viewed as a science. His treatise summarizes the history of the cosmos and reveals the meaning of life, according to holy belief. "It is certain and evident to our senses," he writes,

> that in the world some things are in motion. Now whatever is moved is moved by another...If that by which it is moved be itself moved, then this also must needs be moved by another, and that by another again. But this cannot go on to infinity, because then there would be no first mover and, consequently, no other mover, seeing that subsequent movers move only inasmuch as they are moved by the first mover, as the staff moves only because it is moved by the hand. Therefore it is necessary to arrive at a first mover, moved by no other; and this everyone understands to be God.

Although the last part remained unfinished at Thomas's death in 1274, the document he left behind totaled 3,500 dense pages.

He was canonized in 1323 as Saint Thomas Aquinas.

Hereford Mappa Mundi

(1280–1300)

Drawn on a large hide, the encyclopedic Hereford Mappa Mundi depicts the world as it appears to educated Europeans in the late thirteenth century, showing everything from geography and biblical lore to exotic animals, strange peoples from foreign lands, and images from classical mythology—making it a mapped storehouse of medieval knowledge.

On display in a new library adjoining England's magnificent Hereford Cathedral is one of the world's grandest visual documents—the Hereford Mappa Mundi, the largest medieval map. Measuring 64 by 52 inches, it consists of a single sheet of vellum stretched over an oak framework. The map portion is set in a circle. Most of the writing is in black ink, with a few additional colors—red for the Red Sea, blue or green for other waters, for example.

The map is signed by "Richard of Haldingham and Lafford, prebend of Lafford in Lincoln Cathedral," who was a cosmologist and cartographer in the region. Experts date its origin to somewhere between 1280 and 1300. Many scholars believe the document was originally intended as a decorative altarpiece which may have been designed to educate the local congregation about the world in all of its glory and dangers as the parishioners knelt and prayed.

Like other maps of its time, the Mundi's geography conforms to Church doctrine, showing heaven as well as numerous key biblical sites, with Jerusalem placed at the center of the world. Near the center of the map, Babylon is shown as a multi-storied fortress city near the Tower of Babel. Above it, in gold letters, India appears as an exotic land with dragons, and above that is the glorious Garden of Eden.

The British Isles appear larger in scale than their actual size. The depiction of the areas now called Asia, Africa, Europe, and some of their adjacent islands, also reflects the rudimentary state of knowledge in thirteenth-century England.

In addition to showing 500 cities or towns, a sizable number of the entries depict exotic peoples, animals and plants according to their heralded reputation. The aphrodisiac mandrake, for example, is featured with roots that resemble a human's hair as many informed Englishmen believed in those days.

The map includes more than 1,000 legends, listing the names of certain countries, rivers, cities and other natural features, along with images capturing their perceived essence. The descriptions are in Latin and the Norman dialect of old French.

The map encapsulates how thirteenth-century scholars interpreted the world in religious as well as geographical terms, representing an early form of what today might be called a data map. A virtual map, enabling readers to study the document in depth, is available at Hereford Cathedral's Mappa Mundi Exploration website.

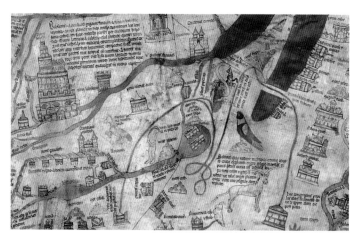

BELOW: *A detail of Mappa Mundi showing the Tower of Babel, Sodom and Gomorrah, and the Red Sea.*

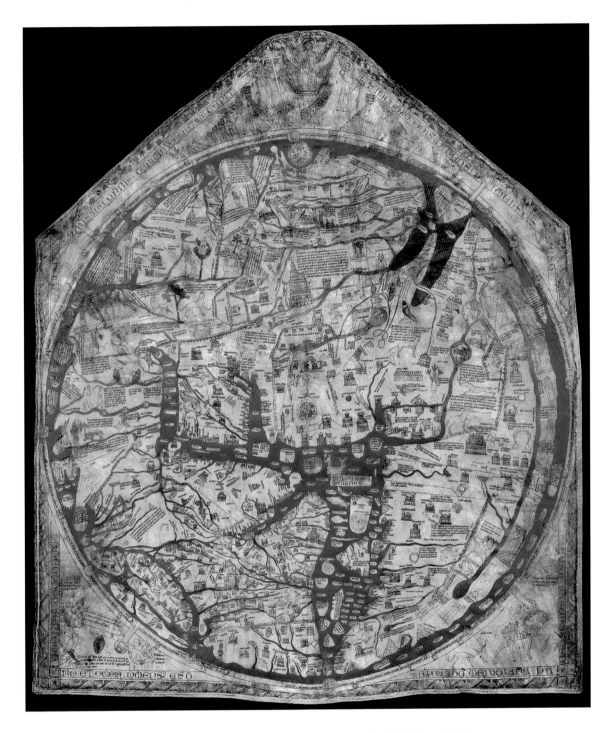

ABOVE: The Mappa Mundi's detailed view of the world is contained within a fifty-two-inch-diameter circle. The map reflects the outlook of the English church in the Middle Ages. Jerusalem is at the center, with countries and oceans squeezed and stretched to fit into the map.

Gutenberg Bible

(1450s)

Although the first inventions occurred much earlier in China and Korea, the genesis of modern printing by means of a printing press using metal movable type is rightly traced to Gutenberg's publication of the Bible, which changed the nature of document production—and transformed the world.

Woodblock printing was invented in China early in the sixth century when a carved board was inked and used to print multiple copies of a page. The Chinese also modified the method to create individual characters in the 1040s, although their use of such technology was limited by the requirement of having to create the thousands of individual characters needed for Chinese writing. Korea was the first country to adopt China's woodblock printing and the first to devise metal movable type for individual characters, which was done to print the Buddhist document *Jikji* in 1377. But the complexities of Asian languages made the use of metal movable type better suited for publishing Western alphabetical languages.

The great breakthrough occurred in the 1450s when a blacksmith and printer in Mainz, Germany named Johannes Gutenberg (1398–1468) spent four years perfecting new printing methods in order to produce an exquisite edition of the Vulgate, the fourth-century Latin-language version of the Bible.

Working with a crew of at least twenty ink-stained assistants, Gutenberg developed his fine printing technology largely from scratch, experimenting with different inks, papers, and processes until he had found the right one. Instead of traditional water-based inks, he chose oil-based ink of the highest quality and mastered its manufacture to the most exacting standards. The best paper was brought in from Italy. Through trial and error, he developed a special metal alloy that would melt at a low temperature but remain strong enough to withstand being squeezed in a press. He found just the right method to make individual letters by casting them in a specially created sand-cast mold, also devising ways to sort, store, and maintain the type so it could be used repeatedly with good effect. His fonts were expertly designed and crafted with absolute precision, with 292 different blocks of type, including as many as six versions of the same letter, made to different widths to enable each to be squeezed to fit in a tight space if needed, down to the millimeter. His custom-made wooden printing press, modeled on a winepress, enabled the operator to print pages at a much faster rate than any woodblock press and the quality of the finished product was excellent.

Notable for its regularity of ink impression, harmony of layout, and other qualities, the 1,286-page Gutenberg Bible (also known as the "forty-two-line Bible," "Mazarin Bible," or "B42") was hailed as a masterpiece.

Scholars today think that somewhere between 160 and 185 copies were printed, of which forty-eight have survived. The Gutenberg Bible had a profound effect on printing and fueled an information revolution.

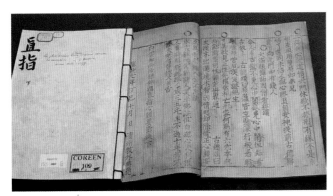

LEFT: The Korean Jikji, *a book of Buddhist teachings, was first printed in 1377. It is the oldest extant book produced with movable metal type.*

Leonardo da Vinci's Notebooks

(1478–1519)

For most of his later life, the quintessential Renaissance man keeps a daily record of his interests and ideas, abounding with careful illustrations and notes showing that he is far ahead of his time. That is why he furtively writes much of the text by means of his own secretive method—the "da Vinci code."

Leonardo di ser Piero da Vinci (1452–1519), the great Italian Renaissance polymath of all polymaths, possessed boundless creativity, "unquenchable curiosity," and a "feverishly inventive imagination." His mind burst with insights about infants in the womb, helicopters and submarines, the inner-workings of plants, and endless other phenomena.

As Leonardo did not want his ideas pilfered, he had to go to remarkable lengths not to offend the tyrannical hegemony of his day. Knowing that one move deemed threatening to those in power could dearly cost him, he tried to cover at least some of his tracks.

While making extensive notes and drawings to record some of his current pursuits in art and natural philosophy, Leonardo often cloaked his observations by means of a unique backwards-lettered cursive script that he had designed to keep out thieves, inquisitors, and other enemies. His peculiar form of "mirror handwriting" may have been facilitated by his being left-handed, but it drove intruders crazy.

The master would start fleshing out his ideas by making quick sketches on loose sheets of paper, sometimes utilizing miniature paper pads that he stored in his belt. He later would arrange the copious notes according to theme and file them in order in his notebooks.

After Leonardo's death, his longtime student and companion Francesco Melzi received fifty of the notebooks containing 13,000 pages and took them to Milan. Upon Melzi's death, many of the documents eventually ended up getting sold off and some were lost. Many were bound. They became known as "The da Vinci Codex" (a codex being a bound book made up of separate pages).

Leonardo's notebooks later ended up in several of the world's leading collections such as the Louvre, the British Library and the Biblioteca Ambrosiana in Milan. The last possesses the largest notebook, the wide-ranging Codex Atlanticus, consisting of 1,119 leaves that da Vinci compiled between 1478 and 1519. The only major one involving science that is privately owned, the Codex Leicester, was purchased by Bill Gates for $30.8 million in 1994. Written on seventy-two loose sheets of linen paper between 1506 and 1510 it deals mostly with hydrology.

Besides providing clues about the mind that produced some of the world's most treasured art masterpieces, the notebooks are the greatest remaining written representation of Leonardo's genius across a wide range of disciplines.

RIGHT: Above are da Vinci's designs for a flying machine from the Codex Atlanticus. Below are his scientific notes from the Codex Leicester, also known as the Codex Hammer, which was bought by Bill Gates in 1994 for $30.8 million, making it the most expensive manuscript sold at auction.

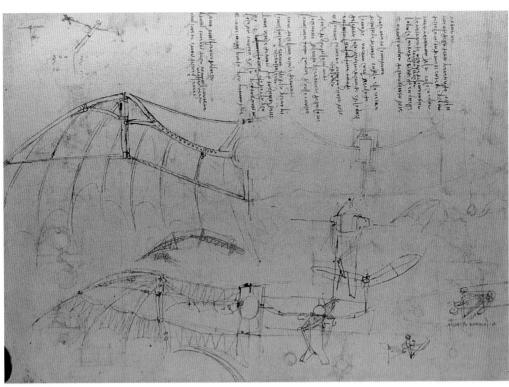

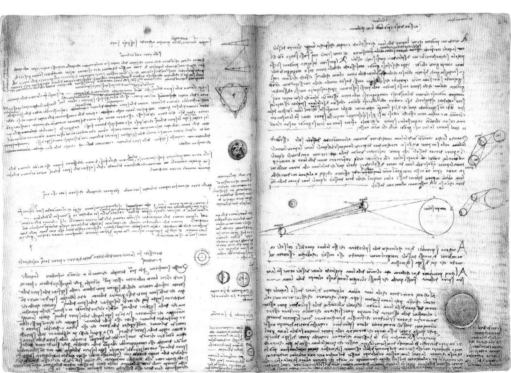

*ABOVE: The document that ordered all Jews to leave Spain
at once, under pain of death, and without trial.*

Alhambra Decree

(1492)

In the most cataclysmic event in Jewish history since the second century AD, Spain's Catholic joint monarchs, Ferdinand and Isabella, issue an edict expelling all of the kingdom's Jews unless they convert to Christianity—a milestone in the history of intolerance.

In 1491 Spanish forces scored their victory in the Battle of Granada, effectively ending 780 years of Muslim rule of the Iberian Peninsula. The region's peaceful coexistence of Muslims, Christians, and Jews came to an end as King Ferdinand II and Queen Isabella I of Spain took steps to drive out a large Jewish population that had lived there under the Moors.

On March 31, 1492 the royal couple (led by Isabella) signed an edict, setting forth a list of purported offenses committed by the Jews. Conversion being a central issue for the Spanish Inquisition, it was claimed that some purported converts to Christianity still secretly practiced Judaism—"wicked" practices, they said, that had "redounded to the great injury, detriment, and opprobrium of our holy Catholic faith." Hence, for these and other alleged offenses, all Jews in the kingdom were ordered to leave the country at once, under pain of death without trial if they remained. Anyone who sheltered or hid Jews stood to forfeit all their property and hereditary privileges.

The expulsion covered all Jews and their servants and supporters living within the entire Spanish kingdom and territories—an estimated population of 250,000 persons.

Ferdinand and Isabella issued the document at the same time they ordered Christopher Columbus to sail for the Indies in what would turn out to be another world-changing event, and Columbus was keenly aware of it, particularly since he too may have had some Jewish ancestry.

The Alhambra Decree was ordered to take effect in precisely four months—an impossibly short time frame given what was required. As a result, Dominican priests hounded the Jews to force them to convert. Thousands renounced their Jewish beliefs. Those who did not had to hastily liquidate their homes and businesses (at drastic prices), yet they were forbidden to take away any gold, silver, or minted money. In the frantic effort to flee, tens of thousands of refugees died; others were charged exorbitant sums and betrayed. As many as 100,000 exiles trudged to neighboring Portugal, from which they would be expelled again four years later. Another 50,000 or so crossed into North Africa or they fled by ship to Turkey or other ports. Regardless, by the end of July there were no more Jews left in Spain.

The Vatican finally revoked the edict in 1968 and in 2014 the government of Spain formally recognized its "shameful" treatment of the Jews back in 1492. The Alhambra Decree records one of history's infamous chapters of religious persecution.

ABOVE: A Jewish man pleads for mercy in Emilio Sala's Expulsion of the Jews from Spain (1889), based on the passing of the Alhambra Decree.

Christopher Columbus's Letter

(1493)

On the return leg of his first voyage of discovery to the New World, Christopher Columbus writes a letter describing what he has found. It creates a sensation throughout Europe, and until the nineteenth century, it remains his only known written first-person account of the historic events of 1492–93.

Before returning to Spain from his maiden voyage of 1492–93, the Genoese explorer Cristóbal Colón (Christopher Columbus) penned a report dated February 15, 1493, while aboard his caravel, *La Niña*, off the Canary Islands. In it he described what he had found on his journey in search of an ocean route to Asia.

Columbus wrote that he had headed west across the Atlantic, reaching the first island on the thirty-third day, and other islands after that. At the time he thought he was in the (East) Indies, thus describing the native inhabitants he had encountered as "Indians." In fact, he was describing Caribbean islands now known as San Salvador Island in the Bahamas, as well as Cuba, Haiti, and the Dominican Republic; and the mainland he heard rumors about from the natives was not Cathay (China) but the Americas.

Shortly after Columbus arrived back in Spain, a printed version of the letter in Spanish appeared in Barcelona. A month after that, a Latin translation of a nearly identical version appeared in Rome and was widely distributed by the Church. The document announced, "I discovered many islands inhabited by numerous people. I took possession of all of them for our most fortunate King by making public proclamation and unfurling his standard, no one making any resistance." His letter also provided observations about the natives' vulnerability to conquest, saying "they are destitute of arms, which are entirely unknown to them, and for which they are not adapted; not on account of any bodily deformity, for they are well made, but because they are timid and full of terror." The explorer brought back several of the Indians as prisoners (only eight of twenty-five survived the trip) to demonstrate what such strange peoples were like.

Columbus depicted the New World as a paradise of exotic creatures and abundant fruits, spices, and gold, gushing that the rich territory was Spain's for the taking and its inhabitants could be easily conquered, enslaved, and converted to the Christian faith. His initial account was so enticing that the Crown quickly outfitted him for a return voyage with a massive fleet that departed on September 24, 1493. He made two more return voyages after that.

Since no original handwritten copy of Columbus's letter has ever been found, historians have relied on the multiple printed versions of the 1493 document to help them reconstruct his great discovery.

RIGHT TOP: One of the printed versions of Columbus's letter, published in 1493. Columbus's "Oceanic Classis" (ocean fleet) is depicted in the opening woodcut print. RIGHT: Cartographer Juan de la Cosa accompanied Columbus on his voyage of 1492–93. He produced this remarkable map of the New World in 1500.

Oceanica Classis

Iohana septē vel octo palmaꝛ genera: ꝗ ꝓce
ritate ꝫ pulchꝛitudie (quēadmodū cetere oēs
arboꝛes/herbe/fructusꝗ)nꝫas facile exuperāt
Sūt ꝫ mirabiles pinꝰ/agri/ꝫ pꝛata vastissima/
varie aues/varie mella/variaꝗ metalla:ferro.
excepto. In ea aūt quā Hispanā supꝛa dixim̄ꝰ
nūcupari : maximī sunt mōtes ac pulcri:vasta
rura/nemoꝛa/ cāpi feracissimi/seri/ pacisꝗ ꝫ
cōdendis edificijs aptissimi. Poꝛtuū in hac in
sula cōmoditas: ꝫ p̄stantia fluminū copia salu
bꝛitate admixta hoīm:ꝗ nisi quis viderit: cre
dulitatē supat. Huius arboꝛes pascua ꝫfructꝰ
multum ab illis Iohane differūt. Hec ꝑterea
Hispana diuerso aromatis genere/ auro/ me
tallisꝗ abundat. cuiꝰ quidē ꝫ oīm aliaꝛ quas
ego vidi: ꝫ quaꝛ cognitionē habeo:icole vtri
usꝗ sexus nudi semp̄ incedūt : quēadmodum
edunt in lucem.pꝛeter aliquas feminas. ꝗ fo
lio frondeue aliꝗ: aut bombicino velo: pudē
da operiūt:ꝗd ipe sibi ad id negocij parāt. Ca
rent hi oīes (vt supꝛa dixi) quocunꝗ genere
ferri. carent ꝫ armis:vtpote sibi ignotis nec ad
ea sūt apti.nō ppꝫ coꝛpis defoꝛmitatē (cū sint
bn̄ foꝛmati)sꝫ qꝛ sūt timidi ac pleni formidine.
gestāt tn̄ ꝑ armis arūdines sole pustas:i quaꝛ
radicibꝰ hastile ꝗ ꝺꝺā ligneū siccū ꝫ in mucro
nē attenuatū figūt:neꝗ his audēt iugitervti nā

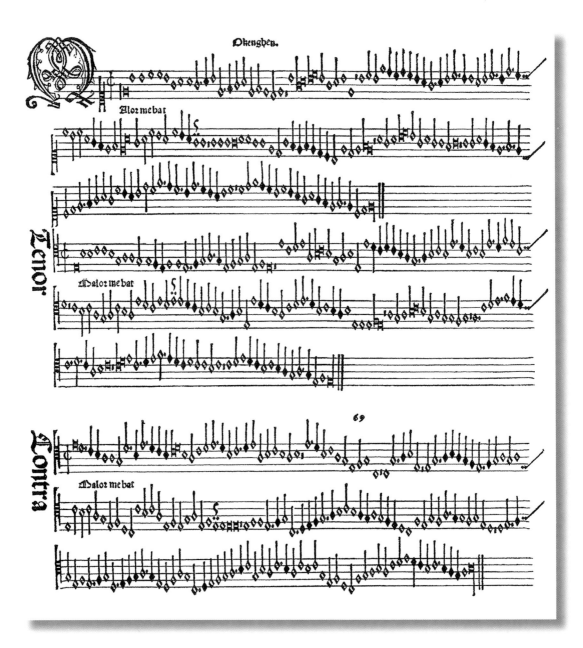

Petrucci's Harmonice Musices Odhecaton A

(1501)

A pioneering Renaissance printer introduces movable type to print the score of complex polyphonic songs, thereby preserving the main international repertoire of his day. His finest collection is a triumph in art and technology.

Ottaviano Petrucci (1466–1539) is remembered for his inventions in fine music printing using movable type. Born and raised in Fossombrone, Petrucci went to Venice to learn the art of printing at the height of the Italian Renaissance. A few years later he petitioned the Venetian Senate for the privilege to market a valuable new invention, saying he had devised a way to print *"canto figurato"* using movable type—something that "many, not only in Italy but also outside of Italy, have long attempted in vain." His efforts bore fruit, for in 1498 he obtained the exclusive twenty-year license to print and sell such music throughout the republic.

Three years later, Petrucci published a magnificent collection of music, mostly Flemish chansons that had been written by leading composers of the time, which he titled *Harmonice Musices Odhecaton A*. The anthology included ninety-six secular and polyphonic songs for three or four voice parts, written in strict fixed forms.

To capture the extraordinarily complex polyphonic sounds of his day, the pioneer had devised an ingenious but demanding technique requiring two separate printing impressions using metal movable type—one for the staves and one for the notes placed on them. When lyrics were involved, each sheet was actually printed three times—for the staves, the music, and the words—all coordinated on the same page. His innovative layout displayed two parts on the right-hand side of a page, and two parts on the left, thereby enabling four singers or instrumentalists to follow the same music sheet during their performance.

Besides showing great technological prowess, his work turned the publication of the most complex music into fine art. His printing was magnificently executed with exquisite typefaces and other fine features, although occasionally the impressions were not perfectly coordinated, resulting in a jumbled display that caused havoc with the musicians. Nevertheless Petrucci managed to turn the mass production of his art form into a commercially successful business—so much so that he later had to compete with rivals.

The first edition of the *Odhecaton*, carrying a dedication date of May 15, 1501, has not survived in its entirety. But the second and third editions of 1503 and 1504 remain. Without it, today's listeners would not be familiar with the music of Petrucci's period.

LEFT: This woodcut from Silvestro Ganassi's musical instruction book of 1535 shows a group of recorder players using printed sheet music.

Martin Luther's
Ninety-Five Theses

(1517)

An Augustinian monk posts a document containing ninety-five criticisms of the practices of the Catholic Church on a church in Saxony—thereby unintentionally providing the catalyst for a series of world-changing events that will become known as Europe's Protestant Reformation.

Born to prosperous parents in Eisleben, Saxony (now Germany), which was part of the Holy Roman Empire, Martin Luther (1483–1546) grew up to be a pious but little-known Augustinian monk and scholar. But he was about to become a major figure in world history as a result of a provocative document he had composed.

On October 31, 1517, Luther used a hammer and nail to post a paper on the side door of the Castle Church of Wittenberg, to alert the parish. Penned in Latin as *Disputatio pro declaratione virtutis indulgentiarum* ("Ninety-Five Theses on the Power and Efficacy of Indulgences"), his offering was intended to prompt discussion within the Church. But it struck a nerve.

"Out of love for the truth and from desire to elucidate it," he began, "the Reverend Father Martin Luther, Master of Arts and Sacred Theology, and ordinary lecturer therein at Wittenberg, intends to defend the following statements and to dispute on them in that place. Therefore he asks that those who cannot be present and dispute with him orally shall do so in their absence by letter." Then Luther proceeded to list his ninety-five theses, one by one. "1. When our Lord and Master Jesus Christ said, 'Repent' (Mt 4:17), he willed the entire life of believers to be one of repentance…"

The litany attacked officials at all levels of the Catholic Church, alleging a stew of clerical corruption and abuses that included nepotism, usury, and the sale of indulgences (defined by the Church as "remissions of temporal punishment, especially purgatorial atonement, due for sins after absolution"). It also questioned some core Catholic practices and beliefs.

Luther sent copies of his thesis to his bishop and the archbishop who was in charge of the indulgence sales. The fact that many Church officials had resorted to selling indulgences as a means of obtaining financial support made it a touchy subject for anyone to raise, even indirectly. Luther brazenly alleged that the practice violated the original intention of confession and penance, and rattled off other embarrassing criticisms as well.

Within a few months his diatribe was being translated into a number of languages and circulated across Europe. Luther's document sparked the schism within Western Christianity that became known as the Protestant Reformation, and Luther and other Christian reformers who were protesting Catholic orthodoxy became known as Protestants.

RIGHT: Although the original manuscript posted on the door has not survived, two broadside editions of the Ninety-Five Theses document—one printed in Nuremberg, the other in Leipzig—remain preserved. There is also a copy of a seven-page quarto edition at Harvard College Library.

Amore et studio elucidande veritatis: hec subscripta disputabuntur Wittenberge. Presidente R. P. Martino Luther: Artiū et S. Theologie Magistro: eiusdemqz ibidem lectore Ordinario. Quare petit: ut qui non possunt verbis presentes nobis cū disceptare: agant id literis absentes. In noie dñi nostri iesu christi. Amē.

1 Dominus et magister noster Iesus christus dicendo. Penitentiā agite, etc. omnē vitam fideliū penitentiam esse voluit.

2 Quod verbū de penitentia sacramentali (id est confessionis et satisfactiōis que sacerdotum ministerio celebratur) non pōt intelligi.

3 Non tñ solam intendit interiorē: immo interior nulla est. nisi foris operetur varias carnis mortificationes.

4 Manet itaqz pena donec manet odiū sui (id est penitentia vera intus) scz vsqz ad introitum regni celoꝝ.

5 Papa nō vult nec pōt villas penas remittere. pter eas: quas arbitrio vel suo vel canonum imposuit.

6 Papa nō pōt remittere villā culpā nisi declarando et approbando remissam a deo. Aut certe remittendo casus reseruatos sibi: quibus ptēptis culpa prorsus remaneret.

7 Nulli prorsus remittit deus culpā: quin simul eū subijciat: humiliatū in omnibus: sacerdoti suo vicario.

8 Canones penitētiales solū viuētibus sunt impositi. nihilqz morituris sm eosdē debet imponi.

9 Inde bñ nobis facit spūssctūs in papa. excipiendo in suis decretis sp articulū mortis et necessitatis.

10 Indocte et male faciūt sacerdotes ij: qui morituris phias canonicas in purgatorium reseruant.

11 Zizania illa de mutanda pena Canonica in penam purgatorij. vident certe dormientibus episcopis seminata.

12 Olim pene canonice nō post: sed ante absolutionem imponebantur: tanqz tentamenta vere contritionis.

13 Morituri morte omnia soluunt. et legibus canonū mortui iam sunt. habentes iure earum relaxationem.

14 Imperfecta sanitas seu charitas morituri: necessario secum fert magnū timorē: tantoqz maiorē: quāto minor fuerit ipsa.

15 Hic timor et horror satis est. se solo (vt alea taceā) facere penā purgatorij: cum sit primus desperationis horrori.

16 Vident infernus: purgatoriū: celum differre: sicut desperatio: ppe desperatio. securitas differunt.

17 Necessariū videt aiabus in purgatorio: sicut minui horrore. ita augeri charitatem.

18 Nec probatum videt vllis: aut rōnibus aut scripturis. qz sint extra statū meriti seu augende charitatis.

19 Nec hoc probatū esse videt: qz sint de sua beatitudine certe et secure saltē oēs. licz nos certissimi sumus.

20 Igitur papa per remissionē plenariā oim penaꝝ. nō simpliciter oim. intelligit: sed a seipso tantūmodo impositaꝝ.

21 Errant itaqz indulgētiaꝝ pdicatores. ij: qui dicūt per pape indulgētias: hoiem ab oĩ pena solui et saluari.

22 Quin nullā remittit aiabus in purgatorio: quā in hac vita debuissent sm Canonē soluere.

23 Si remissio villa oim oino penaꝝ: pōt alicui dari. certū est eā nō nisi pfectissimis. i. paucissimis dari.

24 Falli ob id necesse est: maioꝛē partē popli: per indifferentē illā et magnificam pene solute pmissionem.

25 Qualē ptātem hz papa in purgatoriū gñaliter: talem hz quilibet Episcopus et Curatus in sua diocesi et parochia specialiter.

1 Optime facit papa: qz nō prate clauis (quā nullā hz) sed per modū suffragij dat aiabus remissionem.

2 Hoiem predicāt. qui statim vt iactus nummus in cistam tinnierit: euolare dicunt animā.

3 Certū est. nūmo in cistā tinniente: augeri questū et auaricia posse. suffragium aūt ecclesie: in arbitrio dei soli9 est.

4 Quis scit. si oēs aie in purgatorio velint redimi. sicut de. s. Seuerino et paschali factū narratur.

5 Nullus est securus de veritate sue cōtritiōis. multominus de cōsecutione plenarie remissionis.

6 Quā rar9 est ve penitēs: tā rar9 est ve indulgētias redimens. i. rarissim9.

7 Dānabunt ineternū cū suis magistris: qui p lras veniaꝝ securos sese credunt de sua salute.

8 Cauendi sunt nimis: qui dicūt venias illas Pape: donū esse illud dei inestimabile: quo reconciliatur hōmo deo.

9 Gratie eñ ille venialcs: tantū respiciunt penas satisfactiōis sacramētalis ab homie constitutas.

10 Non christiana predicāt: qui docent. qz redemptoꝝ anias vel cōfessionalia nō sit necessaria contritio.

11 Quilibet christianus vere cōpunctus: hz remissionē plenariā: a pena et culpa. etiam sine lris veniaꝝ sibi debitā.

12 Quilibet verus christianus: siue viuus siue mortu9: hz participationē oim bonoꝝ Chri et Ecclesie. etiā sine lris veniaꝝ a deo sibi datam.

13 Remissio tñ et participatio Pape: nullo mō est spmenda. qz (vt dixi) est declaratio remissionis diuine.

14 Difficillimū est: etiā doctissimis Theologꝝ simul extollere veniaꝝ largitatem: et contritiōis veritatē coram populo.

15 Contritionis veritas penas querit et amat. Veniaꝝ aūt largitas relaxat: et odisse facit saltem occasione.

16 Caute sunt venie apsce pdicande. ne populus false intelligat. eas pferri ceteris bonis opibus charitatis.

17 Docendi sunt christiani. qz Pape mens nō est: redemptione veniaꝝ vlla ex parte cōparandā esse opibus misericordie.

18 Docendi sunt christiani. qz dans pauperi: aut mutuans egenti: meli9 facit: qz si venias redimeret.

19 Quia p opus charitatis crescit charitas: et fit hō melior. sed p venias nō fit melior: sed tm liberior a pena.

20 Docendi sunt chriani. qz qui videt egenū: et neglecto eo. dat p venijs: nō indulgētias Pape: sed indignationē dei sibi vendicat.

21 Docendi sunt chriani. qz nisi sup fluū abundent: necessaria tenenꝝ domui sue retinere: et nequaqz pter venias effundere.

22 Docendi sunt christiani. qz redemptio veniaꝝ est libera: nō precepta.

23 Docendi sunt chriani. qz Papa sicut magis eget: ita magis optat in veniis dandis pro se deuotam orationem: qz pmptam pecuniam.

14 Docendi sunt christiani. qz venie Pape sunt vtiles: si nō in eas confidant. Sed nocentissime: si timorem dei per eas amittant.

15 Docendi sunt chriani. qz si Papa nosset exactiones venialiū pdicatorum: mallet Basilicā. s. Petri in cineres ire: qz edificari. cute carne et ossibus ouium suaꝝ.

1 Docendi sunt chriani. qz Papa sicut debet ita vellet. etiam vendita (si opus sit) Basilica. s. Petri: de suis pecunijs dare illis: a quoꝝ plurimis quidā cōcionatores veniaꝝ pecuniam elciunt.

2 Uana est fiducia salutis p lras veniaꝝ. etiā si Cōmissarius: immo papa ipse suā aiam p illis impigneraret.

3 Hostes chri et Pape sunt ij: qui pter venias pdicandas verbū dei in alijs ecclesijs penitus silere iubent.

4 Iniuria fit verbo dei: dū in eodē sermone: equale vel longius tēpus impenditur venijs qz illi.

5 Mens Pape necessario est. qz si venie (qz minimum est) vna cāpana: vnis pompis: et ceremonijs celebranꝝ. Euangelium (qz maximū est) centū campanis: centū pompis: centū ceremonijs predicetur.

6 Thesauri ecclesie vñ Papa dat indulgētias: neqz satis noiati sunt: neqz cogniti apud christi.

7 Temporales certe nō esse patet. qz nō tā facile eos pfundit: sz tmmō colligunt multi concionatoꝝ.

8 Nec sunt merita Chri et sctoꝝ. qz hec sp sine papa opeꝛnt gram hois interioris: et cruce: morte: infernumqz exterioris.

9 Thesauros ecclesie. s. Laurēt dixit esse: paupes ecclie. sz locutus est vsu vocabuli sui tpe.

10 Sine temeritate dicim9 claues ecclie: merito Chri donatas: esse thesaurum istum.

11 Claꝝ est eñ. qz ad remissionē penaꝝ et casuū sola sufficit ptās Pape.

12 Uerus thesaurus ecclie: est sacrosctā euāgeliū glorie et gratie dei.

13 Hic aūt est merito odiosissimus. qz ex primis facit nouissimos.

14 Thesaurus aūt indulgentiaꝝ merito est gratissimus. qz ex nouissimis facit primos.

15 Igitur thesauri Euangelici rhetia sunt: quibus olim piscabant viros diuitiarum.

16 Thesauri indulgentiaꝝ rhetia sunt: qbus nūc piscanꝝ diuitias viroꝝ.

17 Indulgētie: quas cōcionatores vociferant maximas gras. intelligunt vere tales: quoad questum pmouendum.

18 Sunt tamen re vera minime ad gram dei et crucis pietatē compate.

19 Tenent Epi et Curati venias: apsicaꝝ Cōmissarios cū omni reuerentia admittere.

20 Sed magis tenent oibus oculis intendere: oibus aurib9 aduertere: ne p cōmissione Pape sua illi somnia pdicent.

21 Cōtra veniaꝝ apsicaꝝ vitatē qz loquit. sit ille anathema et maledict9.

22 Qui vero contra libidine ac licentiā verboꝝ Cōcionatoꝛes veniaꝝ curam agit: sit ille benedictus.

23 Sicut Papa iuste fulminat eos: qui in fraudem negocij veniaꝝ quacunqz arte machinantur.

24 Multomagis fulminare intendit eos: qui p veniaꝝ pretextū in fraudem scte charitatis et veritatis machinant.

25 Opinari venias papales tātas esse: vt soluere possint hoiem. etiā si p impossibile dei genitricē violasset. Est insanire.

1 Dicimus contra. qz venie papales: nec minimū venialium pctoꝝ tollere possint quo ad culpam.

2 Qz df. nec s. s. Petrus modo Papa esset: maiores gras donare poss est blasphemia in s. Petrum et Papam.

3 Dicimus contra. qz etiā iste et quilibet papa maiores hz. scz Euangelium: virtutes: gras curationū. etc. vt. i. Co. iij.

4 Dicere. Crucē armis papalibus insigniter erectā: cruci christi equiualere: blasphemia est.

5 Rationē reddent Epi: Curati: et Theologi. Qui tales sermones in populum licere sinunt.

6 Facit hec licētiosa veniaꝝ pdicatio. vt nec reuerentiā Pape facile sit: etiā doctis vir? redimere a calūnijs aut certe argut? qstiōib9 laicoꝝ.

7 Scz. Cur papa nō euacuat purgatoriū pter scrissimā charitatē: et summā aiarū necessitatē: vt cām oīm iustissimā. Si infinitas aias redimit: pter pecuniā funestissimā ad structurā Basilice: vt cās leuissimā.

8 Itē. Cur manent exequie et anniuersaria defunctoꝝ: et nō reddit aut recipi pmittit bñficia p illis instituta. cū iā sit iniuria p redēptꝝ orare.

9 Itē. Que illa noua pietas Dei et Pape. qz impio et inimico. pter pecuniā pcedat: aiam piā et amicā dei redimere. Et tñ pter necessitatē ipsius met pie et dilecte aniae nō redimunt eā gratuita charitate.

10 Itē. Cur Canones phiales re ipa et nō vsu: iā diu in semet abrogati et mortui: adhuc tñ pecunijs redimunt per pcessionē indulgētiaꝝ tanqz viuacissimi.

11 Itē. Cur Papa cui9 opes hodie sunt opulentissimis crassis crassiores: nō de suo pecunijs magz qz paupꝝ fideliū struit vnā tmmō Basilicā sancti Petri.

12 Item. Quid remittit aut participat Papa iis: qui p ptritionē pfectam ius habēt plenarie remissionis et participationis.

13 Item. Quid adderet ecclie boni maioris. Si Papa sicut semel facit: ita cēties in die cuilibz fideliū has remissiōes et pticipationes tribueret.

14 Ex quo Papa salutē querit aiaꝝ: qz venias magz: qz pecunias. Cur suspendit lras et venias iam olim ocessas: cū sint eque efficaces.

15 Hec scrupulosissima laicoꝝ argumēta: sola prate opescere: nec reddita ratione diluere. Est ecclesiā et Papā hostib9 ridendos exponere: et infelices christianos facere.

16 Si ergo venie sm spiritu et mente Pape pdicarentur. facile illa oĩa soluerent: immo nō essent.

17 Valeāt itaqz oēs illi pphetæ. qui dicūt ppro Chri. Pax pax. et nō est pax.

18 Bñ agāt oēs illi pphetæ. qui dicūt ppro Chri. Crux crux. et non est crux.

19 Exhortandi sunt Christiani: vt caput suū chrm per penas: mortes: infernosqz sequi studeant.

20 Ac it magis p multas tribulatiōes intrare celū: qz p securitatē pacis confidant.

W. D. Xvij.

Doctor Martini Luthers offen=
liche Verhör zü Worms im Reichs tag/
Red/ Vnd Widerred Am. 17. tag/
Aprilis/ Jm jar 1 5 2 1
❧ Beschechen ❦

Copia ainer Missiue/ Doctor Martinus Luther nachsei=
nem abschid zü Worms zü rugck an die Chürfür
sten/ Fürsten/ Vñ stend des Reichs da selbst
verschriben gesamlet hatt.

ABOVE: This "tabloid" report issued shortly after the Diet of Worms shows a seated Charles V with Johann Eck on the left and Luther on the right. Luther's books are in the center.

Edict of Worms

(1521)

The Holy Roman Emperor Charles V issues a decree at Worms in Germany, labeling the Church critic Martin Luther as a heretic and banning his writings. But the document has the opposite effect, elevating the dissident's stature within the growing Protestant Reformation.

After Martin Luther posted his Ninety-Five Theses, Pope Leo X initially thought the fracas would blow over, but in June 1520 his advisors convinced him to publicly denounce the defiant monk. The papal bull *Exsurge Domine* ("Arise, O Lord") attacked Luther for forty-one specific "errors" and threatened to excommunicate him unless he recanted within sixty days. Pope Leo also had some of Luther's problematic writings publicly burned.

But Luther refused to comply and instead issued his own polemical tracts attacking the papacy; then he publicly torched a copy of the bull—acts of rebellion that were unprecedented in Church history.

For this he was subsequently summoned to appear before an imperial diet (formal deliberative assembly) that was called to examine the matter. The Diet of Worms was held at the Heylshof Garden, with Emperor Charles V presiding.

After Luther stated his views, the emperor's agent, Johann Eck, called him a heretic and private conferences were started to determine Luther's fate. But before a decision had been reached, and knowing he faced likely conviction and execution, Luther absconded.

On May 25, 1521, Emperor Charles V issued a formal decree, known as the Edict of Worms, in which he labeled Luther a "reviver of the old and condemned heresies" and an "inventor of new ones." The document ordered Luther's books burned and his property confiscated. It severed him from the Church, called for his arrest, and forbade anyone from harboring or sustaining the fugitive. Anyone who failed to obey or opposed the decree in any way, it said, "will be guilty of the crime of *lese majeste* and will incur our grave indignation as well as each of the punishments mentioned above."

Luther, however, continued to flaunt the pope's authority and get away with it. After spending some time in hiding, he returned to Wittenberg where he devoted himself to building a new church based on his reformist ideas. He also married a nun and the couple had six children.

Luther's church became the leading faith in his region and its popularity spread. Consequently, the secular authorities concluded that it would not be wise to attempt to enforce the Edict of Worms. Lutheranism continued to spread throughout northern Europe and planted the seeds of dissent for Calvinism and other varieties of Protestantism.

Martin Luther died in 1546 and was buried beneath the pulpit of the church where he had posted his famous document, the Ninety-Five Theses.

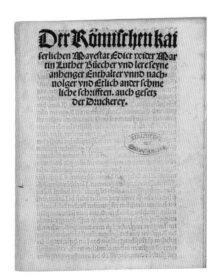

LEFT: The title page of the Edict of Worms. This formal notice called for the excommunication of Luther from the Catholic Church. It stripped him of the right to a fair trial and prohibited the dissemination of his teachings.

Journal of Magellan's Voyage

(1522–25)

A scholarly shipmate of Ferdinand Magellan documents the events of their epic around-the-globe voyage that have cost the explorer his life and changed the course of world history. Of the 237 mariners who embarked, only eighteen have survived the three-year ordeal.

Ferdinand Magellan (1480–1521) was a Portuguese-born explorer sailing at the service of Spain by order of King Charles I on a major expedition to the Indies. A total of 237 men set out from Seville in five vessels in August 1519. Although most of the crew were Spaniards, their ranks also included a mixture of Portuguese, Italians, Greeks, and Frenchmen, as well as different classes. Among those closest to Magellan were his brother-in-law, his indentured servant, and Antonio Pigafetta (1490/91–1534), a Venetian scholar who would serve as Magellan's assistant and act as the explorer's liaison to the natives when they established first contact. He was also the official chronicler of the expedition.

Pigafetta had kept a meticulous daily journal of the voyage around the world in 1519–22, recording their discoveries and hardships in rich detail. Although Magellan would end up being largely credited for leading the first successful voyage to circumnavigate the globe, he had been slain in combat with natives in the Philippines midway through the odyssey—an event that Pigafetta recounts with deep sadness, ending with the passage, "they killed our mirror, our light, our comfort, and our true guide."

After the commander's death it fell to Juan Sebastián Elcano to captain the rest of their exploration, which he managed to do. Only 7 percent of the voyagers would survive the nightmare of fear, hunger, disease, storms, warfare, mutiny, and homicide. A feeble Elcano and his skeleton crew, including Pigafetta, arrived back in Seville on the only remaining vessel almost exactly three years after they had started.

Many historians consider Magellan's expedition the greatest in history. It was the first to reach Asia by sailing westward from Europe—achieving what Columbus had failed to do in 1492—and was the first voyage to circumnavigate the globe, covering an astonishing 43,400 miles under rough conditions in what was probably the greatest feat of seamanship in history.

Although the original log was later lost, Pigafetta's extraordinary account, which he wrote between 1522 and 1525, has survived in four manuscript versions. The finest copy, written in French in numbered chapters and richly illustrated with beautiful maps, is held in the Beinecke Library of Yale University. Remarkably, the *Journal of Magellan's First Voyage around the World* was not published in its entirety until the late eighteenth century. Pigafetta's straightforward and readable narrative includes fascinating descriptions of some of the places and cultures the explorers encountered around the globe. Little is known about his own fate after he penned the document.

RIGHT: A page from the Beinecke Library manuscript version of Pigafetta's log. Pigafetta's chronicle of Magellan's voyage around the world included twenty-three maps. This one shows the southern tip of South America and the eponymous Strait of Magellan, which was discovered on their expedition.

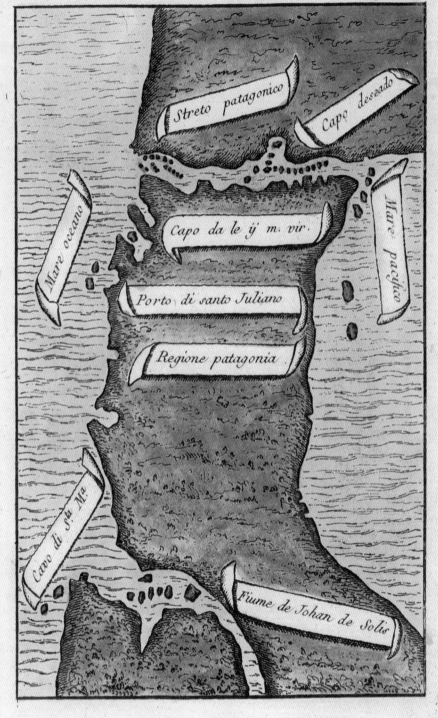

Parecer de fray br.me de las Casas

çerca delos yndios

q en lo q toca al remedio delos yndios de todas las yndias y
a la manera q se deve tener p̃a q sean x̃panos y se conser
uen en las vidas y en su libertad y no los acaben de
destruir los españoles: no ay otro rremedio ni modo ni
orden sino q su mag.t los encorpore en su real coro
na como sus vasallos q son quitando todas las encomie
das q estan hechas en todas las yndias y no dando
vno ni ningun yndio a español por encomienda ni
por vasallo ni en feudo ni de otra qualquiera manera
porq segun la larga y muy cierta experiencia q se tiene
de qualquiera m̃a q de españoles se den los an
de matar y destruir por sus ardias de oro y riquezas
y por tanto hazer el contrario es contra la ley de dios
y gran pecado mortal, y en gradissimo perjuizio y
destruicion del patrimonjo real de su mag.t

çerca dela bivienda delos españoles

y la poblacion y bivienda de españoles en las yndias
es muy necessaria asi p̃a la conversion y policia delos yndios
como p̃a sustentar el estado y señorio q su mag.t y delos
reyes de castilla en las yndias. Esta poblacion y bivienda
delos españoles en aqllos reynos y t̃ras se puede muy
bien hazer y sustentar sin encomiendas ni serujcio de
yndios como en todas las otras partes del mundo se hi
zieron las poblaçones sin serujrse de yndios porq no
se lee en njnguna escriptura q los q yvan a poblar el
t̃ras nuevas tyranjzasen y opprimjesen alas gentes que
en ellos hallavan y se sirviesen dellas contra su ṽlad
volutad y en perjuizio y detrimeto de su libertad
y de sus vidas proprias y sus mugeres y hijos: sino
fuesen tyranos y crueles y robadores como lo era
nembroth q opprimja los pobres y como hasta oy se an
avido y haze en las yndias /. es pues la manera q en
sustentar la d̃a poblacion y bivienda delos españoles se
deve tener, q su mag.t haga muchas m̃des alos t̃ales
pobladores espeçialmente labradores y gente trabajadora
y provechosa dandoles muchas y muy largas t̃ras y
aguas y m̃tes no quitando los alos yndios las q
tiene y oviere menester p̃a sus sementeras y sustento.

Destruction of the Indies

(1542)

A conquistador undergoes a change of heart regarding his nation's brutal colonial policies in the Americas. His documentation of Spanish genocide and enslavement of the indigenous peoples helps to prevent the Indians' extinction but contributes to another atrocity: the rise of the African slave trade.

Bartolomé de las Casas (1484–1566) was a Spanish-born colonist who immigrated to Hispaniola (now the Dominican Republic and Haiti) in 1502. His father Pedro had sailed with Columbus. The son participated in slave raids and slaughters against the native peoples there and in other parts of the West Indies. But he became appalled by many of the atrocities he had witnessed and later confessed, "I saw here cruelty on a scale no living being has ever seen or expects to see."

By 1515, Las Casas had become so convinced that Spain's actions in the New World were illegal and unjust, that he began to openly criticize the *encomienda* system that legitimized such treatment. He became a Dominican friar in 1523 and began documenting acts of horrific mistreatment of the Indians, based on events he had witnessed firsthand, and then took his litany to Spain to make a direct appeal before the Holy Roman Emperor and King, Charles V.

In the official proceedings held in 1542, Las Casas presented his passionate eyewitness narrative of the abuses along with sweeping proposals for radical reform.

ABOVE: *The cover of Las Casas's* Short Account of the Destruction of the Indies.

LEFT: *Bartolomé de las Casas's "Statement of Opinion" was sent to Charles V in 1542. In this document, Las Casas questioned Spanish policies to the "Indians of the New World," including conquest, conversion, servitude, and slavery.*

"It is my fervent hope," he wrote, "that, once Your Highness perceives the extent of the injustices suffered by these innocent peoples and the way in which they are being destroyed and crushed underfoot, unjustly and for no other reason than to satisfy the greed and ambition of those whose purpose it is to commit such wicked atrocities, Your Highness will see fit to beg and entreat His Majesty to refuse all those who seek royal licence for such evil and detestable ventures."

His pleas were so effective that on November 20, 1542, the Emperor signed a series of measures known as the New Laws, which forbade all taking of Indians as slaves, set in motion the gradual abolition of the *encomienda* system, and exempted the few surviving Indians of Hispaniola, Cuba, Puerto Rico, and Jamaica from compulsory servitude. The Emperor also removed certain oppressive colonial officials. But the reforms were met by intense resistance among the slaveholders back in the New World.

Published in Seville in 1552 by Sebastian Trugillo, *A Short Account of the Destruction of the Indies* broke new ground in exposing Spain's hideous treatment of native peoples during the early stages of conquest. The impassioned firsthand account was widely translated and republished by Spain's adversaries and rivals. Although some critics have blamed Las Casas for contributing to the African slave trade—he had once advocated the use of African slaves instead of West Indian natives—he eventually spoke out against that practice as well. Today he has become widely regarded as an early opponent of slavery and one of the founding fathers of universal human rights.

Gregorian Calendar (Inter Gravissimas)

(1582)

After detecting an error in the existing civil calendar from Julius Caesar's time, the Pope issues a document of enormous practical and political significance. But his order has no power beyond the Catholic Church and the Papal States—so how and when will others respond?

Since becoming Pope Gregory XIII in 1572, Ugo Boncampagni (1502–85) had sought to reform the Catholic Church according to the recommendations of the Council of Trent that had been spurred by the Protestant Reformation. His most far-reaching action was the attempt to correct mistakes of the calendar that Caesar had introduced in 46 BC.

Although the Julian calendar had proved far superior to the lunar calendar, astronomers had since determined that it turned out to be slow by one day every 128 years because its calculation of 365.25 days to a year was eleven minutes, ten seconds too great. This posed theological problems for the Church, in part because the scheduling of the crucial holiday of Easter was based on the vernal equinox and the moon's phases. Gregory's counselors wanted him to suppress ten days, in order to adjust Easter's timing and prevent other problems. He ended up relying on two leading astronomers, Aloysius Lilius and Christopher Clavius, to advise him in the calculations.

On February 24, 1582, Pope Gregory XIII issued a bull "to restore" the calendar so that seasonal events critical for the calculation of Easter dates would be back in their "proper places."

The document precisely explained in Latin what needed to be done and why. The number of leap years was reduced and the date of Easter was to be set according to a new method—"To the greater glory of God." Of greatest practical concern was the fact that in order to make the adjustment, October 4, 1582 was to be followed by October 15, 1582.

Although the pope's text ordered Church officials to carry out his plan, his language was careful to merely ask, exhort, or recommend such changes to the civil authorities, who after all were not beholden to papal control. In fact, the rulers of several non-Catholic countries initially refused to adopt the provisions. The British Parliament did not accept them until 1750 and they only took effect in England and its colonies in 1752.

Many English subjects didn't like hearing that the government was going to remove eleven days from the calendar. But the American scientist and statesman Benjamin Franklin endorsed the idea, saying, "It is pleasant for an old man to be able to go to bed on September 2, and not have to get up until September 14."

LEFT: Christopher Clavius (1538–1612), the mathematician and astronomer who helped modify the proposal for the Gregorian calendar after the death of its primary author Aloysius Lilius (1510–76).

RIGHT: The original papal bull is kept in the Vatican archives. The Latin title Inter Gravissimas *is an abbreviation of the opening line of the document, which translates as "Among our gravest concerns."*

CALENDARIVM GREGORIANVM PERPETVVM.

Orbi Christiano vniuerso à Gregorio XIII. P. M. propositum. Anno M. D. LXXXII.

GREGORIVS EPISCOPVS

SERVVS SERVORVM DEI

AD PERPETVAM REI MEMORIAM.

NTER grauissimas Pastoralis officij nostri curas,ea postrema non est,vt quæ à sacro Tridentino Concilio Sedi Apostolicæ reseruata sunt, illa ad finem optatum, Deo adiutore, perducantur. Sane eiusdem Concilij Patres, cum ad reliquam cogitationem Breuiarij quoque curam adiungerent, tempore tamen exclusi rem totam ex ipsius Concilij decreto ad auctoritatem, & iudicium Romani Pontificis retulerunt. Duo autem Breuiario præcipue continentur;quorum vnum preces , laudesq. diuinas festis, profestisque diebus persoluendas complectitur,alterum pertinet ad annuos Paschæ, festorumque ex eo pendentium recursus, Solis, & Lunæ motu metiendos: Atque illud quidem felicis recordationis Pius V. prædecessor noster absoluendum curauit, atque edidit. Hoc vero, quod nimirum exigit legitimam Calendarij restitutionem, iam diu à Romanis Pontificibus prædecessoribus nostris, & sæpius tentatum est, verum absolui, & ad exitum perduci ad hoc vsque tempus non potuit; quod rationes emendandi Calendarij,quæ à cælestium motuum peritis proponebantur, propter magnas, & fere inextricabiles difficultates, quas huiusmodi emendatio semper habuit, neque perennes erant, neque antiquos Ecclesiasticos ritus incolumes (quod in primis hac in re curaudum erat) seruabant. Dum itaque nos quoque credita nobis, licet indigni, à Deo dispensatione freti in hac cogitatione,curaque versaremur,allatus est nobis liber à dilecto filio Antonio Lilio artium,& medicinæ doctore, quem quondam Aloysius eius germanus frater conscripserat , in quo per nouum quendam Epactarum Cyclum ab eo excogitatum, & ad certam ipsius Aurei numeri normam directum,atque ad quamcumque anni solaris magnitudinem accommodatum,omnia,quæ in Calendario collapsa sunt, constanti ratione , & seculis omnibus duratura,sic restitui posse ostendit : vt Calendarium ipsum nulli vnquam mutationi in posterum expositum esse videatur. Nouam hanc restituendi Calendarij rationem exiguo volumine comprehensam ad Christianos Principes , celebrioresq. vniuersitates paucos ante annos misimus, vt res, quæ omnium communis est , communi etiam omnium consilio perficeretur ; illi cum, quæ maxime optabamus,concordes respondissent, eorum nos omnium consensione adducti,viros ad Calendarij emendationem adhibuimus in alma Vrbe harum rerum peritissimos, quos longe ante ex primarijs Christiani orbis nationibus delegeramus : Ii cum multum temporis , & diligentiæ ad eam lucubrationem adhibuissent , & Cyclos tam veterum , quàm recentiorum vndique conquisitos, ac diligentissime perpensos inter se contulissent ,suo, & doctorum hominum qui de ea re scripserunt , iudicio hunc præ cæteris elegerunt Epactarum Cyclum, cui nonnulla etiam adiecerunt, quæ ex accurata circumspectione visa sunt ad Calendarij perfectionem maxime pertinere .

Considerantes igitur nos, ad rectam Paschalis festi celebrationem iuxta sanctorum Patrum, ac veterum Romanorum Pontificum , præsertim Pij & Victoris primorum, nec non magni illius œcumenici Concilij Nicæni , & aliorum sanctiones , tria necessario coniungenda, & statuenda esse, primù certam Verni æquinoctij sedem , deinde rectam positionem xiiij. lunæ primi Mensis,quæ vel in ipsum æquinoctij diem incidit , vel ei proxime succedit, postremo primum quemque diem Dominicum , qui eandem xiiij. lunam sequitur,curauimus non solum æquinoctium Vernum in pristinam sedem, à qua iam à Concilio Nicæno decem circiter diebus recessit,restituendum; & xiiij. Paschalem suo in loco , à quo quatuor , & eo amplius dies hoc tempore distat, reponendam;sed viam quoque tradendam, & rationem, qua caueatur,vt in posterum æquinoctium,et xiiij.luna à proprijs sedibus nunquam dimoueatur.

B   tur

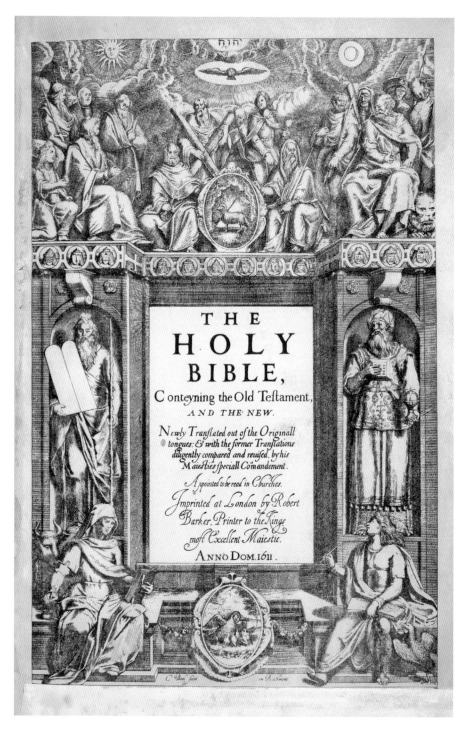

ABOVE: The engraved title page of the King James Bible was the first bible in the English language to include an illustration of the Trinity: the Father, the Son, and the Holy Ghost.

62_____100 Documents that Changed the World

King James Bible

(1611)

Although the revision derives from a ruler's largely political considerations, and the translation is produced by committee, the King James Bible is a literary masterpiece as well as one of the most influential documents ever created—a triumph of language.

Shortly after taking England's throne following the death of Queen Elizabeth, King James I (1566–1625) met at Hampton Court Palace with Church of England representatives and Puritan leaders regarding certain thorny matters of church doctrine.

The Scotsman struck some observers as vulgar and impatient, with a tongue that was "too big for his mouth." But James was also a clever politician, and he floated the notion of making a new translation of the Bible to replace the existing English-language version of 1568, believing that this might serve to bring together different Protestant factions and help him to achieve other political objectives. The idea was well received.

James ordered a new translation from the Greek, Hebrew, Aramaic, and Latin, calling for a committee of forty-seven elite and approved scholars from Oxford, Cambridge, and Westminster to carry out the task. Their diligent work would require shading certain meanings here and there to suit the King's purpose, making the process as much a revision as a translation. It was also perfectly timed to take advantage of new advancements in printing and English colonization and hegemony.

Each working group used as its base an identical unbound copy of the Bishops' Bible, 1602 edition, which had been specially printed for them to duly record their committee's precise revisions in the margins, which would later be copied into the other committee's copy, one by one, according to a strictly uniform procedure. Issues of grammar, spelling, and biblical meaning all had to be minutely scrutinized, which was in itself a monumental undertaking.

Two partial transcripts by John Bois (1560–1643), lead secretary of the committee, have survived. Dating from 1608, they were discovered in 1964, along with a bound set of marked-up corrections to one of the forty bibles used. They are held at Oxford University.

Work on the new translation took place during a literary Renaissance in England when authors such as William Shakespeare, Ben Jonson, and Sir Francis Bacon were producing some of their finest works. The committee's final version of the King James Bible rivals these greats in its masterful language.

After its approval, the book was first issued by the King's printer, Robert Barker, in 1611 as a complete folio Bible. Measuring 16 inches high, the loose-leaf version was sold for ten shillings and the bound version cost twelve.

Known as the King James Bible or the Authorized Version, the work exerted a profound influence on the English language, culture, and politics.

ABOVE: This rare leather-bound edition of the Bible belonged to King James's own son, Henry Frederick, Prince of Wales. It is held at Washington National Cathedral Rare Book Library.

Mayflower Compact

(1620)

Before venturing ashore into an unsettled and lawless land in America, a majority of passengers aboard the Mayflower form a compact that binds the signers into a "Civil Body Politic" that will enact "just and equal Laws . . . for the general good of the Colony"—an agreement to live together under the rule of law.

The *Mayflower*'s stormy 3,000-mile crossing of the Atlantic had not been easy. To make matters worse, upon reaching the North American coast in late autumn the captain realized they were at Cape Cod, not near the mouth of the Hudson River as stipulated by their charter. Rather than risking more dangerous time at sea, he decided they would have to land there instead.

The change of plan posed many problems. The 102 persons aboard were divided over what to do next. There were forty-one English Pilgrims—families of Calvinist religious dissenters calling themselves "Saints"—who had fled Europe to escape persecution. The rest (whom the Pilgrims called "Strangers") included English merchants, craftsmen, skilled workers and indentured servants, and four young orphans.

Some of the Strangers now argued that, once they set foot on the land, they would no longer be subject to any law, since both maritime rules and the jurisdiction of the Virginia Company no longer applied there. Hence, upon leaving the ship they would not be under anyone's legal authority. Servants, for example, could legally become free, and there were many other implications. The prospects were terrifying.

The Pilgrim leaders, realizing that they urgently needed to create some alternate government authority, convinced nearly all of the adult males aboard (Pilgrims and Strangers alike) to form a written agreement among themselves. Basing their document on a social compact idea found in some separatist church covenants, the Pilgrims set forth that this agreement would form a "civil body politic" to establish "just and equal laws… for the general good of the Colony," by which all of the signers would be bound.

Forty-one adult males crammed the ship's tiny cabin to sign the document. Their agreement, which historians named the Mayflower Compact, amounted to one of the first and best-known expressions of self-government in American history. Shortly before forming their new colony, the signers elected a governor, and when that governor died, another governor was selected to succeed him and procedures were established for subsequent elections, thereby ensuring continuity. Born of necessity, the Mayflower Compact represented both the idea of the rule of law and some basic principles of democracy.

Although the original manuscript of the compact has been lost, versions of the text and a list of the signers were later printed in several early histories. The most famous transcript, written by *Mayflower* passenger William Bradford, is contained in a collection of his journals entitled *Of Plimoth Plantation*. Based on his handwritten accounts, the book was not published until 1856. Bradford's manuscripts are held in a vault at the Massachusetts State Library.

RIGHT AND BELOW: William Bradford's journal contains the only transcript of the Mayflower Compact written by a passenger of the famous ship. Below is a late nineteenth-century painting of the Mayflower signatories.

fets by them done (this their condition considered) might be as firme as any patent; and in some respects more sure. The forme was as followeth.

In ȳ name of god Amen. We whose names are underwriten, the loyall subiects of our dread soueraigne Lord King Iames, by ȳ grace of god, of great Britaine, franc, & Ireland king, defender of ȳ faith, &c.

Haueing vndertaken, for ȳ glorie of god, and aduancemente of ȳ christian faith, and honour of our king & countrie, a voyage to plant ȳ first colonie in ȳ Northerne parts of Virginia. doe by these presents solemnly & mutualy in ȳ presence of god, and one of another, couenant, & combine our selues togeather into a civill body politick; for ȳ our better ordering, & preseruation & further-ance of ȳ ends aforsaid; and by vertue hearof to enacte, constitute, and frame shuch just & equall Lawes, ordinances, Acts, constitutions, & offices, from time to time, as shall be thought most meete & conuenient for ȳ generall good of ȳ Colonie: vnto which we promise all due submission and obedience. In witnes wherof we haue here vnder subscribed our names at Cap-Codd ȳ ·11· of Nouember, in ȳ year of ȳ raigne of our soueraigne Lord king Iames of England, franc, & Ireland ȳ eighteenth and of Scotland ȳ fiftie fourth. An: Dom. 1620.]

After this they chose, or rather confirmed Mr Iohn caruer (a man godly & well approued amongst them) their Gouernour for that year. And after they had prouided a place for their goods, or comone store, (which were long in vnlading for want of boats, foulnes of ȳ winter weather, and sicknes of diuers) and begune some small cottages for their habitation; as time would admitte they mette and consulted of lawes, & ordors, both for their civill, & military gouermente, as ȳ necessitie of their condi-tion did require, still adding thervnto as vrgent occasion in seuerall times, and as cases did require.

In these hard & difficulte beginings they found some discontents & murmurings arose amongst some, and mutinous speeches & cariags in other; but they were soone quelled, & ouercome, by ȳ wis-dome, patience, and just & equall carrage of things, by ȳ Gour: and better part wth claue faithfully togeather in ȳ maine. But that which was most sadd, & lamentable, was, that in 2. or .3. monthes time halfe of their company dyed, espetialy in Ian: & febuary, being ȳ depth of winter, and wanting houses & other comforts; being ynfected with ȳ Scurvie &

SHAKESPEARES

COMEDIES,
HISTORIES, &
TRAGEDIES.

Published according to the True Originall Copies.

To the Reader.

This Figure, that thou here seest put,
It was for gentle Shakespeare cut;
Wherein the Grauer had a strife
with Nature, to out-doo the life :
O, could he but haue drawne his wit
As well in brasse, as he hath hit
His face ; the Print would then surpasse
All, that vvas euer vvrit in brasse.
But, since he cannot, Reader, looke
Not on his Picture, but his Booke.

B. I.

LONDON
Printed by Isaac Iaggard, and Ed. Blount. 1623.

*ABOVE: Martin Droeshout's portrait of Shakespeare is believed
to be the most accurate likeness. Shakespeare's friend and
contemporary Ben Jonson writes on the facing page that the
engraver had "a strife with Nature, to out-doo the life."*

Shakespeare's First Folio

(1623)

Seven years after his death, two of William Shakespeare's closest stage friends strive to preserve his amazing legacy. The resulting collection of his masterful plays will go on to become what one appraiser will call the "most documented book in the world," without which the playwright's work may have sunk into obscurity.

William Shakespeare (1564–1616) may have been the greatest writer in the history of the English language, but that reputation never would have come about without the effort of his two fellow actors and closest friends, John Heminges and Henry Condell, who labored for years "onely to keepe the memory of so worthy a Friend, & Fellow alive, as was our Shakespeare, my humble offer of his playes."

Heminges and Condell spent years gathering and editing thirty-six of the late writer's plays (but not the sonnets or poems). Before that point, only half of the dramatic works had been published, and those that had were issued in a small format and rife with errors. Some versions didn't even credit Shakespeare as the playwright. As managers in Shakespeare's company, however, Heminges and Condell had access to his surviving handwritten scripts and prompt-books. At last, they wrote, readers would have the great dramatist's plays as they were actually performed, "where before, you were abused with diverse, stolen and surreptitious copies, maimed, and deformed by the frauds and stealths of injurious impostors... ."

So in 1621 his friends began to supervise a fine printing that was done by Isaac Jaggard and Edward Blount. *Mr. William Shakespeares Comedies, Histories, & Tragedies* first appeared in 1623. Scholars called it the First Folio, in reference to its original appearance and its large page size.

Given that Shakespeare's original play manuscripts do not survive, the pair's scrupulously prepared version of his comedies, histories and tragedies remain the closest thing to Shakespeare's original words for the stage. Without the Folio the world would not have *Macbeth, Julius Caesar, Antony and Cleopatra, Coriolanus, Twelfth Night, As You Like It, Measure for Measure, The Comedy of Errors, The Winter's Tale,* and *The Tempest.* The book's portrait of Shakespeare (engraved by Martin Droeshout) on the title page may have also been the most authentic likeness extant, so his face was preserved as well.

The book's original price was £1 for an unbound copy and £2 or £3 for a bound version, a substantial amount in those days.

About 30 percent of the approximately 800 copies printed are known to have survived. The Folger Shakespeare Library in Washington, Meisei University in Japan, and the British Library all have multiple copies. Considered one of the world's most valuable printed books, a copy sold at auction in 2001 for $6.16 million, when Stephen Massey the book appraiser called it "the most documented book in the world."

Although Shakespeare's work has undergone continual new translations to make it more understandable to contemporary audiences, this would not have been possible without the First Folio.

Galileo's Dialogue

(1632)

In presenting the theory that the Sun, not the Earth, is the center of the universe, the greatest scientist of his day tries to dramatize his argument as a witty dialogue poking fun at Church dogma. But Galileo ends up being brought before the Roman Inquisition.

By 1632 the great Tuscan astronomer, mathematician, and philosopher Galileo Galilei (1564–1642) was already famous for his telescope design and his amazing planetary discoveries. Yet his support for Copernicus's almost century-old theory of a heliocentric universe (with the Sun, not the Earth, as the center of the solar system) didn't square with rigid Church doctrine, so he held off writing down his conclusions until he thought it was safe to do so. Following the election of his most powerful admirer, Maffeo Cardinal Barberini, as Pope Urban VIII, Galileo assumed he would not be persecuted for expressing his scientific view, particularly if he couched his case in humor.

Writing in his native Tuscan dialect rather than Latin, Galileo penned a 500-page book in the form of a witty and irreverent dialogue between three fictional characters, who engage in a four-day-long rational discussion about the Earth's motion, the organization of the heavenly bodies, and the ebb and flow of the sea. The conversation takes place in Venice, where the action of the tides is a major concern. Salviati, the "Academician," expresses Galileo's own views; Sagredo is a wealthy layman in search of the truth who is initially neutral on such questions until he becomes convinced by reason; and Simplicio is a conservative follower of Ptolemy and Aristotle, who stubbornly adheres to Church dogma. Ptolemy's view of the universe, which remained unchallenged until Copernicus published his theories

in 1543, placed Earth, not the Sun, at the center of the universe.

Told in common language that is both poetic and didactic, the amusing encounter is laced with barbed remarks about narrow-minded and irrational thinkers. The final part of the dialogue, about the tides, especially offended the Catholic hierarchy because it refuted Church doctrine and put the Pope's words in a fool's mouth, thereby subjecting the pontiff to ridicule.

When Pope Urban was informed that Galileo had written such a work that was contrary to Church teachings, he became enraged and ordered the seventy-year-old professor hauled before the Holy Office to face possible torture. Following a lengthy trial in Rome, Galileo was found in "grave suspicion of heresy" and forced to publicly recant; his writings and teachings were banned and he was sentenced to house arrest for the rest of his life. Although the book was placed on the Index of Forbidden Books, unauthorized copies of his explosive *Dialogue Concerning the Two Chief World Systems (Dialogo sopra i due massimi sistemi del mondo)* became a bestseller on the black market and went on to become regarded as one of the most earth-shaking books in Western thought.

Humiliated and discredited by the Church, Galileo went blind and died in 1642. Copies of his trial proceedings and recantation are in the Vatican's collection; copies of the first published edition of the book are owned by several major libraries.

RIGHT: Galileo's diagram of the Copernican system shows the Sun at the center of the universe. The difference between this diagram and Copernicus's heliocentric model of 1543 is that this drawing includes the four moons of Jupiter, which Galileo discovered in 1610.

SIMP. Sia questo segnato A. il luogo del globo terrestre.

SALV. Bene stà. So secondariamente, che voi sapete benissimo, che essa terra non è dentro al corpo solare, nè meno a quello contigua, ma per certo spazio distante, e però assegnate at Sole qual altro luogo più vi piace remoto dalla terra a vostro beneplacito, e questo ancora contrassegnate.

SIMP. Ecco fatto: Sia il luogo del corpo solare questo segnato O.

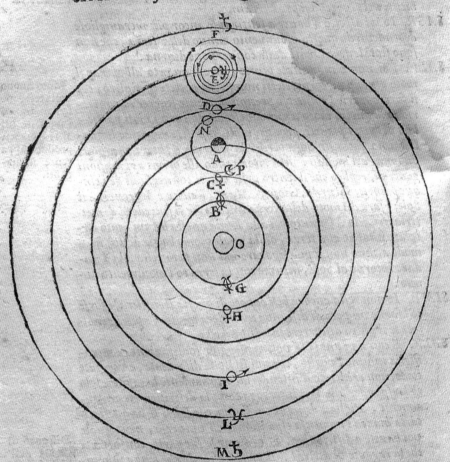

SALV. Stabiliti questi due, voglio, che pensiamo di accomodar il corpo di Venere in tal maniera, che lo stato, e movimento suo possa sodisfar a ciò, che di essi ci mostrano le sensate apparenze.

Execution Warrant of Charles I

(1649)

The most dramatic document in Britain's Parliamentary Archives appears tinged with blood, which is fitting given that it is that lawmaking body's execution warrant for Charles I's beheading in the wake of the bloody English Civil War. Ten of the warrant's signatories would later be executed as revenge.

The English Civil War claimed as many as 200,000 lives. After Oliver Cromwell's victory, Puritans claimed that King Charles I had carried out "a wicked design totally to subvert the ancient and fundamental laws and liberties of this nation," and "levied and maintained a civil war in the land." The Rump Parliament put him on trial for high treason and his son went into exile. Amid the chaos, a group of the commissioners condemned the king to death, though the death warrant had already been drawn up, with blanks provided for the time and place of the execution. In the end, fifty-nine of the sixty-seven commissioners who had pronounced judgment signed the warrant. Many would live to regret it.

On the bitterly cold afternoon of January 30, 1649 the doomed king bent down over the chopping block, behaving with such strength and dignity that the crowd groaned when his head toppled away from the executioner's axe.

Following the regicide, eleven more years of fighting ensued until the rebel government fell, whereupon the slain king's son, Charles II, set about using Parliament's death warrant as a guide for exacting his revenge. The document consists of a piece of parchment measuring 17 x 8 inches, containing wax seals and handwriting in iron gall ink. Although parts appeared damaged, the writing—namely, its fifty-nine signatures—were sufficiently legible to guide the king's agents.

Three of the main conspirators, including Oliver Cromwell, were already dead, so their bodies were exhumed and hanged in their shrouds, with the heads later displayed on spikes. Ten others who had fled were tracked down, convicted of treason, then hung, drawn, and quartered. Another was murdered. Nineteen others were imprisoned for life.

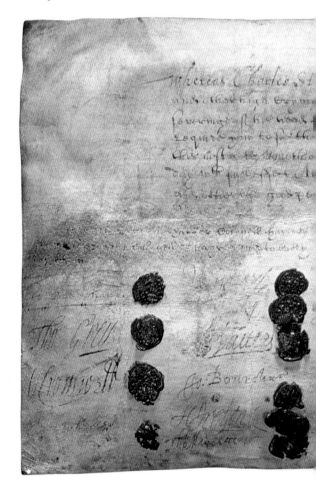

RIGHT: The document that sealed Charles I's fate and led to the subsequent rule of Oliver Cromwell as Lord Protector of the Commonwealth of England, Scotland, and Ireland. Cromwell's signature can be seen far left. Following the restoration of the monarchy in 1660, the death warrant was used to identify and prosecute all of the "regicides" who had signed it.

Charles I's beheading changed the way the English viewed themselves, their king, the Civil War, and their country. Historians contend that the shocking execution shattered the image of an all-powerful monarch. The Church of England established the date of January 30 for perpetual lamentation—in memory of the events recorded in the reddish execution warrant of 1649 and as a warning of the dangers of "unnatural rebellion, usurpation, and tyranny of ungodly and cruel men, and from the sad confusions and ruin thereupon ensuing."

Today the warrant is preserved in the care of the House of Lords Record Office. Scholars continue to speculate about the way the document was constructed, particularly the timing of the warrant and its signatures.

Samuel Pepys's Diary

(1660–69)

An urbane and very observant Londoner keeps a private daily diary covering everything from his most mundane activities to some of the greatest events of the age, leaving an intimate and fascinating record of life under England's Restoration.

Samuel Pepys (1633–1703), the son of a London tailor, was born into modest circumstances but rose to become a member of England's privileged class. He attended the execution of Charles I in 1649, was educated at Magdalene College, Cambridge, dined in splendor, and enjoyed London's high arts and society. Through patronage he held several posts, including Chief Secretary to the Royal Navy under King Charles II and James II. Pepys suffered from painful bladder stones and other ailments that left him sterile. Although married, he and his wife often lived apart and he engaged in extramarital affairs.

No one would know this today except for the fact that from 1660 to 1669, a crucial period in Britain's history, Pepys kept an extraordinarily detailed personal record of every aspect of his life and times. First published in 1825, Pepys's diary is considered one of history's finest eyewitness accounts.

On January 1, 1660 he recorded his first entry:

Blessed be God, at the end of the last year I was in very good health, without any sense of my old pain but upon taking of cold. I lived in Axe yard, having my wife and servant Jane, and no more in family than us three. My wife, after the absence of her terms for seven weeks, gave me hopes of her being with child, but on the last day of the year she hath them again.

Besides providing a vivid, firsthand view of Restoration London, and a rare peep into a gentleman's intimate private musings and affairs, Pepys's diary is notable for its detailed and colorful reportage about several major historical events of the period. During the Great Plague of London (1665–66), Pepys reports having to "buy some roll tobacco to smell to and chaw" in order to take away "the apprehension" of infection, writing, "But Lord! How everybody's looks, and discourse in the street, is of death, and nothing else; and few people going up and down, that the town is like a place distressed and forsaken." After a maid awakens him early in the morning of September 2, 1666 to warn him of a blaze spreading in the distance, Pepys heads to the Tower of London to see "the houses at the end of the bridge all on fire, and an infinite great fire on this and the other side"—the Great Fire of London.

The diary recounts his rich cultural activities, detailing his tastes in books, music, the theater, and science (including his correspondence with Isaac Newton). "The truth is," he wrote, "I do indulge myself a little the more in pleasure, knowing this is the proper age of my life to do it; and, out of my observation that most men that do thrive in the world do forget to take pleasure during the time that they are getting their estate, but reserve that till they have got one, and then it is too late for them to enjoy it." His descriptions of the dramatic stage of the period are especially keen.

Although encroaching blindness prevented him from writing after May 31, 1669, Pepys kept his diary well preserved. For these reasons, and its fine style, the work has long been a favorite among historians and general readers alike.

Although written in a form of shorthand known as Tachygraphy, the six volumes of bound manuscripts were later deciphered, and published in 1825 and several times since. The original manuscript and first transcription lie in the Samuel Pepys Library at Magdalene College, Cambridge.

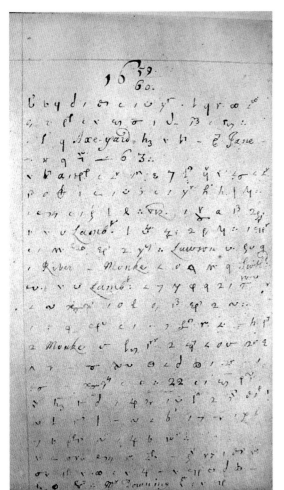

ABOVE: The first page of Pepys's diary, from Sunday January 1, 1659/1660. Written in shorthand, and covering everything from politics and national events to the trials and tribulations of married life, his diary offers an invaluable insight into life in London in the 1660s. The six leather-bound volumes of his original handwritten diaries are kept at the Pepys Library in Cambridge.

ABOVE: These two pages are taken from a notebook dating from the mid-to-late 1660s and show Newton's early mathematical thinking that would eventually develop into his theories of calculus. His detailed notes and calculations are sometimes written on small scraps of paper that he had to hand.

Isaac Newton Papers

(1660s–1727)

The most influential scientist in history leaves behind one of the world's largest collections of precious original scholarly manuscripts, but the gatekeepers for centuries restrict access to some of the papers because they don't like Newton's ideas about certain subjects.

Sir Isaac Newton (1642–1727) was far and away the greatest scientist, mathematician, and natural philosopher of the Enlightenment. Best known for his mathematical description of universal gravitation, but also revered for his achievements in calculus, classical mechanics, optics, color, and countless other domains, Newton is credited with so many important discoveries and inventions that he is regarded as probably the most influential scholar in the history of science. Yet many of his less well known writings delved into other subjects that complicated his legacy.

The story of Isaac Newton's papers is interesting for a number of reasons. Newton left behind an enormous stack of manuscripts, letters and other papers that was estimated in size at ten million words. His celebrated works of scientific and mathematical genius were and are highly prized. But a large portion of his archives, dealing with alchemy, theology, and chronology, remained under wraps for centuries.

Newton's wide range of unorthodox interests turned off some persons who had access to the papers. His forensic analysis of the Bible, for example, along with his pursuit of "heretical" religious ideas—such as his rejection of the Holy Trinity—startled many religious conformists. And his obsession with alchemy and other "strange" notions made others question his scientific judgment. As a result, the full breadth of Newton's massive paper trail was kept out of bounds for centuries, continuing through the squeamish Victorian age, for what might be termed political reasons. One discriminating historian was aghast to find some of Newton's pristine mathematical notes intermingled with worrisome theological materials, not appreciating, perhaps, the interdisciplinary nature of Newton's genius. "I frame no hypotheses," he wrote, "for whatever is not deduced from the phenomena is to be called an hypothesis; and hypotheses, whether metaphysical or physical, whether of occult qualities or mechanical, have no place in experimental philosophy."

Newton was closely associated with Cambridge University, where he was a student and holder of the Lucasian Chair of Mathematics. So it is not surprising that the bulk of his mathematical and scientific manuscripts were bequeathed to the University of Cambridge Library by one of his relatives in 1872. Another important collection of Sir Isaac Newton's scientific manuscripts was donated to the university in 2000.

The longstanding skittishness and censorship which has surrounded Newton's papers appears to be changing in the digital age. A huge archive of classic Newton works is being posted online by Cambridge University. And another web-based initiative, the Newton Project based at Sussex University, has dedicated itself to publishing in full an online edition of all of Newton's writings. Thus far, the project has transcribed 6.4 million words. It is also making available translations of his most important Latin texts. The Newton documents keep growing. Now readers will be able to gain a fuller understanding of one of history's most extraordinary minds.

First Printed Newspaper in English

(1665)

First printed as the *Oxford Gazette*, and later moving to become the *London Gazette*, the first English-language broadsheet was being read years before the term "newspaper" was coined—and it is still in publication today as Britain's official organ of record.

O n November 7, 1665, the first issue of the *Oxford Gazette* came off the press, authorized by King Charles II to tell the privileged classes what he wanted them to know. He had it printed 60 miles west of London in an effort to escape the Great Plague that was killing so many residents of that city, and the inaugural issue contained the government's "Bill of Mortality" listing the epidemic's latest victims. Oxford University's Leonard Litchfeld was authorized to serve as its printer.

A well-known politician, Joseph Williamson, wrote the first edition, stating that its publication was, "For the Use of some Merchants and Gentlemen who desire them." The first article announced the appointment of a new Bishop of Oxford, reporting: "This day the Reverend Doctor Walter Blandford, Warden of Wadham Colledge in this University, was Elected Lord Bishop of this See; vacant by the death of Dr. Paul, late Bishop here."

Samuel Pepys in London got hold of a copy on November 22, and wrote in his diary: "This day the first of the *Oxford Gazettes* came out, which is very pretty, full of news, and no folly in it."

After three months in Oxford, Charles II judged London safe enough to return with his court and the useful broadsheet was moved with him as the *London Gazette*.

Consisting of a single page broadsheet, measuring 7.25 x 11 inches and printed on both sides, the text was arranged in a visually

pleasing two-column format known as coranto, with the paper's distinctive title on top along with the date and the line, "Published by Authority." It was issued twice a week, on Mondays and Thursdays, and widely distributed—at first to other neighboring towns and soon to foreign lands via ocean vessels—becoming the leading source of news in Britain and the colonies. The *Gazette* was not a newspaper in the modern sense: it was sent by post to subscribers, not printed for sale to the general public. By 1670 or so, some readers took to calling it a "newspaper."

As the Crown's first official journal of record and newspaper, the *London Gazette* occupied a special place in British affairs, providing the most authoritative information about military actions, political events, and legal proceedings. On January 4, 1666, it was noted that "Seventeen prisoners from Newgate, who were aboard a Barbados ship, got off...went ashore...[and the] master of the ship made pursuit after them."

The newspaper has been continuously published to this day and its back issues are now available in digital form over the Internet.

LEFT: The first edition of the Oxford Gazette *(November 7, 1665) included a "bill of mortality" for the Great Plague.*

The London Gazette.

Published by Authority.

From Monday, Septemb. 3. to Monday, Septemb. 10. 1666.

White-Hall, Sept. 8.

The ordinary course of this Paper having been interrupted by a Sad and Lamentable Accident of Fire lately hapned in the City of *London* : It hath been thought fit for satisfying the minds of so many of His Majesties good Subjects, who must needs be concerned for the Issue of so great an Accident, to give this short, but true Accompt of it.

On the Second instant at One of the Clock in the Morning, there hapned to break out a Sad & Deplorable Fire, in *Pudding-Lane* near *New Fish-Street*, which falling out at that hour of the night, and in a quarter of the Town so close built with wooden pitched houses, spread it self so far before day, and with such distraction to the Inhabitants and Neighbours, that care was not taken for the timely preventing the farther diffusion of it by pulling down houses, as ought to have been ; so that this lamentable Fire in a short time became too big to be mastered by any Engines or working neer it. It fell out most unhappily too, That a violent Easterly Wind fomented it, and kept it burning all that day, and the night following spreading it self up to *Grace-Church-street*, and downwards from *Cannon-street* to the Water-side as far as the *Three Cranes in the Vintry*.

The People in all parts about it distracted by the vastness of it, and their particular care to carry away their Goods, many attempts were made to prevent the spreading of it, by pulling down Houses, and making great Intervals, but all in vain, the Fire seising upon the Timber and Rubbish, and so continuing it self, even through those Spaces, and raging in a bright Flame all Monday and Tuesday, notwithstanding His Majesties own, and His Royal Highness's indefatigable and personal pains to apply all possible remedies to prevent it, calling upon and helping the people with their Guards ; and a great number of Nobility and Gentry unweariedly assisting therein, for which they were requited with a thousand blessings from the poor distressed people. By the favour of God the Wind slackned a little on Tuesday night, and the Flames meeting with Brick-buildings at the Temple, by little and little it was observed to lose its force on that side ; so that on Wednesday morning we began to hope well, and his Royal Highness never dispairing or slackning his Personal Care, wrought so well that day, assisted in some parts by the Lords of the Council before and behind it, that a stop was put to it at the *Temple-Church*, neer *Holborn-Bridge*, *Pie-Corner*, *Aldersgate*, *Cripple-gate*, neer the lower end of *Coleman-street*, at the end of *Basing-Hall-street*, by the *Postern*, at the upper end of *Bishopsgate* street, and *Leaden-Hall-street*, at the *Standard* in *Cornhill*, at the Church in *Fan-Church-street*, neer *Clothworkers-hall* in *Mincing-Lane*, at the middle of *Mark-Lane*, and at the *Tower-Dock*.

On Thursday by the blessing of God it was wholly beat down and ex inguished ; but so as that Evening it unhappily burst out again afresh at the *Temple*, by the falling of some sparks (as is supposed) upon a Pile of Wooden Buildings , but his Royal Highness, who watched there that whole night in Person, by the great Labours and Diligence used, and especially by applying Powder to blow up the Houses about it, before day most happily mastered it.

Divers Strangers, *Dutch* and *French*, were, during the Fire, apprehended, upon suspition that they contributed mischievously to it, who are all imprisoned, and Informations prepared to make a severe Inquisition thereupon by my Lord Chief Justice *Keeling*, assisted by some of the Lords of the Privy Council, and some principal Members of the City ; notwithstanding which suspitions, the manner of the burning all along in a Train, and so blown forwards in all its way by strong Winds, makes us conclude the whole was an effect of an unhappy chance, or to speak better, the heavy hand of God upon us for our Sins, shewing us the terrour of his Judgment in thus raising the fire ; and immediately after, his miraculous and never enough to be acknowledged Mercy, in putting a stop to it, when we were in the last despair, and that all attempts for the quenching it, however industriously pursued, seemed insufficient. His Majesty then sat hourly in Council, and ever since hath continued taking rounds about the City in all parts of it, where the danger and mischief was greatest, till this Morning that he hath sent his Grace the Duke of *Albemarle*, whom he hath called for to assist him in this great occasion, to put his Happy and Successful Hand to the finishing this memorable Deliverance.

About the *Tower*, the seasonable Orders given for plucking down Houses to secure the Magazins of Powder, was more especially successful, that Part being up the Wind, notwithstanding which, it came almost to the very Gates of it, so as by this early provision, the severall Stores of War lodged in the Tower were entirely saved : And we have further this infinite cause particularly to give God thanks that the fire did not happen in any of those places where his Majesties Naval Stores are kept, so as though it hath pleased God to visit us with his own hand, he hath not, by disfurnishing us with the means of carrying on the War, subjected us to our Enemies.

It must be observed, That this Fire happened in a part of the Town, where though the Commodities were not very rich, yet they were so bulky, that they could not well be removed, so that the Inhabitants of that part where it first began have sustained very great loss : But by the best Enquiry we can make, the other parts of the Town, where the Commodities were of greater value ; took the Alarm so early, that they saved most of their Goods of value, which possibly may have diminished the loss ; though some think, that if the whole industry of the Inhabitants had been applyed to the stopping of the Fire, and not to the saving of their particular Goods, the success might have been much better, not only to the Publick, but to many of them in their own Particulars.

Through this sad Accident it is easie to be imagined how many persons were necessitated to remove themselves and Goods into the open Fields, where they were forced to continue some time, which could not but work compassion in the beholders ; but His Majesties Care was most Signal in this occasion, who, besides his Personal Pains, was frequent in Consulting all wayes for relieving those distressed persons, which produced so good effects, aswell by His Majesties Proclamations, and the Orders issued to the Neighbour Justices of the Peace to encourage the sending in Provisions to the Markets, which are publickly known, as by other Directions, that when His Majesty, fearing lest other Orders might not yet have been sufficient, had Commanded the Victualler of his Navy to send Bread into *Moor-Fields* for the relief of the Poor, which for the more speedy supply, he sent in Biskets out of the Sea Stores ; it was found that the Markets had

Qqq   been

ABOVE: When the Great Plague had subsided, the Oxford Gazette *relocated to the capital and became the* London Gazette. *The first edition was published on February 5, 1666. Until that time, no one would touch a London newspaper for fear of contamination.*

English Bill of Rights

(1689)

After decades of bloody conflict, the most important document of the Glorious Revolution is an act of Parliament that spells out new limits on the powers of the Crown and establishes the supremacy of Parliament, proclaiming that all Englishmen possess certain inalienable rights under law.

As James II (England's last Roman Catholic monarch) was being deposed and William III and Mary II were about to accept the crown as joint monarchs in culmination of the Glorious Revolution of 1688, a small commission of Parliament members drew up papers to resolve several core issues that had long plagued British rule.

The commission drafted a document declaring that since James II had "abdicated" the throne, Parliament was naming his successors and moving to prohibit further monarchial abuses of the kind that James II had committed. The act was also designed to clarify the powers of Parliament and the civil rights of the people, reflecting some of the political ideas proposed by the Enlightenment philosopher John Locke, who had been in exile in Holland during James II's reign.

Passed on December 16, 1689, the Bill of Rights recounted twelve specific wrongs that James II had committed, and by doing so it helped to establish the rights that Parliament said must be upheld. The act imposed certain limits on royal power, stating that Parliament's consent is required for the king to suspend or create laws, raise taxes, or raise a standing army in peace time; the people are entitled to petition the king without being prosecuted; Parliaments should be held frequently; and that Roman Catholics are barred from the throne.

The new standards held that "excessive bail ought not to be required, nor excessive fines imposed, nor cruel and unusual punishments inflicted"; "jurors ought to be duly impanelled and returned, and jurors which pass upon men in trials for high treason ought to be

RIGHT: An eighteenth-century engraving showing "The Bill of Rights ratified at the Revolution by King William and Queen Mary previous to their Coronation."

freeholders"; and "all grants and promises of fines and forfeitures of particular persons before conviction are illegal and void."

The new monarchs were required to swear they would obey Parliament's laws, including the Bill of Rights, which they did, saying, "We thankfully accept what you have offered to us." They also had to swear to uphold the Protestant religion.

The document joined the Magna Carta as a fundamental pillar of British rights and liberties and later helped inspire the creation of the American Declaration of Independence, the French Declaration of Rights of Man and the Citizen, the US Bill of Rights, and other landmarks of civil liberties. It is still in effect in all Commonwealth realms.

The original document is held at the National Archives in Kew.

Samuel Johnson's Dictionary

(1755)

An eccentric genius spends eight years compiling a mammoth and innovative original dictionary, complete with more than 40,000 word definitions and numerous illustrative literary quotations, making for the most engaging lexicographic treasure house of the English language yet devised.

Many of the most erudite writers and intellectuals of mid-eighteenth-century London called Samuel Johnson (1709–84) the most brilliant man of his era. Adam Smith said, "Johnson knew more books than any man alive," and Edmund Burke thought that if Johnson had gone to Parliament he would have been certainly "the greatest speaker that ever was."

Although he was a man of modest means and odd mannerisms, Johnson was commissioned by London booksellers to create an authoritative English dictionary, and he spent more than eight years immersed in the Herculean task. One of his few assistants was a former Jamaican slave, Francis Barber.

The dictionary's 42,773 word entries included rarities such as *odontálgick* (pertaining to toothache) and some of its definitions were as quirky and humorous as Johnson himself. He defines *cough* as "a convulsion of the lungs, vellicated by some sharp serosity," and *lexicographer* as "A writer of dictionaries; a harmless drudge that busies himself in tracing the original, and detailing the signification of words."

Another of Johnson's delightful innovations was to illustrate a word's meanings by means of apt literary quotations—114,000 of them—which he had taken from Shakespeare and 500 other authors from every branch of learning in a feat of extraordinary scholarship and erudition.

When it first appeared in 1755, Johnson's *Dictionary of the English Language* was priced for the well-to-do and sold only a few thousand copies in its first decade. Yet readers hailed the author as "England's most distinguished man of letters" and called his compendium the "greatest feat of scholarship" of its time. Later marketed in a cheaper abridged edition, the work became a big seller. Until the completion of the *Oxford English Dictionary* in 1928, Johnson's gem was generally viewed as the leading English-language dictionary, and literary scholars have long considered it one of the most influential works in the English language.

Some of Johnson's original manuscripts, including his diary and drafts of his *Plan for a Dictionary of the English Language*, are housed at Harvard University's Houghton Library. Copies of the original first edition of the dictionary have sold for as much as $250,000. Allen Reddick has written extensively about the original documents in *The Making of Johnson's Dictionary, 1746-1773*.

Johnson is recognized for other literary achievements and he is also the subject of one of the greatest single works of biography: James Boswell's *The Life of Samuel Johnson* (1791).

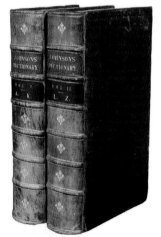

LEFT: The stupendous two-volume tome, measuring nearly 18 inches tall and weighing roughly 20 pounds, ran to 2,300 pages.

RIGHT: The title page of the first edition. Taking eight years to compile, the dictionary was Johnson's attempt to stabilize the rules governing the English language, in which "there was perplexity to be disentangled, and confusion to be regulated."

A

DICTIONARY

OF THE

ENGLISH LANGUAGE:

IN WHICH

The WORDS are deduced from their ORIGINALS,

AND

ILLUSTRATED in their DIFFERENT SIGNIFICATIONS

BY

EXAMPLES from the best WRITERS.

TO WHICH ARE PREFIXED,

A HISTORY of the LANGUAGE,

AND

AN ENGLISH GRAMMAR.

BY SAMUEL JOHNSON, A. M.

IN TWO VOLUMES.

VOL. I.

Cum tabulis animum censoris sumet honesti:
Audebit quæcunque parum splendoris habebunt,
Et sine pondere erunt, et honore indigna ferentur.
Verba movere loco; quamvis invita recedant,
Et versentur adhuc intra penetralia Vestæ:
Obscurata diu populo bonus eruet, atque
Proferet in lucem speciosa vocabula rerum,
Quæ priscis memorata Catonibus atque Cethegis,
Nunc situs informis premit et deserta vetustas.   HOR.

LONDON,

Printed by W. STRAHAN,

For J. and P. KNAPTON; T. and T. LONGMAN; C. HITCH and L. HAWES;
A. MILLAR; and R. and J. DODSLEY.

MDCCLV.

IN CONGRESS, JULY 4, 1776.

The unanimous Declaration of the thirteen united States of America.

Declaration of Independence

(1776)

Drafted in the language of the Enlightenment by Thomas Jefferson between June 11 and June 28, 1776, the Declaration of Independence formally dissolves Great Britain's political control over the American colonies, advancing a revolutionary charter intended to unite Americans under the banner of liberty and the consent of the governed.

When armed conflict between bands of rebellious American expatriates and British soldiers began in Massachusetts in April 1775, the rebels were ostensibly opposing perceived incursions against their rights as subjects of the British crown. But as the rebellion burgeoned into the Revolutionary War, delegates of the Continental Congress assembled in Philadelphia to create a charter for their movement. In mid-June 1776, a small committee was tasked with crafting a motivational political statement explaining the colonies' decision to formally declare their independence.

Thomas Jefferson of Virginia, a gifted designer and polymath who had earned a reputation as an eloquent voice for the patriotic cause after his publication of "A Summary View of the Rights of British America" (1774) and "Declaration of the Causes and Necessity of Taking Up Arms" (1775), drafted the document that would become the Declaration of Independence. The language was intended to galvanize support for the cause.

Jefferson's draft was made up of an introduction, a preamble, a body (divided into two sections) and a conclusion. The introduction effectively stated that it had become "necessary for one people to dissolve the political bands" to Britain, and thus they needed to "declare the causes." While the body of the document outlined a list of grievances against the British crown, the preamble includes its most famous passage:

We hold these truths to be self-evident; that all men are created equal; that they are endowed by their Creator with certain unalienable Rights; that among these are Life, Liberty and the pursuit of Happiness. That to secure these rights, Governments are instituted among Men, deriving their just powers from the consent of the governed, that whenever any Form of Government becomes destructive of these ends, it is the Right of the People to alter or to abolish it, and to institute new Government.

The Congress adopted the Declaration of Independence in Philadelphia on July 2 and formally declared it on July 4, the date celebrated as the birth of American independence. As the first formal statement by a nation's people asserting their right to choose their own government, the Declaration of Independence became a significant landmark in the history of democracy. In addition to its importance in the fate of the fledgling American nation, it would also exert a tremendous influence outside the United States, most memorably in France during the French Revolution. Together with the Constitution and the Bill of Rights, the Declaration of Independence is considered the first of the three essential founding documents of the United States government—and the one proving hardest to live up to.

LEFT: The most famous signature on the Declaration of Independence is that of John Hancock, President of the Continental Congress. Hancock's flamboyant signature became iconic, and "John Hancock" emerged in the United States as an informal synonym for "signature."

The Wealth of Nations

(1776)

After studying the economic and social impact of the early Industrial Revolution, the Scottish political economist and moral philosopher Adam Smith provides a revolutionary new theory of the nature and causes of wealth—arguing that if people are simply allowed to better themselves without government interference, everyone will benefit.

During the late eighteenth century the dominant theory of political economy prevailing in much of Europe including Britain was mercantilism, which held that a nation's wealth derived from the amount of bullion and goods that stayed within its borders. The mercantile system entailed establishing valuable colonies and a strong merchant marine, and developing useful domestic industries that would enable the nation to attain a favorable balance of trade. This required considerable government regulation of a nation's economy in order to increase its power over rival nations.

In 1776, however, the Scottish moral philosopher Adam Smith (1723–90) posited a new theory of political economy which shifted the definition of national wealth to a different standard based on labor. After toiling over the manuscript for more than fifteen years before sending it to press, Smith's 900-page magnum opus, entitled *An Inquiry into the Nature and Causes of the Wealth of Nations,* first appeared on March 9, 1776, at a time of great social and political ferment—the heyday of the Enlightenment, the early Industrial Revolution, and the erupting American Revolution—and his new and systematic analysis of political economy signaled the dawn of modern capitalism and economics, at a critical moment.

Contrary to mercantilist theory, Smith argues that free trade *increases* the wealth of nations by providing more occasion for labor to create more wealth. He contends that the key to improvement for the masses is an increase in labor, productivity, and workforce, by the division of labor and other means. Breaking with many traditional Christian beliefs that self-interested action is immoral, Smith writes, "[M]an's self-interest is God's providence." If government would simply refrain from interfering with free competition, he argues, the marketplace would resolve industrial problems, maximum efficiency would be achieved, and wealth would increase.

Although Smith's document amounted to a capitalist manifesto, he was not uncritical. "Our merchants and masters complain much of the bad effects of high wages in raising the price and lessening the sale of goods," he writes. "They say nothing concerning the bad effects of high profits. They are silent with regard to the pernicious effects of their own gains. They complain only of those of other people."

Five editions of *The Wealth of Nations* were published during Smith's lifetime and it made him rich and famous. He always kept his manuscript close at hand and coveted it above other possessions. But at his request, the original papers were burned upon his death in 1790—an act of self-interest in keeping with his theory.

Few works in economics have had as much influence. Jean-Baptiste Colbert, David Ricardo, and Thomas Malthus all cited it as a major shaper of their thinking. Margaret Thatcher toted a copy in her handbag. The work, and the theory, continues to win both praise and criticism.

LEFT: Adam Smith with a copy of his magnum opus. The first edition sold out in six months.

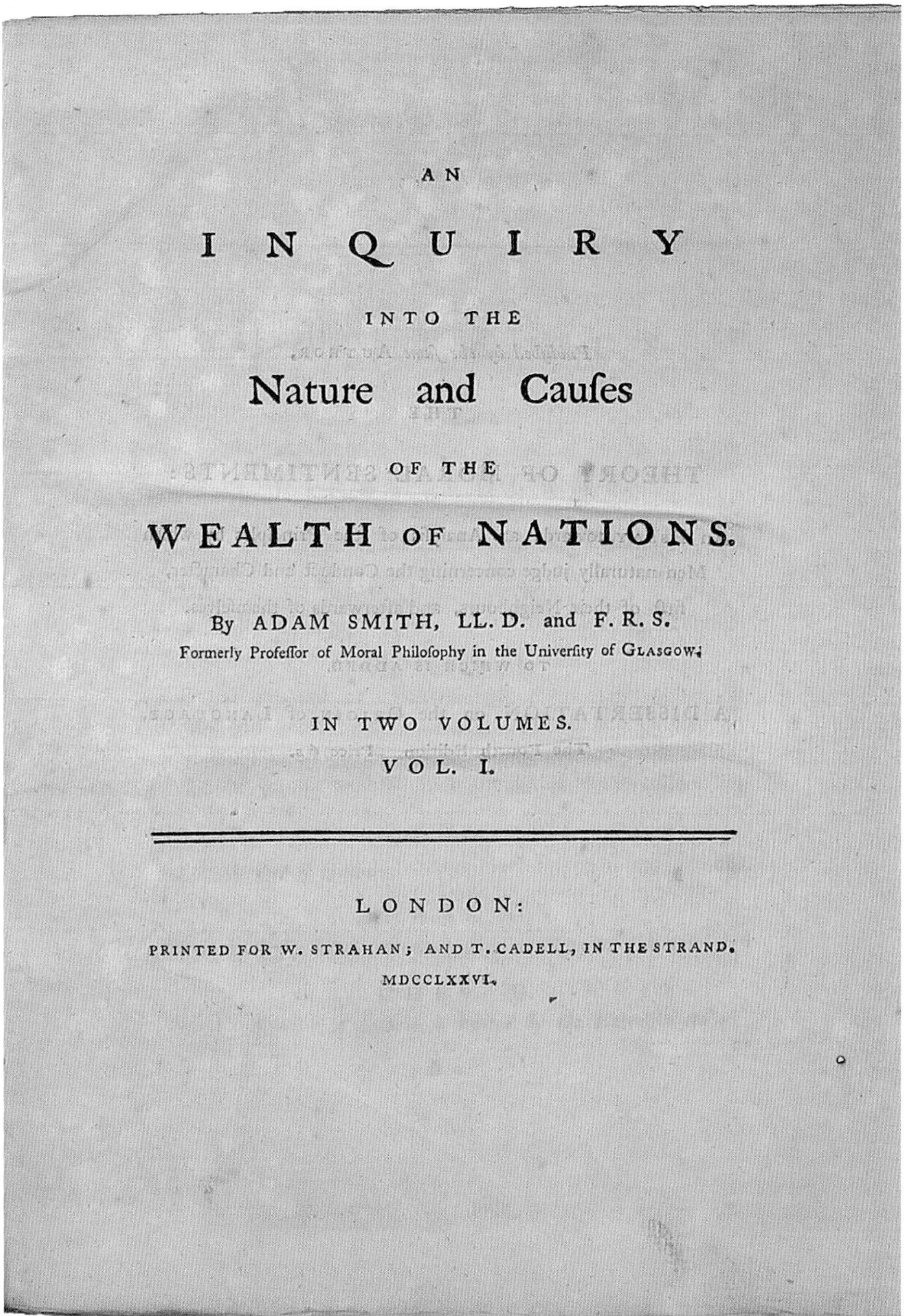

A N

INQUIRY

INTO THE

Nature and Caufes

OF THE

WEALTH of NATIONS.

By ADAM SMITH, LL.D. and F.R.S.

Formerly Profeffor of Moral Philofophy in the Univerfity of GLASGOW.

IN TWO VOLUMES.

VOL. I.

LONDON:

PRINTED FOR W. STRAHAN; AND T. CADELL, IN THE STRAND.

MDCCLXXVI.

ABOVE: The Wealth of Nations *sealed its author's reputation as the father of modern economics. A first edition can sell for as much as $100,000 today.*

We the People *of the United States, in Order to form a more perfect Union, establish Justice, insure domestic Tranquility, provide for the common defence, promote the general Welfare, and secure the Blessings of Liberty to ourselves and our Posterity, do ordain and establish this Constitution for the United States of America.*

Article. 1.

Section. 1. All legislative Powers herein granted shall be vested in a Congress of the United States, which shall consist of a Senate and House of Representatives.

Section. 2. The House of Representatives shall be composed of Members chosen every second Year by the People of the several States, and the Electors in each State shall have the Qualifications requisite for Electors of the most numerous Branch of the State Legislature.

No Person shall be a Representative who shall not have attained to the Age of twenty five Years, and been seven Years a Citizen of the United States, and who shall not, when elected, be an Inhabitant of that State in which he shall be chosen.

Representatives and direct Taxes shall be apportioned among the several States which may be included within this Union, according to their respective Numbers, which shall be determined by adding to the whole Number of free Persons, including those bound to Service for a Term of Years, and excluding Indians not taxed, three fifths of all other Persons. The actual Enumeration shall be made within three Years after the first Meeting of the Congress of the United States, and within every subsequent Term of ten Years, in such Manner as they shall by Law direct. The Number of Representatives shall not exceed one for every thirty thousand, but each State shall have at Least one Representative; and until such enumeration shall be made, the State of New Hampshire shall be entitled to chuse three, Massachusetts eight, Rhode-Island and Providence Plantations one, Connecticut five, New York six, New Jersey four, Pennsylvania eight, Delaware one, Maryland six, Virginia ten, North Carolina five, South Carolina five, and Georgia three.

When vacancies happen in the Representation from any State, the Executive Authority thereof shall issue Writs of Election to fill such Vacancies.

The House of Representatives shall chuse their Speaker and other Officers; and shall have the sole Power of Impeachment.

Section. 3. The Senate of the United States shall be composed of two Senators from each State, chosen by the Legislature thereof, for six Years; and each Senator shall have one Vote.

Immediately after they shall be assembled in Consequence of the first Election, they shall be divided as equally as may be into three Classes. The Seats of the Senators of the first Class shall be vacated at the Expiration of the second Year, of the second Class at the Expiration of the fourth Year, and of the third Class at the Expiration of the sixth Year, so that one third may be chosen every second Year; and if Vacancies happen by Resignation, or otherwise, during the Recess of the Legislature of any State, the Executive thereof may make temporary Appointments until the next Meeting of the Legislature, which shall then fill such Vacancies.

No Person shall be a Senator who shall not have attained to the Age of thirty Years, and been nine Years a Citizen of the United States, and who shall not, when elected, be an Inhabitant of that State for which he shall be chosen.

The Vice President of the United States shall be President of the Senate, but shall have no Vote, unless they be equally divided.

The Senate shall chuse their other Officers, and also a President pro tempore, in the Absence of the Vice President, or when he shall exercise the Office of President of the United States.

The Senate shall have the sole Power to try all Impeachments. When sitting for that Purpose, they shall be on Oath or Affirmation. When the President of the United States is tried, the Chief Justice shall preside: And no Person shall be convicted without the Concurrence of two thirds of the Members present.

Judgment in Cases of Impeachment shall not extend further than to removal from Office, and disqualification to hold and enjoy any Office of honor, Trust or Profit under the United States: but the Party convicted shall nevertheless be liable and subject to Indictment, Trial, Judgment and Punishment, according to Law.

Section. 4. The Times, Places and Manner of holding Elections for Senators and Representatives, shall be prescribed in each State by the Legislature thereof; but the Congress may at any time by Law make or alter such Regulations, except as to the Places of chusing Senators.

The Congress shall assemble at least once in every Year, and such Meeting shall be on the first Monday in December, unless they shall by Law appoint a different Day.

Section. 5. Each House shall be the Judge of the Elections, Returns and Qualifications of its own Members, and a Majority of each shall constitute a Quorum to do Business; but a smaller Number may adjourn from day to day, and may be authorized to compel the Attendance of absent Members, in such Manner, and under such Penalties as each House may provide.

Each House may determine the Rules of its Proceedings, punish its Members for disorderly Behaviour, and, with the Concurrence of two thirds, expel a Member.

Each House shall keep a Journal of its Proceedings, and from time to time publish the same, excepting such Parts as may in their Judgment require Secrecy; and the Yeas and Nays of the Members of either House on any question shall, at the Desire of one fifth of those Present, be entered on the Journal.

Neither House, during the Session of Congress, shall, without the Consent of the other, adjourn for more than three days, nor to any other Place than that in which the two Houses shall be sitting.

Section. 6. The Senators and Representatives shall receive a Compensation for their Services, to be ascertained by Law, and paid out of the Treasury of the United States. They shall in all Cases, except Treason, Felony and Breach of the Peace, be privileged from Arrest during their Attendance at the Session of their respective Houses, and in going to and returning from the same; and for any Speech or Debate in either House, they shall not be questioned in any other Place.

No Senator or Representative shall, during the Time for which he was elected, be appointed to any civil Office under the Authority of the United States, which shall have been created, or the Emoluments whereof shall have been increased during such time; and no Person holding any Office under the United States, shall be a Member of either House during his Continuance in Office.

Section. 7. All Bills for raising Revenue shall originate in the House of Representatives; but the Senate may propose or concur with Amendments as on other Bills.

Every Bill which shall have passed the House of Representatives and the Senate, shall, before it become a Law, be presented to the President of the

Constitution of the United States

(1787)

After a five-month-long discussion, a Federal Convention at Philadelphia's Independence Hall produces a four-page parchment document which is signed by thirty-nine of the fifty-five attending delegates. The Constitution of the United States, describing how the new national government shall operate, begins with the words, "We the people..."

The most important document in United States history, and one of the key legal-governmental documents that changed the world, was signed on September 17, 1787, four years after the Treaty of Paris ended the American War of Independence. The signers included representatives of all of the original Thirteen Colonies (except Rhode Island) as well as the convention's impoverished secretary, William Jackson, who attested to the document's authenticity and became its fortieth signer. Entitled the Constitution of the United States, its purpose was to delineate a proper federal government representing each state.

Based on extensive debate, the delegates to the Constitutional Convention in Philadelphia had concluded that mere amendment of the existing Articles of Confederation would not be sufficient for the new nation, so therefore they would need to build an entirely new structure of supreme law from scratch.

The resulting document comprised seven articles. The first three delineated the doctrine of separation of powers, to be exercised by three branches of government—legislative, executive and judicial; articles four to six spelled out the concept of federalism and the rights and responsibilities of the states in relationship to the central body; and article seven established the procedures for ratification of the Constitution.

Since the Constitution has come into force, it has added twenty-seven amendments. The first ten, known

as the Bill of Rights, enacted in 1791, established specific protections of individual liberty and justice and placed restrictions on the powers of government. Most of the others have defined new civil rights, such as the right to be free from slavery and the right of women to vote. The courts have also built a huge and ever-changing body of constitutional interpretation which has further added to the document's meaning and made it a "living document" by which the United States has continued to function (although some justices want to keep it lifeless—frozen in its original meaning of centuries ago). The Constitution has also influenced the development of other constitutions and declarations around the world.

Yet despite its importance as the nation's foundational document, the original parchment was mislaid for several years until a publisher tracked it down in 1846. Luckily it had escaped destruction when the British burned Washington in the War of 1812. In 1883, another searcher discovered the rolled-up parchment stored in a small tin box on a closet floor at the State, War, and Navy Building. It eventually ended up with the Declaration of Independence in the Library of Congress, and was later moved to Fort Knox.

Since 1952 the document (which is also known as the "Charters of Freedom") has been displayed in the National Archives in Washington, DC, encased in inert helium gas under optimum conditions of temperature, light, and humidity.

LEFT: Jacob Shallus, an assistant clerk of the Pennsylvania State Assembly, was paid thirty dollars "to transcribe & engross" all 4,543 words of the document.

Declaration of the Rights of Man and of the Citizen

(1789)

Inspired by the American Revolution, a group of French nobles led by General Lafayette drafts a political manifesto declaring universal rights built upon liberty, property, security, and resistance to oppression—the founding text of the French Revolution.

On July 11, 1789 Paris was on the verge of armed revolt against King Louis XVI. General Marquis de Lafayette (1757–1834), the French military commander who had aided the victorious rebels in the American Revolution, carried a brief handwritten document into the new National Assembly. He had drafted it with assistance from a few other Frenchmen and his close personal friend, then the American ambassador to France, Thomas Jefferson.

Jefferson, besides being the primary author of the Declaration of Independence, had long been advocating a bill of rights for the American Constitution—an effort that was now bearing fruit, as James Madison had introduced some of its provisions in New York on June 8. Jefferson and Lafayette had been discussing similar options for France as well when Jefferson was in Paris.

France's Declaration of the Rights of Man and of the Citizen embodied many of Rousseau's and Montesquieu's ideas; and like America's Declaration of Independence and Constitution, it laid down certain "natural, unalienable and sacred" rights along with "simple and incontestable principles" upon which citizens could rely.

First among its seventeen articles was the tenet that "Men are born and remain free and equal in rights." The document declared that "[s]ocial distinctions may be founded only upon the general good," and "The aim of all political association is the preservation of the natural and imprescriptible rights of man," which were defined as "liberty, property, security, and resistance to oppression." Sovereignty resides in the nation, not an individual. "Liberty consists in the freedom to do everything which injures no one else" and law could "only prohibit such actions as are hurtful to society." "Law is the expression of the general will," and every citizen has the power to participate in government. Arbitrary arrests and imprisonments are outlawed. Suspects are presumed innocent until declared guilty. Persons shall not be persecuted for their opinions or religious views. "Every citizen may, accordingly, speak, write, and print with freedom, but shall be responsible for such abuses of this freedom as shall be defined by law." The expense of government must be borne equitably. Citizens have the right to demand accountability from their public agents. The rule of law and separation of powers are both essential. And property is deemed "an inviolable and sacred right."

The declaration was approved by the National Assembly on August 26, 1789, becoming the foundational document of revolutionary France and the first step toward a new national constitution. The original handwritten copy is in the Louvre.

RIGHT: This 1789 painting of the Declaration by Jean-Jacques-François Le Barbier is the most widely reproduced version of the document.

DÉCLARATION DES DROITS DE L'HOMME ET DU CITOYEN,

Décretés par l'Assemblée Nationale dans les séances des 20, 21, 23, 24 et 26 août 1789, acceptés par le Roi.

PRÉAMBULE

LES représentans du peuple François constitués en assemblée nationale, considérant que l'ignorance, l'oubli ou le mépris des droits de l'homme sont les seules causes des malheurs publics et de la corruption des gouvernemens ont résolu d'exposer dans une déclaration solemnelle, les droits naturels, inaliénables et sacrés de l'homme, afin que cette déclaration constamment présente à tous les membres du corps social, leur rappelle sans cesse leurs droits et leurs devoirs, afin que les actes du pouvoir législatif et ceux du pouvoir exécutif, pouvant être à chaque instant comparés avec le but de toute institution politique, en soient plus respectés; afin que les réclamations des citoyens, fondées désormais sur des principes simples et incontestables, tournent toujours au maintien de la constitution et du bonheur de tous.

EN conséquence, l'assemblée nationale reconnoit et déclare, en présence et sous les auspices de l'Etre suprême les droits suivans de l'homme et du citoyen.

ARTICLE PREMIER

LES hommes naissent et demeurent libres et égaux en droits, les distinctions sociales ne peuvent être fondées que sur l'utilité commune.

II.

LE but de toute association politique est la conservation des droits naturels et imprescriptibles de l'homme; ces droits sont la liberté, la propriété, la sureté, et la résistance à l'oppression.

III.

LE principe de toute souveraineté réside essentiellement dans la nation, nul corps, nul individu ne peut exercer d'autorité qui n'en émane expressement.

IV.

LA liberté consiste à pouvoir faire tout ce qui ne nuit pas à autrui. Ainsi, l'exercice des droits naturels de chaque homme, n'a de bornes que celles qui assurent aux autres membres de la société la jouissance de ces mêmes droits; ces bornes ne peuvent être déterminées que par la loi.

V.

LA loi n'a le droit de défendre que les actions nuisibles à la société. Tout ce qui n'est pas défendu par la loi ne peut être empêché, et nul ne peut être contraint à faire ce qu'elle n'ordonne pas.

VI.

LA loi est l'expression de la volonté générale; tous les citoyens ont droit de concourir personnellement, ou par leurs représentans, à sa formation; elle doit être la même pour tous, soit qu'elle protège, soit qu'elle punisse. Tous les citoyens étant égaux à ses yeux, sont également admissibles à toutes dignités, places et emplois publics, selon leur capacité, et sans autres distinction que celles de leurs vertus et de leurs talens.

VII.

NUL homme ne peut être accusé, arrêté ni détenu que dans les cas déterminés par la loi, et selon les formes qu'elle a prescrites, ceux qui sollicitent, expédient, exécutent ou font exécuter des ordres arbitraires, doivent être punis; mais tout citoyen appelé ou saisi en vertu de la loi, doit obéir à l'instant, il se rend coupable par la résistance.

VIII.

LA loi ne doit établir que des peines strictement et évidemment nécessaire, et nul ne peut être puni qu'en vertu d'une loi établie et promulguée antérieurement au délit, et légalement appliquée.

IX.

TOUT homme étant présumé innocent jusqu'à ce qu'il ait été déclaré coupable, s'il est jugé indispensable de l'arrêter, toute rigueur qui ne serait pas nécessaire pour s'assurer de sa personne doit être sévèrement réprimée par la loi.

X.

NUL ne doit être inquiété pour ses opinions, mêmes religieuses pourvu que leur manifestation ne trouble pas l'ordre public établi par la loi.

XI.

LA libre communication des pensées et des opinions est un des droits les plus precieux de l'homme; tout citoyen peut dont parler écrire, imprimer librement sauf à répondre de l'abus de cette liberté dans les cas déterminés par la loi.

XII.

LA garantie des droits de l'homme et du citoyen nécessite une force publique; cette force est donc instituée pour l'avantage de tous, et non pour l'utilité particuliere de ceux à qui elle est confiée.

XIII.

POUR l'entretien de la force publique, et pour les dépenses d'administration, une contribution commune est indispensable; elle doit être également répartie entre les citoyens en raison de leurs facultées.

XIV.

LES citoyens ont le droit de constater par eux même ou par leurs représentans, la nécessité de la contribution publique, de la consentir librement, d'en suivre l'emploi, et d'en déterminer la quotité, l'assiette, le recouvrement et la durée.

XV.

LA société a le droit de demander compte à tout agent public de son administration.

XVI.

TOUTE société, dans laquelle la garantie des droits n'est pas assurée, ni la séparation des pouvoirs déterminée, n'a point de constitution.

XVII.

LES propriétés étant un droit inviolable et sacré, nul ne peut en être privé, si ce n'est lorsque la nécessité publique, légalement constatée, l'exige évidemment, et sous la condition d'une juste et préalable indemnité.

AUX REPRESENTANS DU PEUPLE FRANCOIS

lumières et de sagacité, dans l'ignorance la plus crasse, il veut commander en despote sur un sexe qui a reçu toutes les facultés intellectuelles ; il prétend jouir de la révolution, et réclamer ses droits à l'égalité, pour ne rien dire de plus.

DÉCLARATION DES DROITS DE LA FEMME ET DE LA CITOYENNE,

A décréter par l'Assemblée nationale dans ses dernières séances ou dans celle de la prochaine législature.

PRÉAMBULE.

Les mères, les filles, les soeurs, représentantes de la nation, demandent d'être constituées en assemblée nationale. Considérant que l'ignorance, l'oubli ou le mépris des droits de la femme, sont les seules causes des malheurs publics et de la corruption des gouvernemens, ont résolu d'exposer dans une déclaration solemnelle, les droits naturels, inaliénables et sacrés de la femme, afin que cette déclaration, constamment présente à tous les membres du corps social, leur rappelle sans cesse leurs droits et leurs devoirs, afin que les actes du pouvoir des

femmes, et ceux du pouvoir des hommes pouvant être à chaque instant comparés avec le but de toute institution politique, en soient plus respectés, afin que les réclamations des citoyennes, fondées désormais sur des principes simples et incontestables, tournent toujours au maintien de la constitution, des bonnes moeurs, et au bonheur de tous.

En conséquence, le sexe supérieur en beauté comme en courage, dans les souffrances maternelles, reconnaît et déclare, en présence et sous les auspices de l'Etre suprême, les Droits suivans de la Femme et de la Citoyenne.

ARTICLE PREMIER.

La Femme naît libre et demeure égale à l'homme en droits. Les distinctions sociales ne peuvent être fondées que sur l'utilité commune.

I I.

Le but de toute association politique est la conservation des droits naturels et imprescriptibles de la Femme et de l'Homme : ces droits sont la liberté, la propriété, la sûreté, et sur-tout la résistance à l'oppression.

I I I.

Le principe de toute souveraineté réside

A 4

ABOVE: Olympe de Gouges based her feminist manifesto on the official Declaration of 1789. She challenged the Revolution's unequal treatment of women by addressing each point of the earlier Declaration and making the language gender-equal. "Man," she asked, "are you capable of being just?"

Declaration of the Rights of Woman and of the Female Citizen

(1791)

Angry that France's lofty Declaration of the Rights of Man and of the Citizen and the new Constitution both ignore women's rights, a courageous feminist writer and activist presents her own radical declaration demanding equal treatment. And how will the Revolution respond?

When France's National Assembly failed to extend civil and political equality to women, even despite a feminist outcry, the actress, playwright, and pamphleteer Olympe de Gouges (1748–93) decided to press the case.

Born into a petit bourgeoisie household in southwest France, and later widowed, de Gouges had become romantically involved with a wealthy man who supported her activism in antislavery and other risky political causes. This had enabled her to pen many political pamphlets and socially-conscious plays that championed human rights for all.

Considering the vital role that women had performed in the French Revolution and French society, de Gouges was disenchanted that the revolution's all-male leadership had turned their backs on women's rights. She and other feminists wanted action on suffrage, legal equality in marriage, the right of abused women to divorce their spouses, and other pressing issues.

So in 1791 de Gouges took a risk by publishing a brief manifesto, the Declaration of the Rights of Woman and of the Female Citizen, stating what her male counterparts had omitted. She even demanded that the National Assembly immediately enact her declaration as law. De Gouges's trenchant polemic parodied the sacrosanct Declaration of the Rights of Man and of the Citizen, using similar Enlightenment reasoning to expose the Revolution's continuing unequal treatment of women—an act of extraordinary boldness given the dangerous climate at that time.

In a scathing preamble, de Gouges blamed much of France's misfortune and corruption on its oppression of women and their rights. Following the same outline as the previous declaration, she went down the list of rights point by point to make the language gender-equal.

Article I, for example, now stated: "Woman is born free and remains equal to man in rights." Article VI established: "All citizens including women are equally admissible to all public dignities, offices and employments, according to their capacity, and with no other distinction than that of their virtues and talents."

In a rousing postscript, de Gouges exhorted women to wake up and discover they too had the rights proclaimed in the Declaration of the Rights of Man and of the Citizen. "What have women gained from the French Revolution?" she asked. "This revolution will only take effect when all women become fully aware of their deplorable condition, and of the rights they have lost in society."

Contrary to her demands, the National Assembly didn't immediately enact her brave declaration. Instead, under the Reign of Terror Olympe de Gouges was condemned as an "unnatural woman" and sent to the guillotine in November 1793. The rights she proposed were not granted until the Constitution of the French Fourth Republic was adopted in 1946.

Louisiana Purchase

(1803)

By means of fortuitous circumstances, the young United States stands to double its size by acquiring from Napoleon a vast expanse of France's colonial holdings in North America for a bargain sum—but will President Jefferson's unprecedented purchase document stand up in the Supreme Court and Congress?

Shortly after taking office in 1801, one of the major national security and trade concerns confronting the new president, Thomas Jefferson, involved the strategic importance of the Mississippi River, and especially the port of New Orleans—areas that belonged to France, not the United States.

Upon learning that Napoleon was secretly considering the revival of a French colonial empire in North America, Jefferson wished to avoid any future conflict regarding that region, particularly as it might involve America's natural friend and ally, France.

So he instructed his minister in Paris, Robert Livingston, to try to negotiate a deal to buy a tract of land on the lower Mississippi, or, if that failed, to seek an irrevocable guarantee from France for America's free navigation and the right of deposit. Jefferson also dispatched his friend James Monroe as Minister Plenipotentiary to France in an effort to negotiate for the purchase of New Orleans and west Florida for an amount ranging from $2 million to $10 million.

Monroe arrived in France to find that Napoleon—stunned by his losses in the bloody slave revolt in Haiti, and in anticipation of his coming war with Great Britain—had abandoned his dreams of a North American empire in favor of obtaining funds for other needs. As the negotiations got underway, the Americans were dumbfounded when the French asked how much the US was willing to pay for France's entire Louisiana territory.

An agreement was quickly reached. The formal document known as the Louisiana Purchase Agreement was made up of the Treaty of Cession and two Conventions setting forth the financial aspects of the transaction. The treaty was signed in Paris on April 30, 1803, by Citizen Francis Barbé Marbois of France and Livingston and Monroe.

Instead of spending up to $10 million for the port of New Orleans and the Floridas, the US ended up paying $15 million for an enormous territory of more than 828,000 square miles of land stretching west from the Mississippi River to the Rocky Mountains. The area was larger than most of Western Europe and amounted to a virtual doubling of the nation's total size, at a price of about four cents an acre.

It took several weeks for word of the deal to reach Washington by sea and the action was not announced until July 4.

Because the new nation's Constitution contained no provision for such a purchase, the Louisiana Purchase treaty had to undergo close scrutiny before it was eventually upheld by Chief Justice John Marshall and ratified by the Senate. The House also approved the appropriation, finalizing the greatest nonviolent land acquisition in American history.

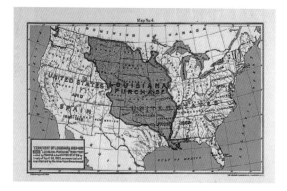

ABOVE AND RIGHT: A map showing the extent of the Louisiana Purchase. The territory secured by the treaty included the present-day states of Louisiana, Arkansas, Oklahoma, Missouri, Kansas, Colorado, Iowa, Nebraska, Wyoming, Montana, and North and South Dakota.

Treaty

Between the United States of America
and the French Republic

The President of the United States of America and the First Consul of the French Republic in the name of the French People desiring to remove all Source of misunderstanding relative to objects of discussion mentioned in the Second and fifth articles of the Convention of the { 8th Vendémiaire an 9 / 30 September 1800 } relative to the rights claimed by the United States in virtue of the Treaty concluded at Madrid the 27 of October 1795 between His Catholic Majesty, & the Said United States, & willing to strengthen the union and friendship which at the time of the Said Convention was happily reestablished between the two nations have respectively named their Plenipotentiaries to wit The President of the United States, by and with the advice and consent of the Senate of the Said State; Robert R. Livingston Minister Plenipotentiary of the United State and James Monroe Minister Plenipotentiary and Envoy extraordinary of the Said State near the Government of the French Republic; And the First Consul in the name of the French people, Citizen Francis Barbé Marbois Minister of the public treasury who after having respectively exchanged their full powers have agreed to the following articles

√ Mathematical Instruments . . . . . . √412.95
√ Arms, Ammunition & Accoutrements . . √182.08
√ Medicine &c . . . . √ 94.49
Clothing . . . . √317.73
√ Provisions &c . . . . √366.70
                                        √669.50
√ Indian Presents (see below) 663.84
                                        116.68
√ Camp Equipage ————   148.30
                                        2145.99
Indian Presents additional ————   15.67
                                        2,161.66
                                        2160.13
                                        ————
                                        1.53
                                        2160.13

Israel Whelen Esqr   Philadᵈ. June 1ˢᵗ 1803
for Cap Lewis —   Dᵗ. of David Jackson
  30 Gallons Strong Spt. Wine @ 233/3 $ 70
   6 Iron Bound Kegs ——— 1.20   7.20
                            $ 77.20

Duplicate,   Received the above articles.
                        Meriwether Lewis
                        Capt 1ˢᵗ US Regt Infty.

ABOVE: *The $116.68 allocated for "Indian Presents" in this early shopping list (top) rose to $696 in Lewis's final list of expenses. Despite alcohol being a precious commodity, Lewis purchased thirty gallons of "Strong Spt. Wine" (brandy) in Philadelphia before embarking on his expedition. This was in addition to his crew's main refreshment—120 gallons of whiskey.*

Meriwether Lewis's List of Expenses

(1803)

Before setting off with William Clark on his epic overland expedition westward to the Pacific, Jefferson's protégé prepares a detailed list of all the equipment and supplies that Congress will need to authorize for purchase. Nearly one-third of the total projected cost is for "Indian presents."

While final negotiations were still going on for the Louisiana Purchase, President Jefferson proceeded with another audacious plan—this one involving exploration of the vast, uncharted North American continent west of the Mississippi River. In the fall of 1802 he picked his secretary and disciple, Meriwether Lewis (1774–1809), to head an expedition of discovery. Specially trained in astronomy, navigation, surveying, geography, botany, zoology, engineering, biology, medicine, writing, politics, and art, Lewis also received instruction in the use of a cipher to enable him to secretly communicate with the President in order to safeguard their activities from foreign powers.

Lewis was ordered to keep meticulous records of the expedition, and for starters, in order to receive federal funding for the mission, he had to draw up an estimate of costs, based on his projected expenses for equipping and supporting an officer and ten to twelve soldiers across the wilderness.

His detailed accounting added up to $2,500 for clothing, guns, ammunition, medical supplies, camp gear, and scientific instruments, with $696 earmarked for "gifts to the Indians." The latter underscored Jefferson's recognition of the mission's importance in opening diplomatic relations between the United States and the as-yet-unknown Native American nations of the West, in hopes of gaining their favor in trade over the English, French, or Spanish. The President told Lewis, "it will now be proper you should inform those through whose country you will pass...that henceforth we become their fathers and friends."

Based on his limited understanding of Native American affairs, Jefferson anticipated this would entail the giving of ceremonial gifts to establish cordial relations. But there was no way of telling what kind of reception they might encounter. Lewis's list of gifts included pocket mirrors, sewing needles and thread, steels for striking fire, scissors, glass beads, silk scarves, ivory combs, rolls of tobacco, tomahawks, knives, fishhooks, and other items considered enticing and appropriate.

With Congressional approval in early 1803, Lewis and Capt. William Clark were officially appointed to head the venture, to be called the Corps of Discovery. The expedition began at the Mississippi River in May 1804 and proceeded west until they crossed the Rockies and came within sight of the Pacific Ocean on November 7, 1805. Then they returned to St. Louis, Missouri on September 23, 1806. At the time the results were considered mixed. On one hand they had proved the feasibility of an overland crossing of the continent and met with more than two dozen indigenous nations, mapping and establishing their presence for a legal claim to the land. But their mission failed to find an easy water route across the western expanse.

Lewis died of gunshot wounds in 1809. He had been on his way to Washington, DC, to reclaim payment of drafts he had drawn against the War Department. It was never established whether he committed suicide or was murdered.

The Meriwether Lewis records are held by the National Archives.

Napoléonic Code

(1804)

Napoléon Bonaparte establishes a comprehensive civil code that abolishes feudalism, fosters religious tolerance, and enacts other liberal reforms across Europe. Building on Roman law and principles of the French Revolution, it proves to be one of the most influential legal codes in world history.

The French military commander and political leader Napoléon Bonaparte (1769–1821) dominated European affairs from 1799 to 1815, serving much of that time as supreme ruler over a vast and growing empire. His ambitious, hands-on style and attention to detail extended to a sweeping reform of the French legal system, which under the *ancien régime* had long suffered from a welter of problems including an excessive number of privilege-based courts with overlapping jurisdictions that conducted slow and exorbitantly expensive proceedings to produce rampant injustice.

To remedy the situation, Napoléon appointed a commission of experts who spent more than two years discussing the subject. Napoléon himself attended many of the meetings and astounded the jurists with his deep knowledge of ancient Roman law and his ability to get things done.

The result was a sweeping new French civil code (*Code civil des français*), known as the Napoléonic Code or Code Napoléon, which took effect on March 21, 1804, shortly before the ruler would be declared Emperor of France.

Modeled on Justinian's sixth-century codification of Roman law and other exemplars, Napoléon's comprehensive structure was highly rational and lacking in religious content. It also incorporated the French Revolution's ideas of liberty, equality, and fraternity in clear vernacular French. In keeping with the Revolution, vestiges of feudalism and royal privilege were seemingly abolished. The Code required that for laws to be properly applied, they first had to be duly promulgated and enacted. Secret laws were ended. *Ex post facto* laws were invalidated. And procedures were required to make the application of the laws just and fair.

Not everything about the Code represented a step forward, however, as Napoléon's act also reinforced patriarchal power by making the husband the ruler of the household, with supremacy over his wife and minor children; and its abolition of divorce by mutual consent actually amounted to a significant regression for French women. (Notwithstanding the revolt in Saint-Domingue, in 1802 he had already restored hideous black slavery in France's colonies.)

But Napoléon was pleased that his new laws had been disseminated throughout the empire, and said late in his life: "Waterloo will wipe out the memory of my forty victories; but that which nothing can wipe out is my Civil Code. That will live forever."

An original copy of the Napoléonic Code is housed in the Historisches Museum der Pfalz in Speyer, Germany.

ABOVE AND RIGHT: Napoléon's weighty tome is divided into three books that comprise 2,281 clauses, 1,570 of which are related to property. He wrote into law what the Revolution had promised or practiced. Feudalism and royal privilege were seemingly abolished.

CODE CIVIL

DES

FRANÇAIS.

ÉDITION ORIGINALE ET SEULE OFFICIELLE.

GRAND JUGE ET MINISTRE DE LA JUSTICE.

À PARIS,

DE L'IMPRIMERIE DE LA RÉPUBLIQUE.

An XII. — 1804.

Tableau des Signes Phonétiques des Écritures Hiéroglyphique et Démotique des anciens Égyptiens — Pl. IV

Deciphering the Rosetta Stone

(1822)

After more than a decade of obsessive work studying the mysterious hieroglyphics on the famous Rosetta Stone, a young Frenchman has an epiphany that he describes in a letter to the head of the country's leading scholarly organization. He has cracked the code.

At age ten, Jean-François Champollion (1790–1832) became enchanted by stories of Napoléon's Egyptian campaign, the pyramids, and the strange ancient hieroglyphs that no European had been able to decipher. Upon visiting an exhibition of antiquities decorated with the odd-looking inscriptions, he vowed that one day he would solve the mystery and decode them.

In the 1810s, Champollion closely followed the exacting empirical work of the English polymath Thomas Young, who was publishing his theories about Egyptian hieroglyphs that were based on his study of the Rosetta Stone. The ancient stele from the days of the pharaohs had been recovered by French soldiers in the Nile Delta in 1799. But efforts to decipher its extensive script, apparently written in three different languages, had thwarted Young and everyone else. Champollion was determined to crack the code.

On September 14, 1822, while in Paris, Champollion made a crucial breakthrough that revealed the phonetic nature of hieroglyphics. He proclaimed *"Je tiens l'affaire!"* ("I've got it!"), before fainting on the spot.

He immediately sent a letter to the secretary of the French Académie des Inscriptions et Belles-Lettres regarding his discovery. On September 27, Champollion read the eight-page document before a packed room at the Académie. "I am certain," he wrote, that the same hieroglyphic-phonetical signs used to represent the sounds of Greek or Roman proper names, are also employed in hieroglyphic texts inscribed far prior to the arrival of the Greeks in Egypt, and that they at that earlier time already had the same representative sound or articulations as in the cartouches inscribed under the Greeks or Romans.

Shortly afterward, Champollion published his findings in a booklet of forty-four pages containing four illustrated plates. His work was instrumental in showing that the Rosetta Stone, dating from 196 BC, had announced a decree issued on behalf of King Ptolemy V, in three different languages. The lowest text was written in Ancient Greek, the middle one in Demotic (Egyptian) script, and the top version was written in Ancient Egyptian hieroglyphs. Because the stone presented essentially the same text in all three scripts, and one of the languages (Ancient Greek) could be understood, this held the key to decoding two forgotten languages.

Based on his discoveries, Champollion became known as the "Father of the Decipherment of Hieroglyphs." His original papers are displayed at the Champollion Museum in Figeac, France.

LEFT: Champollion's phonetic table held the key to the Rosetta Stone, showing that hieroglyphs recorded the sound of the Egyptian language. His discovery laid the foundation for our understanding of ancient Egyptian language and culture.

First Photograph

(1826)

A brilliant French inventor labors for more than a decade to capture real-life images as lasting records by means of a process he calls Heliographie; his first surviving effort, depicting the country scene outside his workshop window, is considered the first permanent photographic image.

Joseph Nicéphore Niépce (1765–1833) was an ingenious French inventor who had created a number of amazing mechanical devices, including the Pyréolophore (the world's first internal combustion engine), a hydraulic Marly machine for pumping water, and the delightful Velocipede (an early version of the bicycle). Some of his longtime fascinations converged around his dream of capturing sunlight and a desire to develop improved processes in the emerging art of lithography. Although he was not an artist, he saw great commercial potential in such pursuits, provided he could make it work.

In April 1816 using a camera obscura he managed to capture small images on paper he had coated with silver chloride, which excited him. But the strange results were darkest where they should have been brightest and vice versa—what we now know as negatives—and the images quickly faded. After countless experiments with different light-sensitive materials and techniques, in 1822 he succeeded in copying a copperplate engraving by laying it on a glass plate coated with bitumen of Judea, although that achievement also proved rather primitive.

Four years later, on a sunny spring day at his country estate Le Gras at Chalon-sur-Saone, Niépce conducted an eight-hour-long experiment using a professionally crafted camera made by the Parisian optician Charles Chevalier to capture an image upon a pewter plate. With cotton swabs he coated the plate with an emulsion of bitumen of Judea. The coating, dissolved in oil of lavender, hardened in the brightly lit parts, whereas the dimly lit areas remained soluble and

the coating was washed away with a solvent consisting of oil of lavender and white petroleum (turpentine). The result was a permanent positive picture in which the light was preserved by bitumen and the darker shades by bare pewter.

There, preserved on the pewter, was the image of the view from his high workroom window. It showed the pigeon-house on the left, a pear-tree with a patch of sky showing through its branches; at the center one could clearly see the barn's slanting roof, and another wing of the house on the right-hand side.

Niépce believed he had made a major discovery, which he called *Heliographie* (for sun drawing). But he was never able to capitalize on it. Upon his death in 1833, Niépce's notes were passed on to his associate, Louis-Jacques-Mandé Daguerre (1787–1851), the creator of the daguerreotype, who made further improvements. In 1839, the new art form became known as "photography."

Niépce's original picture from 1826, meanwhile, was rediscovered in 1952 when the historian Helmut Gernsheim credited Niépce as the inventor of photography and "View from the Window at Le Gras" was identified as the world's oldest surviving photograph. The original plate belongs to the Ransom Center at the University of Texas at Austin.

LEFT: This daguerreotype is the earliest surviving photographic self-portrait. It was taken in 1839 by Philadelphia-based photographer Robert Cornelius.

ABOVE: This is the earliest surviving photograph. Taken in 1826 by Joseph Nicéphore Niépce, it is a view from the photographer's studio window in Le Gras, France. BELOW: Louis Daguerre's 1838 photograph of Boulevard du Temple in Paris is the earliest known photograph to include people.

ANNO TERTIO & QUARTO

GULIELMI IV. REGIS.

****

C A P. LXXIII.

An Act for the Abolition of Slavery throughout the *British* Colonies; for promoting the Industry of the manumitted Slaves; and for compensating the Persons hitherto entitled to the Services of such Slaves.　　　　[28th *August* 1833.]

WHEREAS divers Persons are holden in Slavery within divers of His Majesty's Colonies, and it is just and expedient that all such Persons should be manumitted and set free, and that a reasonable Compensation should be made to the Persons hitherto entitled to the Services of such Slaves for the Loss which they will incur by being deprived of their Right to such Services: And whereas it is also expedient that Provision should be made for promoting the Industry and securing the good Conduct of the Persons so to be manumitted, for a limited Period after such their Manumission: And whereas it is necessary that the Laws now in force in the said several Colonies should forthwith be adapted to the new State and Relations of Society therein which will follow upon such general Manumission as aforesaid of the said Slaves; and that, in order to afford the necessary Time for such Adaptation of the said Laws, a short Interval should elapse before such Manumission should take effect: Be it therefore enacted by the King's most Excellent Majesty, by and with the Advice and Consent of the Lords Spiritual and Temporal, and Commons, in this present Parliament assembled, and by the Authority of the same, That from and after the First Day of *August* One thousand eight hundred and thirty-four

All Persons who on the 1st August 1834 shall

10 Y

ABOVE: The Act made an exception for "Territories in the Possession of the East India Company, or to the Island of Ceylon, or to the Island of Saint Helena." Slavery continued there until the Indian Slavery Act of 1843. OPPOSITE: William Wilberforce, a key figure in the fight for abolition, died in July 1833, a month before the Act received its Royal Assent.

Slavery Abolition Act

(1833)

Pressured by slave revolts and abolitionist agitation, Parliament finally outlaws slavery in the British Empire, with some exceptions and caveats. The act includes a provision for huge compensation, not for the slaves, but for the slave owners—reparations for the wealthy.

By the time Parliament outlawed the international slave trade in 1807, British ships had carried more than three million Africans into bondage and slavery was booming in the colonies. Although judicial action in 1772 had ended the practice of slavery in Great Britain, and slave trading in the British Empire was ceased in 1807, a growing anti-slavery movement was demanding the abolition of British slavery anywhere.

Slave resistance and rebellion fueled the unrest. During Jamaica's Christmas holiday of 1831, a slave preacher named Sam Sharpe led a peaceful protest in the island's sugarcane fields that escalated into a full-fledged revolt. The Jamaican planters suppressed the uprising at a cost of hundreds of slaves and fourteen whites killed, prompting many abolitionists to escalate their campaign.

In response to the furor, the British Parliament conducted two inquiries, which contributed to the passage of an "Act for the Abolition of Slavery throughout the British Colonies; for promoting the Industry of the manumitted Slaves; and for compensating the Persons hitherto entitled to the Services of such Slaves." The Act received Royal Assent in August 1833 and came into force on August 1, 1834.

In practical terms, the Anti-Slavery Act only freed slaves below the age of six. Those who were older were redesignated as "apprentices" and their servitude was gradually abolished in two stages: the first set of apprenticeships were to end in 1838, while the final (exceptional) apprenticeships were scheduled to cease in 1840. All "apprentices" were expected to continue serving their former owners until their apprenticeships expired. In the words of the Act: "it is just and expedient that all such Persons should be manumitted and set free."

A crucial provision for the slave owners addressed the issue of compensation for those who would be losing their "property." Under the Act, the British government authorized £20 million to compensate the registered owners for the loss of their business assets. Although the sum for reparations amounted to a staggering 40 percent of the government's total annual expenditure, it didn't offer a penny to the former slaves or their descendants.

The Act also provided for a Parliamentary Return listing of the names of those who had been compensated. Records showed that hundreds of wealthy British families were considerably enriched by the payoffs. The awardees included Henry Phillpotts, the Bishop of Exeter; John Gladstone (the father of nineteenth-century Prime Minister William Gladstone); ancestors of British Prime Minister David Cameron, and many others.

Records of the original documents are preserved in Britain's National Archives. A database bearing the names of the plantation owners and the compensation they received is kept by University College London.

Charles Darwin on Natural Selection

(1837–59)

Twenty-two years after his first epiphany on the subject and seventeen years after he coins the term "natural selection," an English naturalist finally gets around to publishing his revolutionary theory. Documents show how his thinking has evolved, providing a paper trail of his development.

Charles Darwin (1809–82), the English naturalist and geologist, often documented his field observations and ruminations in notebooks that recorded his newest discoveries as they were unfolding. The first expressions of his powerful new ideas were brimming with excitement.

In mid-July of 1837, for example, shortly after returning home from his five-year-long, life-changing voyage of discovery aboard the *Beagle*, the then-twenty-eight-year-old scientist drew an abstract sketch of a tree to symbolize some of his embryonic thoughts about evolution, along with the words, "I think." He recorded it on page thirty-six of his First Notebook on Transmutation of Species (Notebook B).

In September 1838, while reading Thomas Malthus's famous *An Essay on the Principle of Population* with its supposed statistical proof that human populations breed beyond their means and ability to survive, Darwin noted a similarity he perceived in the struggle for existence among different species of plants. On page 135e of his Transmutation Notebook D, he described "a force like a hundred thousand wedges" pushing well-adapted plant variations into "gaps in the economy of nature," so that the survivors would somehow pass on their stronger qualities while lesser variations would simply die out.

In a pencil sketch of 1842, Darwin wrote the words "Natural Means of Selection," and he later coined the phrase "natural selection" in another entry. These and other day-by-day writings recorded how Darwin developed his theory of natural selection over a long period but held back from publishing the results until he was ready. Scholars still speculate about why he waited, but clearly he recognized how astronomers and other scientists over the ages had suffered persecution for their new ideas. He also realized that his theory would upset many religious authorities who had adopted a literal version of the Creation from the Bible.

At last Charles Darwin's theory of evolution was published as *On the Origin of Species by Natural Selection* on November 24, 1859. "I have called this principle, by which each slight variation, if useful, is preserved, by the term of Natural Selection," he wrote. Although the work seemed fresh and revolutionary to most readers, it wasn't new to him. He had developed it over many years and by then was fifty years old; the initial excitement had mellowed. Yet his thinking transformed the way that scientists viewed the natural world. "The expression often used by Mr. Herbert Spencer," he wrote, "of the Survival of the Fittest, is more accurate, and in some times equally convenient."

Darwin's papers reside at Cambridge University, where today readers can study them on the Internet via Darwin Online.

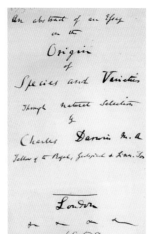

LEFT AND RIGHT: The original handwritten manuscript of On the Origin of Species *(1859) and the now-iconic sketch from Notebook B, showing a prototype of the evolutionary tree that formed the basis of Darwin's theory of natural selection.*

I think

Case must be that one generation then should be as many living as now. To do this & to have many species in same genus (as is) requires extinction.

Thus between _A_ & B. immense gap of relation. C & B. the finest gradation, B & D rather greater distinction Thus genera would be formed. — bearing relation

LEFT: *Morse's drawings of overhead telegraph poles from his notebooks of 1844. In a letter from the same year, Morse raises a note of caution about this new form of communication: "Be especially careful not to give a partisan character to any information you may transmit." His warning is just as relevant in today's age of instant messaging and social media.*

RIGHT: *An illustration of a Morse Telegraph Receiver from 1844.*

BELOW: *The first telegram, sent from Washington to Baltimore at 8:45 AM on Friday, May 24, 1844.*

First Telegram

(1844)

Samuel F.B. Morse's introduction of the telegraph seems to have fizzled until a young girl with a crush on the widower-inventor rekindles his hopes and also comes up with the famous text of the message that is transmitted as the world's first telegram.

By 1843 the gifted portrait painter Samuel F.B. Morse (1791–1872) had spent more than a decade trying to realize his idea for a revolutionary new communications system using electricity to transmit message signals for long distances over wires. Working with his assistant Alfred Vail, his old college friend Henry Ellsworth and others, the self-taught scientist struggled to gain the necessary funding and technical support to achieve his goal. The financial Panic of 1837 and other hardships didn't help in his endeavors. After overcoming countless obstacles, Morse asked Congress for $30,000 that would allow him to build an overhead telegraph line from Washington to Baltimore, 40 miles away. At last he managed to get an appropriation bill through the House of Representatives but it had languished in the Senate through the final closing hours of the session, leaving him exhausted and bereft. In the bewitching hours of March 3, he left the Senate Chamber with less than a dollar to his name, resigned to his ruin.

Ellsworth, however, managed to pull off a last-minute approval of the legislation and President John Tyler immediately signed it into law. When an ebullient

Ellsworth informed his family at the breakfast table, his seventeen-year-old daughter agreed to alert Morse before their friend's scheduled departure back to New Haven. A part-time copyist at the Patent Office, Annie Ellsworth had long revered the fifty-two-year-old widower and secretly had a crush on him, so she welcomed the chance to deliver the good news on her way to work. Morse was so thankful he said he would give her the honor of selecting the first message over his new telegraph line.

That day came on May 24, 1844 when she gave Morse the words she had taken from Numbers 23:23: "What hath God wrought?" From his station in the old Supreme Court chamber of the Capitol, Morse sent it to Alfred Vail at the Mount Clare depot in Baltimore, by means of his dot-and-dash code. The dits and dahs flashed over the wire as coded electrical impulses.

At his telegraph station in Baltimore, Vail received the signals that the machine had converted to raised dots and dashes on a paper tape, which he translated to their corresponding letters of the alphabet. The resulting document proved the success of the experiment and inaugurated a world-changing new form of rapid long-distance communication. Proving relatively cheap to install and easy to use, the telegraph linked stations throughout the country.

Yet the initial success received little notice. Only fifteen persons were present with Morse when he sent off his first telegraph message from Washington that day and the only newspaper coverage occurred in Baltimore, three days later. Annie Ellsworth's text wasn't mentioned.

The Communist Manifesto

(1848)

A 12,000-word pamphlet written by two young German philosophers offers a radical new interpretation of history and political economy—and forms the basis for a movement which will later sweep the world. "WORKERS OF THE WORLD UNITE!"

"The history of all hitherto existing societies is the history of class struggle." So begins *The Communist Manifesto*, a brief statement of purpose that was written in late 1847 by two young German intellectuals and militants, Karl Marx and Friedrich Engels, and first published in German as *Manifest der Kommunistischen Partei* in London in February 1848. Shortly after its appearance, and their prompt expulsion from England, the pair participated in the ill-fated Revolution of 1848 while serving as newspaper editors in Cologne.

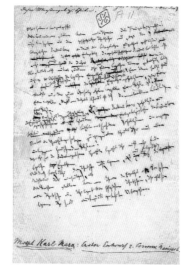

The first English translation of the *Manifesto* appeared two years later and numerous more editions were published in German, Russian, French, and English over the next three decades. The first American publication occurred in 1872, a decade after Marx ended his assignment as a foreign correspondent for the *New York Daily Tribune*. It was not until the twentieth century that the work would reach its largest audience and give rise to numerous communist revolutions across the globe.

According to the pair's analysis (written mostly by Marx over a frantic six-week period), the nature of history's ongoing class struggle unfolds according to the nature of the principal form of production. Thus, in agrarian societies the class struggle was between the landowners and those who worked the fields—lords versus serfs. Marx and Engels posited that during the Industrial Revolution a third class—the bourgeoisie—had emerged to own the means of production, whereas the proletariat (working class) owned nothing except their own ability to work. "Of all the classes that stand face to face with the bourgeoisie today," he wrote, "the proletariat alone is a really revolutionary class."

Marx coined the term "capitalism" for the mode of production developed by the bourgeoisie—saying it was a profit-driven system that was constantly forced to expand, which it did by the "constant revolutionizing of production [and] uninterrupted disturbance of all social conditions." *The Communist Manifesto* offered a penetrating analysis of capitalism along with the prediction that such an economic system would eventually be replaced by socialism and ultimately communism.

"You are horrified at our intending to do away with private property," they write. "But in your existing society, private property is already done away with for nine tenths of the population; its existence for the few is solely due to its non-existence in the hands of those nine tenths."

The work listed several short-term demands, such as the abolition of private land, state takeover of the means of production, a hefty progressive income tax, free public education, and the abolition of child labor.

No original copy of the manuscript has been found, except for a single page in Marx's frenzied script, which is kept in a Moscow archive.

THESAURUS

OF

ENGLISH WORDS AND PHRASES,

CLASSIFIED AND ARRANGED

SO AS

TO FACILITATE THE EXPRESSION OF IDEAS

AND ASSIST IN

LITERARY COMPOSITION.

BY PETER MARK ROGET, M.D., F.R.S., F.R.A.S., F.G.S.

FELLOW OF THE ROYAL COLLEGE OF PHYSICIANS;

MEMBER OF THE SENATE OF THE UNIVERSITY OF LONDON;

OF THE LITERARY AND PHILOSOPHICAL SOCIETIES ETC. OF MANCHESTER, LIVERPOOL,
BRISTOL, QUEBEC, NEW YORK, HAARLEM, TURIN, AND STOCKHOLM.

AUTHOR OF

THE "BRIDGEWATER TREATISE ON ANIMAL AND VEGETABLE PHYSIOLOGY,"

ETC.

"It is impossible we should thoroughly understand the nature of the SIGNS, unless
we first properly consider and arrange the THINGS SIGNIFIED."—Ἔπεα Πτερόεντα.

LONDON:

LONGMAN, BROWN, GREEN, AND LONGMANS.

1852.

*ABOVE: Roget's handwritten lists of synonyms,
which he started to compile in 1805, formed a
personal treasure trove of words that helped
him "facilitate the expression of ideas."*

*RIGHT: Roget, photographed in the early
1860s, some ten years after the publication
of his* Thesaurus. *His intense work on the
project offered a distraction from the bouts of
depression that plagued his adult life.*

*ABOVE: In the preface to the first edition, Roget explained how
the publication of his* Thesaurus *absorbed all of his spare
time: "Since my retirement from the duties of Secretary to
the Royal Society, however, finding myself possessed of more
leisure ... I resolved to embark in an undertaking which, for the
last three or four years, has given me incessant occupation."*

Roget's Thesaurus

(1852)

In an effort to aid himself in finding the proper word when he needs it, an English polymath invents his own classification system, and forty-seven years later he has it published as his "thesaurus." The work has remained in print ever since, and become a standard reference tool for millions of writers.

Peter Mark Roget (1779–1869) was a brilliant British physician and polymath. Like others in his family, he often suffered from bouts of depression, some of it stemming from a traumatic incident in which his beloved uncle had committed suicide by slashing his throat in the young man's presence. Yet he was a high achiever, gaining election as a Fellow of the Royal Society in 1815 and serving as that organization's secretary for over twenty years. He also held many other esteemed posts.

As the author of innumerable scientific papers on a host of subjects, Roget was never one to sit idly by, however, and in an effort to keep himself on track and escape from melancholia, he became a compulsive list-

maker. Obsessed with compiling indices, tables, catalogs and sorting schemes of many sorts, he was particularly influenced by Carl Linnaeus's zoological classification system.

Blessed with an insatiable hunger for knowledge and an inexhaustible appetite for work, Roget always strived to use the precise word for what he wished to convey. To aid himself in this task, in order to "supply my own deficiencies," in 1805 he set about expanding this list-making to create a system whereby he could organize his word lists by meaning in order to efficiently find the right word when he needed it. He worked feverishly on the scheme for a year, calling the finished manuscript his "thesaurus" from the Greek word for treasury or storehouse.

Over the next forty-four years, Roget often consulted his personal classification system of related words and found it useful in his writing. But he never shared the system with other writers. When he turned seventy his daughter suggested that he publish the document as a retirement project and he agreed.

Three years later in 1852 Roget published his *Thesaurus of English Words and Phrases Classified and Arranged so as to Facilitate the Expression of Ideas and Assist in Literary Composition.* The book listed 15,000 words. Roget did not consider them synonyms because he believed every word was unique, but over time, the very name Roget would come to signify synonym for many readers.

The book has been reprinted and expanded countless times, making it one of the standard desk reference works for students, teachers, and writers of all kinds. The latest edition contains over 250,000 words. Millions of copies of the book remain in use.

A collection of Roget's manuscripts can be found in the Karpeles Manuscript Library in Illinois.

John Snow's Cholera Map

(1854)

An independent-minded physician uses empirical methods to identify the source of a deadly cholera outbreak, thereby revolutionizing theories about the way that some diseases are transmitted. His findings prompt sweeping changes in public health and help to establish the new life-saving field of epidemiology.

London in the mid-nineteenth century was terrorized by a series of lethal cholera epidemics that turned its sufferers "dead-blue." While the prevailing wisdom attributed the cause to everything from bad weather and foul smells to poverty, the source of the disease and an effective remedy remained unknown.

John Snow (1813–58) was an empirically-minded English physician whose groundbreaking research sought to improve the public health in such matters as anesthesia and medical hygiene. His scientific studies had led him to doubt the then-dominant "miasma" theory which attributed such diseases as bubonic plague and cholera to "bad air." So when London's Soho district near his home was struck by another deadly wave of cholera, Snow began compiling detailed evidence about the incidence and path of the disease.

Using interviews, skilled reasoning, graphs, and maps to record data about the victims' locations, the investigator soon focused his interest on the Broad Street water pump. "I found that nearly all the deaths had taken place within a short distance of the pump," he wrote. He established that there had not been an outbreak of cholera throughout Soho, just among people who were in the habit of using the Broad Street pump.

Research later revealed that the well from which the pump drew its water had indeed been dug only three feet from an old cesspit, causing it to leak deadly bacteria into the water supply.

Snow published his findings, complete with maps showing the incidence of recorded deaths in Soho, which clustered around the suspicious water pump. The graphic results eventually convinced the authorities to shut down the pump in question, which brought an end to the epidemic. Snow's findings regarding water-borne disease inspired fundamental changes in London's public water and waste systems, which quickly led to similar improvements in other cities throughout the world.

Snow died young from a stroke. But his work lived on. Known today as the "father of modern epidemiology," his work is also credited with making some of the foundational contributions to the new field of data mapping and data visualization.

Copies of Snow's early cholera documents are widely published.

LEFT: *John Snow received many posthumous accolades for his pioneering work. A statue of a water pump was erected on Broad Street (now Broadwick Street) in his memory and a nearby public house was named after him.*

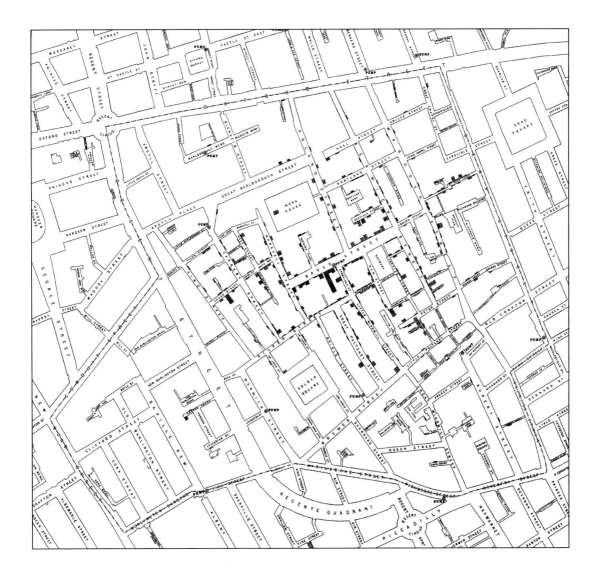

ABOVE: Snow's map showed that the majority of cholera-related deaths were concentrated around the Broad Street water pump. He concluded: "The result of the inquiry, then, is that there has been no particular outbreak or prevalence of cholera in this part of London except among the persons who were in the habit of drinking the water of the above-mentioned pump well."

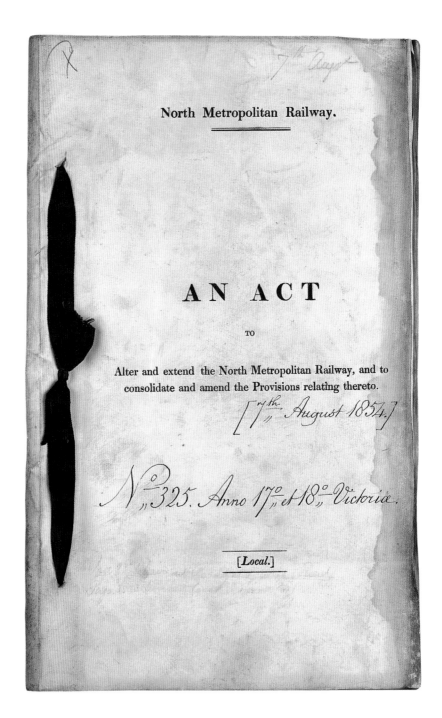

North Metropolitan Railway.

AN ACT

TO

Alter and extend the North Metropolitan Railway, and to
consolidate and amend the Provisions relating thereto.

[7th August 1854.]

No. 325. Anno 17° et 18° Victoriæ.

[Local.]

ABOVE: Charles Pearson helped draft the North Metropolitan Railway Act that led to the opening of the first underground train system. He did not live to see the completion of the project, however, having died of dropsy in September 1862. The original Act of 1854 is kept in London's Parliamentary Archives.
RIGHT: An engraving showing the construction of the Metropolitan Railway around King's Cross.

First Underground Train System

(1854–63)

A visionary reformer recognizes the need for improved public transportation to and from London, and his relentless campaign to build a subterranean iron road beneath the teeming city finally becomes realized only a few months after his death. The world's first subway is a huge success.

With a population of more than 2.5 million, London by the 1850s had developed into the world's first megalopolis, stretching out from its ancient core on the Thames to distant suburbs, the hub of a mighty, imperial empire. As the seat of international commerce, it was both the richest city on the globe and one of the most congested, its roadways clogged each day with more than a quarter million commuters and horses that left more than 3 million tons of droppings amid the puddles and grime. The traffic to and fro was a nightmare.

A Londoner from birth, Charles Pearson (1793–1862) was a dutiful member of the middle class who had entered public service in 1816 and spent his whole life engaged in various social causes. Being old enough to remember what the city had been like before the industrial revolution, he sought a way to clear the streets. Although railroads were still relatively new—the first

locomotive-driven railway between cities, the Liverpool and Manchester Railway, had only begun operating in 1830—by 1845, Pearson, now a solicitor for the City of London, began imagining a new kind of smokeless public rail transportation for the future.

In 1854, he authored a major research report that ascribed much of the city's overcrowding to poor traffic control of the growing "migratory population." Besides helping to gain Royal Assent to the North Metropolitan Railway Act on August 7, 1854, he also devised the financing scheme for the construction of the Metropolitan Railway heading northwest from the city's financial heart, at an estimated cost of £1 million.

A variety of approaches were employed to build the railway underground. Some sections involved tunneling beneath the city; others were done by leveling the existing structures, digging a deep trench for the rail bed and later covering it to accommodate future buildings over the railway. Despite a number of accidents, collapses, floods, and other mishaps that occurred during the excavation, the engineering feat was largely accomplished by 1861, when the first of many trial runs were conducted. The first trial trip over the entire line was staged in May 1862 with a party of prominent passengers including William Gladstone, the Chancellor of the Exchequer, aboard.

After a grand opening ceremony on January 9, 1863, the Metropolitan Railway opened to the public the following day, when its steam locomotives hauled gas-lit wooden carriages carrying 38,000 passengers between Paddington and Farringdon Street.

The world's first underground railway was a resounding success, carrying 9.5 million passengers in its first twelve months and 12 million in its second year.

Fort Sumter Telegram

(1861)

The commander of a bombarded Army fort in Charleston Harbor sends a hurried message to the Secretary of War in Washington, informing him of his garrison's surrender. It means that the Confederacy has staged an attack against the United States. The War Between the States has begun.

Following South Carolina's secession from the United States and Abraham Lincoln's inauguration as President, on April 10, 1861 Brig. Gen. Pierre G.T. Beauregard of the provisional Confederate forces demanded the surrender of the besieged US garrison of Fort Sumter in Charleston Harbor.

The rebel forces numbered 10,000 well-equipped men while the defenders had only sixty-eight soldiers with inferior armaments and scant food and supplies. But the fort's commander, US Army Major Robert Anderson, refused to concede.

On Friday, April 12 at 4:30 AM, Confederate Lieutenant Henry S. Farley, commanding a battery of two 10-inch siege mortars on James Island, fired the first shot at the US fort, beginning a long cannonade. At about 7:00 AM, Captain Abner Doubleday, Sumter's second in command, fired the first salvo in response, aware that his guns weren't capable of reaching their target. The Confederates' bombardment continued for thirty-four hours.

Realizing that resistance was futile and lacking hope of immediate reinforcements, Anderson raised a white flag of surrender on April 13 at 2:30 PM. He was allowed to evacuate the following day and escaped to the North.

As soon as he was able to do so, on April 18 at 10:30 AM Anderson telegraphed from the steamship *Baltic* off Sandy Hook to US Secretary of War Simon Cameron in Washington, informing him of what had transpired. "HAVING DEFENDED FORT SUMTER FOR THIRTY FOUR HOURS," he reported, "UNTIL THE QUARTERS WERE ENTIRELY BURNED THE MAIN GATES DESTROYED BY FIRE. THE GORGE WALLS SERIOUSLY INJURED. THE MAGAZINE SURROUNDED BY FLAMES AND ITS DOOR CLOSED FROM THE EFFECTS OF HEAT."

The document's import was immediately clear. Robert Toombs, the Confederate Secretary of State, said at the time, "The firing upon that fort will inaugurate a civil war greater than any the world has yet seen…" Upon receiving the telegram, President Lincoln ordered 75,000 volunteers and called Congress into session. The assault became a rallying cry for the Union cause.

Although the attack resulted in just two Union soldiers killed and two wounded, with no casualties on the other side, the incident marked the opening engagement of the exceptionally bloody Civil War.

The original Fort Sumter telegram is kept in the National Archives in Washington, DC.

ABOVE: Fort Sumter on April 15, 1861, forty-eight hours after Major Robert Anderson's surrender. The Stars and Bars flag of the Confederate States flies high above one of the gutted structures inside the fort. RIGHT: The Fort Sumter telegram documented the first battle of the Civil War. After receiving the telegram, President Lincoln ordered 75,000 volunteers and called Congress into session.

S.S.BALTIC.OFF SANDY HOOK APR.EIGHTEENTH.TEN THIRTY A.M. .VIA NEW YORK. . HON.S.CAMERON. SECY.WAR. WASHN. HAVING DEFENDED FORT SUMTER FOR THIRTY FOUR HOURS UNTIL THE QUARTERS WERE ENTIRELY BURNED THE MAIN GATES DESTROYED BY FIRE.THE GORGE WALLS SERIOUSLY INJURED.THE MAGAZINE SURROUNDED BY FLAMES AND ITS DOOR CLOSED FROM THE EFFECTS OF HEAT .FOUR BARRELLS AND THREE CARTRIDGES OF POWDER ONLY BEING AVAILABLE AND NO PROVISIONS REMAINING BUT PORK.I ACCEPTED TERMS OF EVACUATION OFFERED BY GENERAL BEAUREGARD BEING ON SAME OFFERED BY HIM ON THE ELEVENTH INST.PRIOR TO THE COMMENCEMENT OF HOSTILITIES AND MARCHED OUT OF THE FORT SUNDAY AFTERNOON THE FOURTEENTH INST.WITH COLORS FLYING AND DRUMS BEATING.BRINGING AWAY COMPANY AND PRIVATE PROPERTY AND SALUTING MY FLAG WITH FIFTY GUNS. ROBERT ANDERSON.MAJOR FIRST ARTILLERY.COMMANDING.

By the President of the United States of America:

A Proclamation.

Whereas, on the twenty-second day of September, in the year of our Lord one thousand eight hundred and sixty-two, a proclamation was issued by the President of the United States, containing, among other things, the following, to wit:

"That on the first day of January, in the year of our Lord one thousand eight hundred and sixty-three, all persons held as slaves within any State or designated part of a State, the people whereof shall then be in rebellion against the United States, shall be then, thenceforward and forever free; and the Executive Government of the United States, including the military and naval authority thereof, will recognize and maintain the freedom of such persons, and will do no act or acts to repress such persons, or any of them, in any efforts they may make for their actual freedom.

"That the Executive will, on the first day

ABOVE: *The original of the Emancipation Proclamation of January 1, 1863, is held in the National Archives in Washington, DC.*

Emancipation Proclamation

(1863)

Effective January 1, 1863, President Abraham Lincoln declares forever free all slaves residing in territory that is in rebellion against the federal government. The Emancipation Proclamation doesn't outlaw slavery, but it shows that the Civil War is being fought over slavery and the Confederates will have to pay a price for their assaults against the Union.

The problem of slavery had plagued the United States since its founding, yet the nation had generally skirted the issue, leaving it to individual states to decide. But the Civil War had brought the conflict to a head. After a Union victory at Antietam in September 1862 and for reasons that were largely part of his military strategy against the Southern rebels, President Abraham Lincoln decided to issue an ultimatum declaring that unless the rebel states returned to the Union by January 1, 1863, "all persons held as slaves" within the rebellious states "are, and henceforward shall be free."

Despite its expansive wording, which lacked constitutional authority and superseded more than a century's worth of law and tradition, the Emancipation Proclamation was limited in many ways. It applied only to states that had seceded from the Union, ignoring 425,000 slaves in the loyal border-states. It also expressly exempted parts of the Confederacy that had already come under Northern control. Most important, the freedom it promised depended upon Union military victory.

The Emancipation Proclamation didn't end slavery in the United States, but it provided a moral rationale for the Union cause and fundamentally transformed the character of the war, declaring freedom for 3.5 million slaves. When the Confederate states refused to comply, every advance of federal troops expanded the domain of freedom. The Proclamation also encouraged the acceptance of African American men into the Union Army and Navy, enabling the liberated to become liberators. By the end of the war, almost 200,000 black soldiers and sailors had fought for the Union and freedom.

By insisting that the war for the Union must become a war for freedom, the Emancipation Proclamation defined both the Civil War and Lincoln's presidency.

With the text covering five pages, the document was originally tied with narrow red and blue ribbons. The document was bound with other proclamations in a large volume preserved for many years by the Department of State. With other records, the volume containing the Emancipation Proclamation of January 1, 1863 was transferred in 1936 to the National Archives of the United States.

After the Union won the Civil War, the passage of the Thirteenth Amendment finally ended the practice of chattel slavery throughout the United States. As a key precursor to slavery's final destruction, the Emancipation Proclamation has assumed a place among America's greatest documents of human freedom.

LEFT: Printed editions of the Proclamation were reproduced widely in broadsides and pamphlets. Colorful commemorative prints appeared in Harper's Weekly *and* Frank Leslie's Illustrated Newspaper.

Alaska Purchase Check

(1868)

After many years of negotiations with the Tsar, the United States buys Russia's huge frozen chunk of North America for two cents per acre, leaving some Americans to question if Alaska is worth that much. But the check is, as they say, in the mail—for more than a year.

Imperial Russia was in desperate need of cash, due in part to its costly Crimean War (1853–56) with Britain. The Tsar's brother also feared that Russia would not be able to defend one of his colonies—the frigid expanse now known as Alaska, from future British invasion via Canada. Therefore, in 1857 Russia started trying to sell the 600,000-square-mile territory to the United States.

The Americans were especially attracted by the place's lucrative sealskin industry—and they liked the idea of gaining another piece of North America.

Nothing happened for several years, however, until the aftermath of the American Civil War, when Russia's foreign minister to the United States, Eduard de Stoeckl, resumed negotiations with Secretary of State William Seward. After an all-night session, the talks ended at 4 AM on March 30, 1867. The US and Russia had struck a deal.

The purchase price was set at $7.2 million, or about two cents per acre. The Senate approved the treaty by a vote of 37–2 on April 9, 1867.

In October 1867, Russian and American dignitaries gathered at the governor's house in Sitka for the formal transfer ceremony. Soldiers paraded, cannons were fired, and the Russian flag was lowered and replaced by the Stars and Stripes.

But the appropriation still had to be approved by the House of Representatives, and that didn't occur until July 14, 1868, by a vote of 113–48.

The $7.2-million check, payable to de Stoeckl, wasn't issued until August 1, 1868.

The Americans chose an Aleut name which the Russians had used: Alyaska. With the purchase, the US added 586,412 square miles of virgin territory—an area twice the size of Texas, with a population estimated at about 70,000 persons, most of them Inuit and Alaska natives as well as a few thousand Russian fur traders.

Reaction to the deal was mixed. Opponents called it "Seward's Folly" or "Seward's Icebox" until 1896, when the great Klondike Gold Strike convinced most critics that Alaska was worth the money. Suddenly Seward seemed smarter.

Alaska became a United States territory in 1912 and a state on January 3, 1959. Its strategic importance was first recognized in World War II, when Japanese forces invaded the Aleutians, and that military value was later reinforced during the Cold War when US–Soviet relations were tense.

RIGHT: The Alaska purchase check and receipt for $7.2 million. Alaska had been owned by Russia from the early 1700s until its transfer to the United States in 1868. Critics of the purchase initially referred to it as "Seward's folly," but the Klondike Gold Rush of 1896–99 made Alaska a valuable addition to the American territory.

The undersigned, Envoy Extraordinary and Minister Plenipotentiary of His Majesty the Emperor of all the Russias, do hereby acknowledge to have received at the Treasury Department in Washington _Seven Million Two hundred thousand dollars ($7,200,000)_ in coin, being the full amount due from the United States to Russia in consideration of the cession, by the latter Power to the former, of certain territory described in the Treaty entered into by the Emperor of all the Russias and the President of the United States on the 30th day of March 1867.—

Washington, August 1st 1868.

Stoeckl.

ABOVE: A manuscript page from War and Peace. *It was Tolstoy's wife Sophia who painstakingly transcribed his handwritten drafts.*

War and Peace

(1869)

A Russian count pens what may be the largest book manuscript ever created, but his wife is the only one capable of deciphering the furiously written script, and she helps him transcribe as many as seven drafts until they reach the final version that is more than half a million words long. Many critics call it the greatest epic novel in world literature.

Count Leo Tolstoy (1828–1910) labored for years on a literary work set in the days before he was born, starting during the reign of Tsar Alexander I in 1805 and ending in 1813 shortly after Napoléon's disastrous invasion of Russia in 1812.

The Russian master conducted painstaking research in archives and other sources and incorporated details from his own military experience in the Crimean War to make the actions as realistic as possible. He also created an elaborate fictional narrative about five aristocratic Russian families who become engulfed in actual events of the bloody Napoléonic war.

The work put the author's large cast of invented characters into interaction with as many as 160 real ones, including Napoléon. Part historical chronicle and part novel, his fine poetic writing also included discussions of his own unique philosophy with some passages in French as well as Russian.

But Tolstoy's atrocious handwriting was often so illegible that even he couldn't read it. The only person who could was his inexhaustible wife, Sophia Tolstaya (1844–1919), who served as his copyist and editor. The biographer Henri Troyat later described her "labor of Hercules" as she struggled to "decipher this sorcerer's spellbook covered with lines furiously scratched out, corrections colliding with each other, sibylline balloons floating in the margins, prickly afterthoughts sprawled over the pages." It was she who transcribed each page of the manuscript into draft, working with him along the way to incorporate countless changes.

The first draft was completed in 1863 and the first excerpt appeared two years later in a periodical under the title "1805." More installments followed, but Tolstoy was not satisfied with the story and he wanted an uninterrupted version, so he and Sophia rewrote the entire novel several times between 1866 and 1869—a monumental task.

At last the final version was published in 1869 as *War and Peace*. Its appearance was hailed as a masterpiece by Ivan Turgenev, Fyodor Dostoyevsky, Gustave Flaubert, Victor Hugo and other major writers of the day, although some critics didn't like it at first. Its stature grew with age.

Upon his death in 1910, Tolstoy left behind a gargantuan cornucopia of papers, including 165,000 sheets of manuscripts and 10,000 letters. His greatest masterpiece, *War and Peace* remains one of literature's grandest tomes and it has been brought to stage and screen numerous times.

BELOW: Anton Chekhov (left) with Tolstoy. Chekhov was in awe of Tolstoy's achievements: "When literature has a Tolstoy, it is easy and gratifying to be a writer ... [he] accomplishes enough for everyone." The sentiment was not returned. Tolstoy once told Chekhov, "You know, I hate your plays. Shakespeare was a bad writer, and I consider your plays even worse than his."

Phonograph

(1878)

A prolific young tinkerer, who had lost most of his hearing as a child, conducts countless experiments on an invention he calls his "speaking-machine." His patent application describes the new device "to record in permanent characters the human voice and other sounds, from which characters such sounds may be reproduced and rendered audible again at a future time."

In 1877 the frenetic inventor Thomas Alva Edison (1847–1931) had been conducting endless experiments aimed at improving sound communication via the telegraph and telephone in his laboratory at Menlo Park, New Jersey.

This gave him the idea of trying to build a machine that would record the sound of the human voice on tinfoil-coated cylinders. The concept was that when someone spoke into a mouthpiece and turned a handle of the machine, the sound vibrations of his voice would make a needle shake and the vibrations would then be indented onto the cylinder by a recording needle to make unique impressions, and the reproduced sound could later be played back.

Edison worked with his mechanic, John Kruesi, to develop the device. When it was assembled, the inventor recorded some words that had popped into his head, while cranking the new machine. He was amazed to hear it repeat the recording of his distinctive voice saying, "Mary had a little lamb, its fleece was white as snow…"

"I was never so taken aback in my life," Edison later said. "Everybody was astonished."

After demonstrating the device to the public, on December 24, 1877 he filed an application with the US Patent Office for the invention he called the "phonograph," from the Greek words meaning "sound writing." In the application, he stated: "I have discovered, after a long series of experiments that a diaphragm or other body

capable of being set in motion by the human voice does not give, except in rare instances, superimposed vibrations, as has heretofore been supposed, but that each vibration is separate and distinct, and therefore it becomes possible to record and reproduce the sounds of the human voice."

Edison was awarded US Patent No. 200,521 for the phonograph on February 19, 1878. The patent specified a particular method—embossing—for capturing sound on tinfoil-covered cylinders. The phonograph went through many changes and refinements after that, including the use of wax instead of tinfoil cylinders, but Edison's basic idea quickly gave rise to the modern music recording industry.

At the end of his long career in which he was credited with more than 1,000 US patents for devices that included the incandescent light bulb, the motion picture camera, and many other major inventions, Edison called the phonograph his favorite, his "baby."

Having lost the ability, since he was twelve years old, to hear the birds sing, he said it was particularly satisfying for him to have become the first person in the world to successfully record and reproduce sound.

RIGHT: *Edison was awarded US Patent No. 200,521 for his "Phonograph or Speaking Machine" on February 19, 1878.*

LEFT: *Edison proudly presents his latest invention in this photograph from 1878.*

T A. EDISON.
Phonograph or Speaking Machine.

No. 200,521.   Patented Feb. 19, 1878.

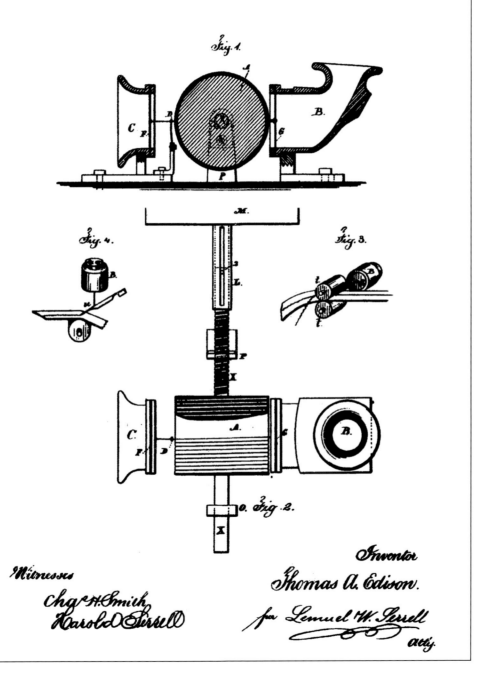

Witnesses
Chas H. Smith
Harold Serrell

Inventor
Thomas A. Edison.
per Lemuel W. Serrell
atty.

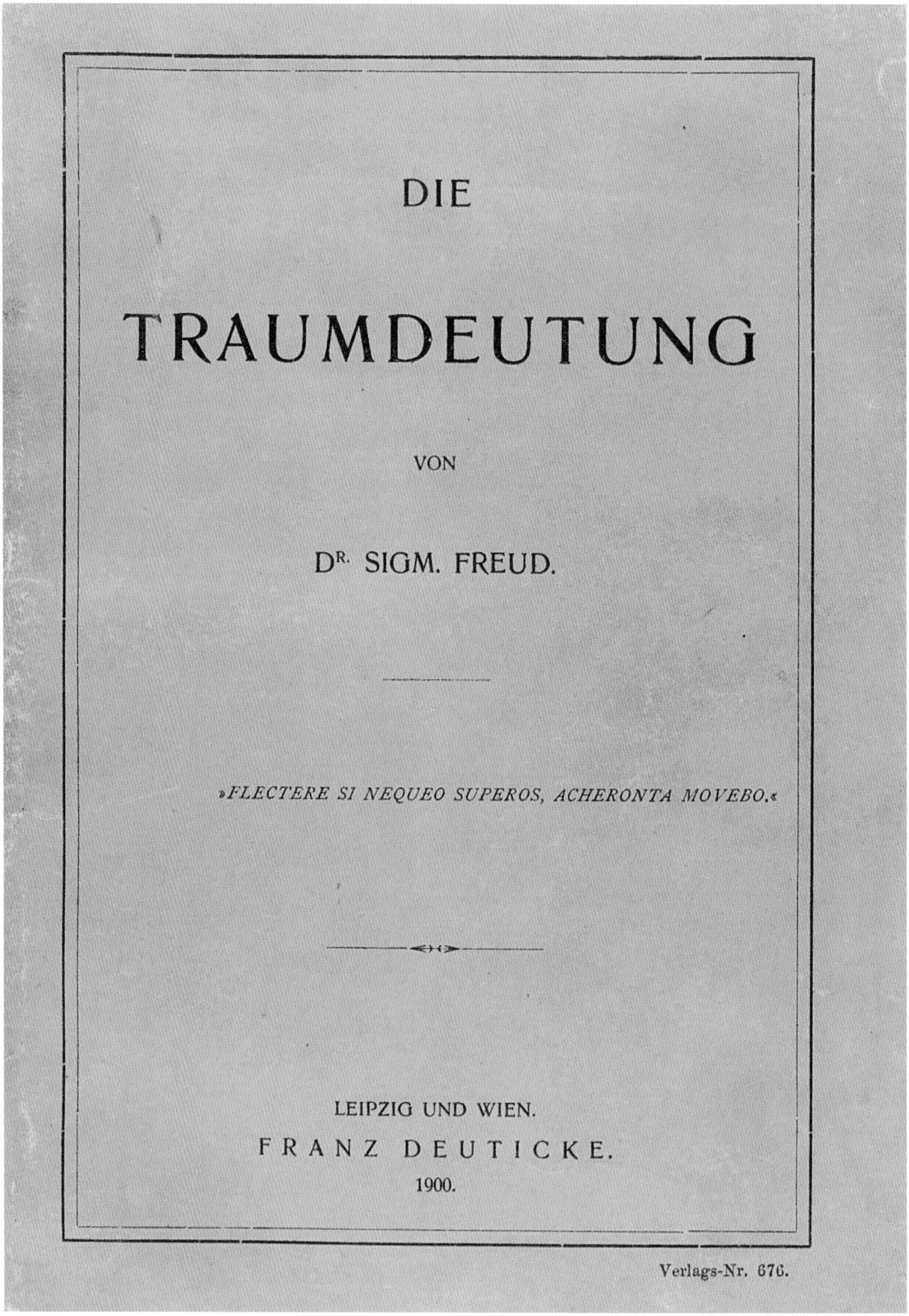

DIE

TRAUMDEUTUNG

VON

DR. SIGM. FREUD.

»FLECTERE SI NEQUEO SUPEROS, ACHERONTA MOVEBO.«

LEIPZIG UND WIEN.

FRANZ DEUTICKE.

1900.

Verlags-Nr. 676.

The Interpretation of Dreams

(1899)

An Austrian neurologist makes an original study of dreams that takes him deep into the human unconscious. After sending the publisher the corrected page proofs, the author discards his handwritten manuscript and notes, leaving behind precious few documents to shed light on an insight that "falls to one's lot but once in a lifetime."

Doctor Sigmund Freud (1856–1939) had a longstanding interest in dreams as a gateway to one's innermost thoughts and desires. In 1889, for instance, he jotted down a note describing his recent dream following the death of his father. "The dream," he wrote, "thus stems from the inclination to self-reproach that regularly sets in among survivors." The Viennese physician also asked his patients to reveal their dreams to him, which he would then analyze.

At the time most educated Europeans considered dreams devoid of psychological importance. But Freud, while on a summer retreat at Bellevue, Austria in the summer of 1895, conceived the idea for a daring new analysis.

In 1899 he published a study on the subject in German, which was entitled *Die Traumdeutung* (*The Interpretation of Dreams*). The gray-covered monograph introduced his complex theory of dream interpretation, involving the "unconscious." Freud said all dreams are forms of "wish fulfillment" or attempts to resolve inner conflicts of one sort or another. He posited that the genesis of a dream often lies in the events of the day preceding the dream—events which he called the "day residue." The work also introduced many other new concepts such as "condensation" (the idea of multiple meanings), and "repression." By far the most controversial parts of his theory involved sexuality, such as his assertion that children had a repressed desire to have sexual relations with the parent of the opposite sex (the "Oedipus complex").

Although very few copies were sold at first and it earned him only $209, Freud considered his theory a breakthrough and said of the original insight, maybe "someday a marble tablet will be placed on the house, inscribed with these words: In this house on July 24, 1895, the secret of dreams was revealed to Dr. Sigm. Freud." Nevertheless, interest in the work was so low that the initial press run didn't sell out for eight years.

Over time, Freud frequently revised the book to keep up with his evolving theory. As it was about to be translated into English, his English publisher, George Allen & Company, required him to remove several sexual references, which he painfully agreed to do. By the 1920s, *The Interpretation of Dreams* was considered the seminal work in psychoanalysis.

After correcting the page proofs, Freud threw away the original manuscript but a number of later editions and letters remain preserved in the Sigmund Freud Collection of the Library of Congress. In keeping with his prediction, a plaque was later erected at the site where he had hatched his momentous theory.

LEFT AND OPPOSITE: Freud at his writing desk and the first edition of Die Traumdeutung. *Although the printed date says 1900, it was actually released on November 4, 1899.*

Sinking of the Titanic

(1912)

On the night of April 14, 1912, the cramped message room of the largest and most luxurious vessel afloat turns into a maelstrom of frantic wireless activity as two young telegraphists issue a flurry of desperate distress calls—the unsinkable ship has struck an iceberg and she is going down.

As the biggest and finest ship of its day, RMS *Titanic* measured 882 feet, 9 inches long with a maximum breadth of 92 feet, 6 inches and a total height from the base of the keel to the top of the bridge of 104 feet. Its pinnacle, a four-wire Marconi 500 kHz antenna suspended between the ship's two masts, standing a full 250 feet above the sea, served the world's most powerful communications equipment, which had a guaranteed working range of 250 miles and a nighttime range of up to 2,000 miles.

In the tiny radio room, two wireless operators, Jack Phillips, aged twenty-five, and his twenty-two-year-old deputy, Harold Bride, kept up a brisk traffic of communications that included both navigational messages and telegrams for passengers that were sent and received as the elegant vessel continued its maiden voyage across the frigid North Atlantic.

ABOVE: An original ticket for the Titanic, *which was launched into Belfast Lough on May 31, 1911 by Harland & Wolff, then the largest shipyard in the world.*

OPPOSITE: The increasingly distressing messages sent from the Titanic *between 11:50 PM and 1:40 AM on April 14–15, 1912.*

At about 11:40 PM on April 14, however, as the ship was cruising about 370 miles south-southeast of the coast of Newfoundland, she struck an iceberg and everything changed. The surviving messages covering the next two hours left behind a dramatic real-time record of what happened that night.

The operators remained at their posts even after the captain released them from their duties, and they continued to transmit distress signals until three minutes before the ship foundered. Just before they fled, Bride's final message reported water flooding into the wheelhouse. He was later pulled from the icy waves just in time to save his life. But Phillips perished and his body was never recovered. He subsequently came under criticism when it was revealed that before the collision another radio operator of the *Californian* had tried to warn him about the approaching ice field, but Phillips had responded, "Shut up! I am busy, I am working Cape Race!"

The sinking resulted in the loss of 1,595 passengers and crew. Only 745 were saved, in part because the ship carried only enough lifeboats for half of those aboard and they were reserved mostly for women and children. The newspapers told how the wealthiest passenger, Col. John Jacob Astor IV, was last seen assisting his pregnant wife into a lifeboat, and calmly smoking a cigarette before the ship went down. Another passenger, Col. Archibald Gracie, also went down with the vessel but he later surfaced and was rescued.

Over the years some of the telegrams from the *Titanic* have fetched high prices at auction. One of the most famous, saying, "We have struck iceberg," along with the *Olympic*'s response, "…are you steaming toward us?" sold for $110,000 at Christie's.

A collection of the *Titanic* messages, translated from Morse code, has been dramatized on stage.

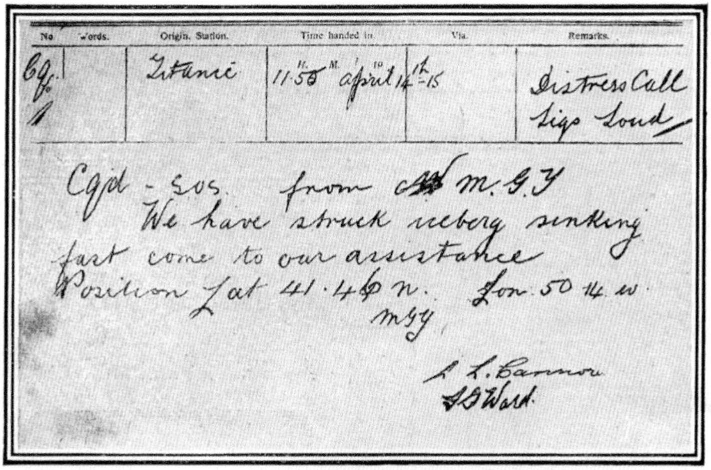

No.	Words.	Origin. Station.	Time handed in.	Via.	Remarks.
69.		Titanic	11.55 ᴴ ᴹ april 14ᵗʰ 15		Distress Call Sigs Loud

Cqd - SOS. from M.G.Y
We have struck iceberg sinking
fast come to our assistance
Position Lat 41.46 N. Lon. 50.14 w.
MGY

S. L. Cannon
F.S Ward.

No.	Words.	Origin. Station.	Time handed in.	Via.	Remarks.
To		Titanic	___H.___M. / 19___		

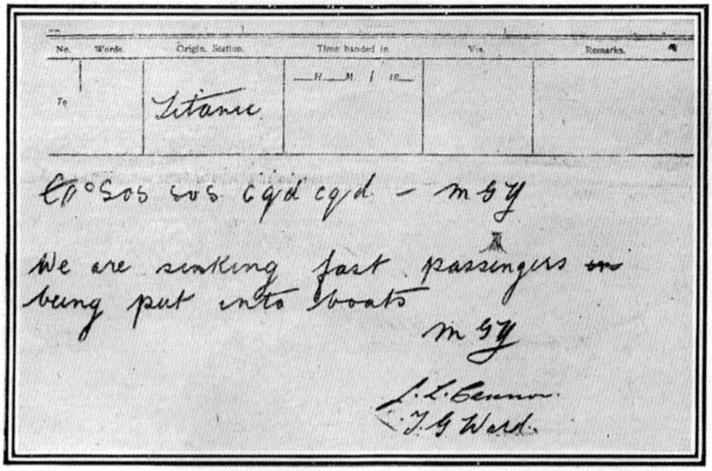

CQ° SOS SOS Cqd cqd - mgy

We are sinking fast passengers are
being put into boats
mgy

S. L. Cannon.
F. G Ward.

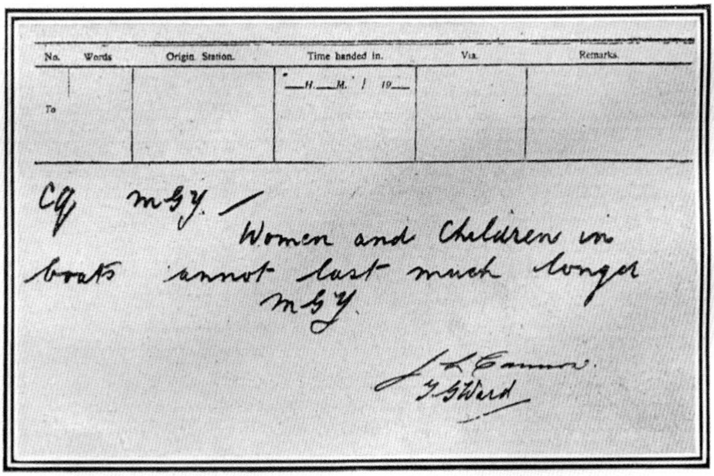

No.	Words.	Origin. Station.	Time handed in.	Via.	Remarks.
To			___H.___M. / 19___		

CQ   mgy.
            Women and Children in
boats   cannot last much longer
            mgy.

S. L. Cannon.
F.G Ward

ABOVE: Sykes and Picot's map (which they signed on May 8, 1916) showed that Britain ("B") would receive control over the red area, which is known today as Jordan, southern Iraq and Haifa in Israel. France ("A") would obtain the blue area (today's Syria, Lebanon, northern Iraq, Mosul and southeastern Turkey, including Kurdistan).

OPPOSITE: A portrait of Colonel Sir Mark Sykes by Leopold Pilichowski. Sykes died in 1919 at the age of thirty-nine after contracting Spanish flu.

Sykes–Picot Agreement

(1916)

Even before the final outcome of the Great War has been determined, Great Britain, France, and Russia secretly discuss how they will carve up the Middle East into "spheres of influence" once the Ottoman Empire is defeated. Their controversial secret treaty will alter the geography of the region for decades to come.

The Ottoman Empire had been in decline for centuries prior to World War I, so the Allied Powers already had given some thought to how they would divide up the considerable spoils in the likely event they defeated the Turks. Britain and France already had some significant interests in the region between the Mediterranean Sea and Persian Gulf, but a victory offered a great deal more. Russia as well hungered for a piece.

From November 1915 to March 1916, representatives of Britain and France negotiated an agreement, with Russia offering its assent. The secret treaty, known as the Sykes–Picot Agreement, was named after its lead negotiators, the aristocrats Sir Mark Sykes of England and François Georges-Picot of France. Its terms were set out in a letter from Sir Edward Grey (British Foreign Secretary) to Paul Cambon (France's Ambassador to Great Britain) on May 16, 1916.

The color-coded partition map and text provided that Britain ("B") would receive control over the red area (known today as Jordan, southern Iraq and Haifa in Israel); France ("A") would obtain the blue area (today's Syria, Lebanon, northern Iraq, Mosul and southeastern Turkey, including Kurdistan); and the brown area of Palestine (excluding Haifa and Acre) would become subject to international administration, "the form of which is to be decided upon after consultation with Russia, and subsequently in consultation with

the other allies, and the representatives of the sheriff of Mecca" (Sayyid Hussein bin Ali). Besides carving the region into British and French "spheres of influence," the arrangement specified various commercial relations and other understandings between them for the Arab lands.

Russia's change of status, brought on by the Revolution and the nation's withdrawal from the war, removed it from inclusion. But when marauding Bolsheviks uncovered documents about the plans in government archives in 1917, the contents of the secret treaty were publicly revealed. The exposé embarrassed the British, since it contradicted their existing claims through Col. T. E. Lawrence ("Lawrence of Arabia") that Arabs would receive sovereignty over Arab lands in exchange for supporting the Allies in the war. Indeed, the treaty set aside the establishment of an independent Arab state or confederation of Arab states, contrary to what had previously been promised, giving France and Britain the rights to set boundaries within their spheres of influence, "as they may think fit."

After the war ended as planned, the terms were affirmed by the San Remo Conference of 1920 and ratified by the League of Nations in 1922. Although Sykes–Picot was intended to draw new borders according to sectarian lines, its simple straight lines also failed to take into account the actual tribal and ethnic configurations in a deeply divided region. Sykes–Picot has affected Arab-Western relations to this day.

Balfour Declaration

(1917)

A brief letter from the British Foreign Secretary to a prominent Jewish leader expresses support for "the establishment in Palestine of a national home for the Jewish people" once the Ottomans are defeated in the Great War. The "scrap of paper" will change history and later lead to the creation of modern Israel.

Chaim Weizmann was a Russian-born Jewish chemist in Britain who had invented a chemical process that provided a vital ingredient needed for artillery shells, without which Britain wouldn't have stood a chance in the deadlocked Great War against chemical-rich Germany.

So, when the British Foreign Secretary and former Prime Minister Arthur James Balfour (1848–1930) asked Weizmann how he wished to be compensated for his contribution to the war effort, the outspoken Zionist responded from the heart. "There is only one thing I want," he replied. "A national home for my people." Balfour knew that for Weizmann, the Jewish "homeland" meant Palestine, the geographic region in Western Asia between the Mediterranean Sea and the Jordan River—the "Holy Land."

Weizmann's advocacy of Zionism was one of the factors that influenced Balfour to draft a letter that would change the course of history. Like several other leading British statesmen of his day, Balfour was a Christian Zionist who identified with the importance of the Holy Land as a spiritual home, albeit for Christians as well as Jews, and he supported the idea of allowing the Jews to settle in their ancient homeland once Britain had defeated the Ottomans in the war. He also wanted funding for the British war effort.

On November 2, 1917, Balfour sent a letter to Weizmann's close friend, Lord Walter Rothschild, the second Baron Rothschild, the financier who was the top leader of Britain's Jewish community and a prominent Zionist. The letter stated the position, recently endorsed

LEFT: Arthur James Balfour, the first Earl of Balfour, became one of the richest men in Britain when he inherited a £4 million fortune at the age of twenty-one.

by the British cabinet, that Britain would support Zionist plans for a Jewish "national home" in Palestine, provided that nothing would be done to infringe the rights of communities already existing there. Thus the reference covered both indigenous Christians and Muslims.

The letter, which soon became famous as the Balfour Declaration, used deliberately vague language for diplomatic reasons. But its message was clear.

The document proved prescient because barely a month later, General Sir Edmund Allenby would lead the British forces in the conquest of Jerusalem, becoming its first Christian conqueror since the Crusades. When Germany and its allies were defeated, the collapse of the Ottoman Empire that had ruled the Middle East since the eleventh century would lead to a redrawing of the map. The notions floated in the Balfour Declaration would later be incorporated into both the Sèvres peace treaty of 1920 that ended the Ottoman Empire and the British Mandate for Palestine of 1923, which established "a national home for the Jewish people," provided that "nothing shall be done which may prejudice the civil and religious rights of existing non-Jewish communities in Palestine, or the rights and political status enjoyed by Jews in any other country."

The anniversary of the Declaration is commemorated in Israel as Balfour Day, and observed as a day of mourning and protest in Arab countries.

Foreign Office,

November 2nd, 1917.

Dear Lord Rothschild,

I have much pleasure in conveying to you, on behalf of His Majesty's Government, the following declaration of sympathy with Jewish Zionist aspirations which has been submitted to, and approved by, the Cabinet

"His Majesty's Government view with favour the establishment in Palestine of a national home for the Jewish people, and will use their best endeavours to facilitate the achievement of this object, it being clearly understood that nothing shall be done which may prejudice the civil and religious rights of existing non-Jewish communities in Palestine, or the rights and political status enjoyed by Jews in any other country"

I should be grateful if you would bring this declaration to the knowledge of the Zionist Federation.

ABOVE: Balfour's brief letter, which expressed support for "a national home for the Jewish people," would lead to the creation of modern Israel.

WESTERN UNION TELEGRAM

NEWCOMB CARLTON, PRESIDENT

CLASS OF SERVICE DESIRED	
Fast Day Message	X
Day Letter	
Night Message	
Night Letter	

Patrons should mark an X opposite the class of service desired; OTHERWISE THE TELEGRAM WILL BE TRANSMITTED AS A FAST DAY MESSAGE.

Send the following telegram, subject to the terms on back hereof, which are hereby agreed to

via Galveston

JAN 19 1917

GERMAN LEGATION

MEXICO CITY

130	13042	13401	8501	115	3528	416	17214	6491	11310
18147	18222	21560	10247	11518	23677	13605	3494	14936	
98092	5905	11311	10392	10371	0302	21290	5161	39695	
23571	17504	11269	18276	18101	0317	0228	17694	4473	
23284	22200	19452	21589	67893	5569	13918	8958	12137	
1333	4725	4458	5905	17166	13851	4458	17149	14471	6706
13850	12224	6929	14991	7382	15857	67893	14218	36477	
5870	17553	67893	5870	5454	16102	15217	22801	17138	
21001	17388	7446	23638	18222	6719	14331	15021	23845	
3156	23552	22096	21604	4797	9497	22464	20855	4377	
23610	18140	22260	5905	13347	20420	39689	13732	20667	
6929	5275	18507	52262	1340	22049	13339	11265	22295	
10439	14814	4178	6992	8784	7632	7357	6926	52262	11267
21100	21272	9346	9559	22464	15874	18502	18500	15857	
2188	5376	7381	98092	16127	13486	9350	9220	76036	14219
5144	2831	17920	11347	17142	11264	7667	7762	15099	9110
10482	97556	3569	3670						

BERNSTORFF.

Charge German Embassy.

The Zimmermann Telegram

(1917)

After British code-breakers discover a secret German plot against the still-neutral United States, and Germany's own ambassador confirms the telegram's authenticity, it pushes America to join the Allied cause in the Great War.

Room Forty of the British Admiralty buzzed with excitement as a team of its best cryptologists used captured German codebooks to decipher a top-secret message dated January 16, 1917 from the German Foreign Minister, Arthur Zimmermann, to the German ambassador of Mexico. The decoded telegram revealed that Germany was planning to carry out unrestricted submarine warfare against US ships, beginning on February 1. Germany presumed that the US would regard such attacks tantamount to a declaration of war, so if hostilities ensued, the German ambassador was instructed to approach Mexico's president with a proposal: Germany would offer Mexico a reward of money plus the territories of Arizona, New Mexico, and Texas in exchange for becoming an ally of the Axis powers against the US. That way, the US would be too busy dealing with Mexico to focus on the war in Europe.

The Zimmermann telegram was hot stuff. But the officer in charge of the intelligence division, Captain Reginald "Blinker" Hall, held back from alerting even his own superiors, fearing that any such disclosure would reveal Britain's code-breaking ability and hamstring his unit's future intelligence activities in the war. So, incredibly, before finally sharing the telegram with anyone, Hall waited for twenty days. By then the German Empire had indeed already commenced unrestricted submarine warfare, which had resulted in the US breaking off diplomatic relations with Germany. In an effort to protect his intelligence, Hall scrambled to concoct an elaborate cover story that would explain how Britain had obtained the text.

On February 19, the decoded telegram was finally shown to an official of the American Embassy in London. Within days, British Foreign Minister Arthur Balfour reported to President Woodrow Wilson regarding the telegram, and Wilson alerted the press. Some editors were wary of falling prey to a propaganda ploy or getting drawn into another "newspaper war." But any such reservations were dispelled by Zimmermann himself, who told an American reporter on March 3, "I cannot deny it. It is true." The German also gave a speech admitting the telegram was genuine.

As a result, and in the face of Germany's deadly submarine attacks on passenger and merchant vessels flying the American flag, American public opinion became inflamed. On April 6, 1917, Congress formally declared war on Germany.

The Zimmermann telegram entered the history books. A copy of the version shared with the United States is held in the US National Archives. The original records from Room Forty are in Britain's National Archives. According to David Kahn, author of *The Codebreakers*, "No other single cryptanalysis has had such enormous consequences."

LEFT: The telegram that changed the course of history. This encrypted message, from German Foreign Minister Arthur Zimmermann to the German Minister to Mexico, Heinrich von Eckhardt, offered US territory to Mexico on the condition that they backed the German cause.

Wilson's Fourteen Points

(1918)

Speaking before a joint session of Congress, President Woodrow Wilson offers his high-minded and detailed plan for ending World War I and establishing a new international order that can ensure postwar peace—but how will the world's powers (and his own country) respond?

By January 1918 the Great War had been raging for three-and-a-half years and the US was nearing the end of its first year of costly combat. Russia's Bolshevik Revolution had also made the need for peace all the more pressing as far as the Western Powers were concerned.

President Woodrow Wilson (1856–1924), a former president of Princeton University and governor of New Jersey, had already convened a group of experts known as The Inquiry to advise him on economic, social, and political factors that might come up in peace discussions, so he was equipped with a huge volume of foreign policy analysis. Wilson tapped these resources to lay the groundwork for an ambitious blueprint for world peace. He also enlisted the aid of the intellectual journalist Walter Lippmann, who as an assistant to the Secretary of War, helped him craft a major political speech.

On January 8, 1918 the President addressed Congress on "War Aims and Peace Terms" by calling for fourteen points as "the only possible programme, as we see it." Confronting what he perceived as the causes for the World War, Wilson responded with a detailed list of proposed solutions including the abolition of secret treaties; absolute freedom of the seas; free trade; reduced armaments; "an absolutely impartial adjustment in colonial claims" in the interests of both native peoples and colonists; evacuation and restoration of all Russian territory, Belgium, Alsace-Lorraine, Romania, Serbia, Montenegro; readjustment of the Italian frontiers; opportunities for autonomous development for the peoples of Austria-Hungary; secure sovereignty for the Turkish portions of the Ottoman Empire; establishment of an independent Poland; and a league of nations to enforce the peace.

"It will be our wish and purpose," Wilson said,

that the processes of peace, when they are begun, shall be absolutely open and that they shall involve and permit henceforth no secret understandings of any kind. The day of conquest and aggrandizement is gone by; so is also the day of secret covenants entered into in the interest of particular governments and likely at some unlooked-for moment to upset the peace of the world.

He continued, "All the peoples of the world are in effect partners in this interest, and for our own part we see very clearly that unless justice be done to others it will not be done to us."

By promising a just peace, Wilson's "Fourteen Points" were designed to lessen the Central Powers' will to fight at a decisive moment in the war. His speech was broadcast on radio throughout the world and German-language copies were dropped behind enemy lines as a propaganda tool.

Wilson's proposal helped to prompt peace discussions leading to the Armistice that would occur eleven months later. In 1919, Wilson was awarded the Nobel Peace Prize for his efforts.

LEFT: Wilson's original shorthand draft of his "Fourteen Points" speech is kept at the Library of Congress.

litical and economic independence and territorial integrity of the several Balkan states should be entered into.

XII. The Turkish portions of the present Ottoman Empire should be assured a secure sovereignty, but the other nationalities which are now under Turkish rule should be assured an undoubted security of life and an absolutely unmolested opportunity of autonomous development, and the Dardanelles should be permanently opened as a free passage to the ships and commerce of all nations under international guarantees.

XIII. An independent Polish state should be erected which should include the territories inhabited by indisputably Polish populations, which should be assured a free and secure access to the sea, and whose political and economic independence and territorial integrity should be guaranteed by international covenant.

XIV. A general association of nations must be formed under specific covenants for the purpose of affording mutual guarantees of political independence and territorial integrity to great and small states alike.

In regard to these essential rectifications of wrong and assertions of right we feel ourselves to be intimate partners of all the governments and peoples associated together against the Imperialists. We cannot be separated in interest or divided in purpose. We stand together until the end.

For such arrangements and covenants we are willing to fight and to continue to fight until they are achieved; but only because we wish the right to prevail and desire a just and stable peace such as can be secured only by removing the chief provocations to war, which this programme does remove. We have no jealousy of German greatness, and there is nothing in this programme that impairs it. We grudge her no achievement or distinction of learning or of pacific enterprise such as have made her record very bright and very enviable. We do not wish to injure her or to block in any way her legitimate influence or power. We do not wish to fight her either with arms or with hostile arrangements of trade if she is willing to associate herself with us and the other peace-loving nations of the world in covenants of justice and law and fair dealing. We wish her only to accept a place of equality among the peoples of the world,—the new world in which we now live,—instead of a place of mastery.

Neither do we presume to suggest to her any alteration or modification of her institutions. But it is necessary, we must frankly say, and necessary as a preliminary to any intelligent dealings with her on our part, that we should know whom her spokesmen speak for when they speak to us, whether for the Reichstag majority or for the military party and the men whose creed is imperial domination.

ABOVE: The last three of Wilson's Fourteen Points and the conclusion that became a blueprint for world peace: "We cannot be separated in interest or divided in purpose. We stand together until the end."

5

Sixty-sixth Congress of the United States of America;

At the First Session,

Begun and held at the City of Washington on Monday, the nineteenth day of May,
one thousand nine hundred and nineteen.

JOINT RESOLUTION

Proposing an amendment to the Constitution extending the right of suffrage
to women.

Resolved by the Senate and House of Representatives of the United States
of America in Congress assembled (two-thirds of each House concurring therein),
That the following article is proposed as an amendment to the Constitution,
which shall be valid to all intents and purposes as part of the Constitution when
ratified by the legislatures of three-fourths of the several States.

"ARTICLE ————.

"The right of citizens of the United States to vote shall not be denied or
abridged by the United States or by any State on account of sex.

"Congress shall have power to enforce this article by appropriate
legislation."

F. H. Gillett

Speaker of the House of Representatives.

Thos. R. Marshall

Vice President of the United States and
President of the Senate.

*ABOVE: The passing of the Nineteenth Amendment was a landmark in American history. Women
were finally able to exercise the same rights and responsibilities of citizenship as men.*

Nineteenth Amendment

(1919)

After eight decades of struggle by women suffragists, an all-male Congress finally passes legislation for a constitutional amendment forbidding the federal government or the states from abridging the right of US citizens to vote based on gender, and it is ratified—yet women are still excluded from a historic signing ceremony.

The original Constitution of the United States granted the right to vote to only a fraction of adult Americans. Exclusions based on property qualifications, race, and gender continued to be permitted for many years, well into the twentieth century.

In 1869 Wyoming became the first state to allow women to vote and in 1871 women's groups began petitioning Congress to amend the Constitution. A constitutional amendment was introduced seven years later by Sen. Aaron A. Sargent of California, but it did not receive a vote by the full Senate until 1887 when it was rejected by a margin of 34 to 16.

The movement was revived in the Progressive Era with increased parades, debates, and strikes that resulted in many protesters being heckled and jailed. But they persisted. After New York adopted women's suffrage in 1917, President Wilson removed his opposition and the climate in Congress became less hostile.

On May 21, 1919, the House of Representatives passed the amendment, and the Senate followed on June 4. When Tennessee approved the measure on August 18, 1920, marking the necessary ratification by three-quarters of the states, suffragists jubilantly prepared to celebrate their greatest victory. Leaders of the two major suffragist factions urged Secretary of State Bainbridge Colby to hold a formal signing ceremony in front of movie cameras and reporters.

But Colby insisted on signing the official certification papers in private, without any women or news media present, claiming that he did not want to detract from the "dignity" of the event.

"It was quite tragic," said Mrs. Abby Scott Baker of the National Woman's Party. "This was the final culmination of the women's fight, and, women,

irrespective of factions, should have been allowed to be present when the proclamation was signed."

For decades at least, the political impact of women's suffrage turned out to be less significant than what many analysts had predicted. African Americans were still excluded in many states and voting remained largely limited to middle-class citizens, with many women voting along the same lines as their spouses. A women's voting bloc did not emerge until the 1950s.

Ratification by the southern states was slow in coming. It did not happen in Maryland until 1941; in Virginia, it was 1952; Alabama, 1953; South Carolina and Florida, 1969; Louisiana and Georgia, 1970; North Carolina, 1971; and Mississippi did not ratify the Nineteenth Amendment until 1984.

BELOW: Suffragists celebrate in Tennessee on August 18, 1920, as it becomes the all-important thirty-sixth state to ratify the amendment. Three-quarters of the states were required for ratification.

Treaty of Versailles

(1919)

After the fighting has stopped, the victors impose harsh settlement terms on Germany for starting the World War; however as one French commander warns, the result is not a recipe for peace, but "an Armistice for twenty years"—and the seeds of German resentment are planted.

By the time the Armistice for the Great War finally occurred at the eleventh hour on November 11, 1918, the number of dead was estimated to have reached 16 million persons and the total wounded was 20 million.

In January 1919 the Paris Peace Conference was convened at Versailles to set the terms of victory and defeat. Although President Wilson's high-minded Fourteen Points had helped to end the fighting, the formal peace agreement proved harder to achieve. While nearly thirty nations participated, the proceedings were dominated by the "Big Four" (Great Britain, France, the United States, and Italy), who often bickered. Russia's new Bolshevik government was excluded, and Germany and the rest of the vanquished Central Powers had no voice. In the end, the domineering English and French delegations retreated from many of Wilson's Fourteen Points in favor of their own nationalistic claims, leaving the Germans feeling they had been tricked.

The Great War Treaty was signed on June 28, 1919. It penalized Germany for waging aggressive war and imposed measures that were intended to prevent future aggression. Germany accepted responsibility for "causing all the loss and damage…as a consequence of the … aggression of Germany and her allies." It also became liable to pay hefty financial reparations to certain Allies, although the actual amount remained to be determined. (The ultimate assessment was 132 billion marks, roughly equivalent to US $442 billion in 2014.)

Germany also had to relinquish 10 percent of its prewar territory in Europe and all of its overseas possessions. The German Army and Navy were greatly reduced in size and the nation was prohibited from keeping an air force and submarines. Several top German officials, including Kaiser Wilhelm II, were subject to trial for alleged war crimes. The treaty also included a plan for an international League of Nations that would serve as a forum and security watchdog in keeping with President Wilson's vision.

One critic, the French Marshal Ferdinand Foch, warned that the treaty was destined to result in future warfare on the continent. "This is not peace," he said. "It is an armistice for twenty years." And many Germans also bitterly resented the terms of the Versailles document and wanted to repudiate it.

Although American public opinion overwhelmingly supported joining the League, Republicans mounted intense opposition in the Senate and Wilson suffered a debilitating stroke that ended his advocacy. Because the final vote fell short of ratification, the US ended up signing a separate treaty with Germany in 1921, never agreeing to the terms of Versailles or joining the international government its own leader had proposed.

RIGHT: The treaty and a photograph of the signing in the Hall of Mirrors at Versailles. It was in the exact same venue, in 1871, that Wilhelm of Prussia was proclaimed Emperor of the German Empire after the French were defeated in the Franco-Prussian War.

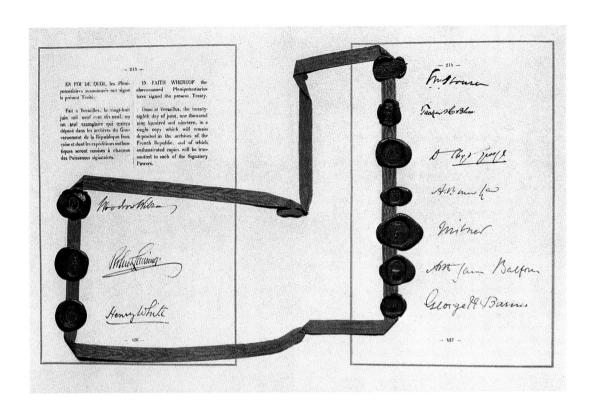

Die Ziele der Nationalsozialisten

Aus dem Programm der NSDAP

Durch bewußte Lügen und Verdrehungen fast der gesamten in Deutschland erscheinenden Zeitungen, die meist nicht von Deutschblütigen geschrieben werden, herrschen vielfach auch heute noch völlig verkehrte Vorstellungen über Wesen und Ziele des Nationalsozialismus.

Die folgenden 25 Programmpunkte wurden Anfang des Jahres 1920 zum ersten Male in München öffentlich bekanntgegeben; sie stehen als Grundformen der Nationalsozialistischen Deutschen Arbeiter=Partei unverrückbar fest.

Die 25 Punkte

Das Programm der Deutschen Arbeiter=Partei ist ein Zeit=Programm. Die Führer lehnen es ab, nach Erreichung der im Programm aufgestellten Ziele neue aufzustellen, nur zu dem Zweck, um durch künstlich gesteigerte Unzufriedenheit der Massen das Fortbestehen der Partei zu ermöglichen.

1. Wir fordern den Zusammenschluß aller Deutschen auf Grund des Selbstbestimmungsrechtes der Völker zu einem Groß=Deutschland.

2. Wir fordern die Gleichberechtigung des deutschen Volkes gegenüber den anderen Nationen, Aufhebung der Friedensverträge von Versailles und St. Germain.

3. Wir fordern Land und Boden (Kolonien) zur Ernährung unseres Volkes und Ansiedlung unseres Bevölkerungs=Ueberschusses.

4. Staatsbürger kann nur sein, wer Volksgenosse ist. Volksgenosse kann nur sein, wer deutschen Blutes ist, ohne Rücksichtnahme auf Konfession. Kein Jude kann daher Volksgenosse sein.

5. Wer nicht Staatsbürger ist, soll nur als Gast in Deutschland leben können und muß unter Fremdengesetzgebung stehen.

6. Das Recht über Führung und Gesetze des Staates zu bestimmen, darf nur dem Staatsbürger zustehen. Daher fordern wir, daß jedes öffentliche Amt, gleichgültig welcher Art, gleich ob im Reich, Land oder Gemeinde, nur durch Staatsbürger bekleidet werden darf.

Wir bekämpfen die korrumpierende Parlamentswirtschaft, einer Stellenbesetzung nur nach Parteigesichtspunkten ohne Rücksicht auf Charakter und Fähigkeiten.

7. Wir fordern, daß sich der Staat verpflichtet, in erster Linie für die Erwerbs= und Lebensmöglichkeit der Staatsbürger zu sorgen. Wenn es nicht möglich ist, die Gesamtbevölkerung des Staates zu ernähren, so sind die Angehörigen fremder Nationen (Nicht=Staatsbürger) aus dem Reiche auszuweisen.

8. Die weitere Einwanderung Nicht=Deutscher ist zu verhindern. Wir fordern, daß alle Nicht=Deutschen, die seit 2. August 1914 in Deutschland eingewandert sind, sofort zum Verlassen des Reiches gezwungen werden.

9. Alle Staatsbürger müssen gleiche Rechte und Pflichten besitzen.

10. Erste Pflicht jedes Staatsbürgers muß sein, geistig oder körperlich zu schaffen. Die Tätigkeit des einzelnen darf nicht gegen die Interessen der Allgemeinheit verstoßen, sondern muß im Rahmen des Gesamten und zum Nutzen aller erfolgen.

Daher fordern wir:

Brechung der Zinsknechtschaft.

11. Abschaffung des arbeits= und mühelosen Einkommens.

12. Im Hinblick auf die ungeheuren Opfer an Gut und Blut, die jeder Krieg vom Volke fordert, muß die persönliche Bereicherung durch den Krieg als Verbrechen am Volke bezeichnet werden. Wir fordern daher restlose Einziehung aller Kriegsgewinne.

13. Wir fordern die Verstaatlichung aller (bisher) bereits vergesellschafteten (Trusts) Betriebe.

14. Wir fordern Gewinnbeteiligung an Großbetrieben.

15. Wir fordern einen großzügigen Ausbau der Altersversorgung.

16. Wir fordern die Schaffung eines gesunden Mittelstandes und seine Erhaltung, sofortige Kommunalisierung der Groß=Warenhäuser und ihre Vermietung zu billigen Preisen an kleine Gewerbetreibende, schärfste Berücksichtigung aller kleinen Gewerbetreibenden bei Lieferung an den Staat, die Länder oder Gemeinden.

17. Wir fordern eine unseren nationalen Bedürfnissen angepaßte Bodenreform, Schaffung eines Gesetzes zur unentgeltlichen Enteignung von Boden für gemeinnützige Zwecke, Abschaffung des Bodenzinses und Verhinderung jeder Bodenspekulation.

(Erklärung.

Gegenüber den verlogenen Auslegungen des Punktes 17 des Programms der NSDAP. von seiten unserer Gegner ist folgende Feststellung notwendig:

Da die NSDAP. auf dem Boden des Privateigentums steht, ergibt sich von selbst, daß der Passus „Unentgeltliche Enteignung" nur auf die Schaffung gesetzlicher Möglichkeiten Bezug hat, Boden, der auf unrechtmäßige Weise erworben wurde oder nicht nach den Gesichtspunkten des Volkswohles verwaltet wird, wenn nötig, zu enteignen. Dieses richtet sich demgemäß in erster Linie gegen die jüdischen Grundspekulationsgesellschaften.

München, den 15. April 1928.   gez. Adolf Hitler.)

18. Wir fordern den rücksichtslosen Kampf gegen diejenigen, die durch ihre Tätigkeit das Gemeininteresse schädigen. Gemeine Volksverbrecher, Wucherer, Schieber usw. sind mit dem Tode zu bestrafen, ohne Rücksichtnahme auf Konfession und Rasse.

19. Wir fordern Ersatz für das dem materialistischen Weltordnung dienende römische Recht durch ein deutsches Gemeinrecht.

20. Um jedem fähigen und fleißigen Deutschen das Erreichen höherer Bildung und damit das Einrücken in führende Stellungen zu ermöglichen, hat der Staat für einen gründlichen Ausbau unseres gesamten Volksbildungswesens Sorge zu tragen. Die Lehrpläne aller Bildungsanstalten sind den Erfordernissen des praktischen Lebens anzupassen. Das Erfassen des Staatsgedankens muß bereits mit Beginn des Verständnisses durch die Schule (Staatsbürgerkunde) erzielt werden. Wir fordern die Ausbildung geistig besonders veranlagter Kinder armer Eltern ohne Rücksicht auf deren Stand oder Beruf auf Staatskosten.

21. Der Staat hat für die Hebung der Volksgesundheit zu sorgen durch den Schutz der Mutter und des Kindes, durch Verbot der Jugendarbeit, durch Herbeiführung der körperlichen Ertüchtigung mittels gesetzlicher Festlegung einer Turn= und Sportpflicht, durch größte Unterstützung aller sich mit körperlicher Jugend=Ausbildung beschäftigenden Vereine.

22. Wir fordern die Abschaffung der Söldnertruppe und die Bildung eines Volksheeres.

23. Wir fordern den gesetzlichen Kampf gegen die bewußte politische Lüge und ihre Verbreitung durch die Presse. Um die Schaffung einer deutschen Presse zu ermöglichen, fordern wir, daß

a) sämtliche Schriftleiter und Mitarbeiter von Zeitungen, die in deutscher Sprache erscheinen, Volksgenossen sein müssen.

b) nichtdeutsche Zeitungen zu ihrem Erscheinen der ausdrücklichen Genehmigung des Staates bedürfen. Sie dürfen nicht in deutscher Sprache gedruckt werden.

c) jede finanzielle Beteiligung an deutschen Zeitungen oder deren Beeinflussung durch Nicht=Deutsche gesetzlich verboten wird und fordern als Strafe für Uebertretungen die Schließung eines Zeitungsbetriebes sowie die sofortige Ausweisung der daran beteiligten Nicht=Deutschen aus dem Reich.

Zeitungen, die gegen das Gemeinwohl verstoßen, sind zu verbieten. Wir fordern den gesetzlichen Kampf gegen eine Kunst= und Literatur=Richtung, die einen zersetzenden Einfluß auf unser Volksleben ausübt und die Schließung von Veranstaltungen, die gegen vorstehende Forderungen verstoßen.

24. Wir fordern die Freiheit aller religiösen Bekenntnisse im Staat, soweit sie nicht dessen Bestand gefährden oder gegen das Sittlichkeits= oder Moralgefühl der germanischen Rasse verstoßen. Die Partei als solche vertritt den Standpunkt eines positiven Christentums, ohne sich konfessionell an ein bestimmtes Bekenntnis zu binden. Sie bekämpft den jüdisch=materialistischen Geist in und außer uns und ist überzeugt, daß eine dauernde Genesung unseres Volkes nur erfolgen kann von innen heraus auf der Grundlage:

Gemeinnutz vor Eigennutz.

25. Zur Durchführung alles dessen fordern wir: Die Schaffung einer starken Zentralgewalt des Reiches. Unbedingte Autorität des politischen Zentralparlaments über das gesamte Reich und seine Organisation im allgemeinen.

Die Bildung von Stände= und Berufskammern zur Durchführung der vom Reich erlassenen Rahmengesetze in den einzelnen Bundesstaaten.

Die Führer der Partei versprechen, wenn nötig unter Einsatz des eigenen Lebens, für die Durchführung der vorstehenden Punkte rücksichtslos einzutreten.

Dieses Flugblatt ist zu beziehen vom Gau Hamburg der NSDAP., Abteilung Propaganda, Hamburg 18, Moorweidenstraße 10. Preis: 100 St. RM. 1.20, 250 St. RM. 2.20, 500 St. RM. 3.50, 1000 St. RM. 5.50, jedes weitere Tausend RM. 5.— porto= oder frachtfrei. Bestellungen gegen Voreinsendung des Betrages auf Postscheckkonto: W. v. Allwörden, Gaupropaganda, Hamburg, Nr. 73 214 oder gegen Nachnahme. Herausgeber: NSDAP Gau Hamburg. — Verantwortlich: Wilh. Schmidt, Hamburg, Moorweidenstraße 10. — Nachdruck verboten. — Rotationsdruck: Berg & Otto, Hbg. 8, Gr. Reichenstr. 63/65.

Hitler's Twenty-Five-Point Program

(1920)

Speaking to a crowd of his cronies in a Munich beer hall, a gaunt and embittered German soldier unveils a list of political demands for his party to follow. Afterwards he comments on the powerful effect he has had on his audience.

On February 24, 1920, Adolf Hitler was still drawing his soldier's pay; his discharge from the army was five weeks away. A veteran of the Great War, who had twice been awarded the Iron Cross, the brooding Austrian seethed with resentment over Germany's ignominious surrender and its "victimization" in the Treaty of Versailles. Blaming foreigners, Jews, and corrupt officials for "betraying" his country, he vowed that strong action must be taken to put the fatherland on the right course.

Working with Anton Drexler, the founder of the German Workers' Party (DAP), Hitler had drafted a list of demands for the party to espouse. Now he was stepping to the speaker's platform to unveil the plan.

The cavernous meeting room of Munich's noisy Hofbrauhäus was crammed with 2,000 beer-guzzling party members, making it difficult for Hitler to make himself heard. But the thirty-year-old Austrian nailed down his twenty-five points. They included: abrogation of the treaty and more land for an expanding population… the denial of German citizenship to Jews and foreigners… the removal of unfit and corrupt officials and death to all traitors and usurers. "[T]he State must assume the responsibility of organizing thoroughly the entire cultural system of the people,"

teaching children the importance of the State… and improving national health. "Newspapers transgressing against the common welfare shall be suppressed." Action must be taken "against those tendencies in art and literature that have a disruptive influence upon the life of our folk." Germans must be guided by the principle of "COMMON GOOD BEFORE INDIVIDUAL GOOD."

To carry out this program, he said, Germany would need to create "a strong central authority in the State." The leaders of the party must stop at nothing to achieve these goals, "if necessary at the sacrifice of their own lives."

No newspaper reported on how Hitler's remarks were received that day. But afterwards the would-be leader confided that he felt his speech had achieved some strong effect, leading to "a new conviction, a new faith, a new will."

Two months later, Hitler advocated that the party change its name to the National Socialist German Workers' Party (NSDAP or Nazi), which it did. Soon after that he was arrested and convicted for his radical activities. While in prison he wrote a longer version of his twisted ideas, which was published as *Mein Kampf.*

The document of 1920 proved to be a harbinger of Hitler's fateful agenda.

LEFT: Hitler's twenty-five points stated that only those born of German blood could be considered German citizens. His plan declared that Jews should be segregated from Aryan society and stripped of all their political, legal, and civil rights.

Uncovering Tutankhamun's Tomb

(1922)

With funding from a wealthy sponsor back in England, a veteran archaeologist and Egyptologist spends years futilely searching for the tomb of a pharaoh known as the "boy king," meticulously recording each step—until he makes a wondrous discovery.

Howard Carter (1874–1939) had spent the last thirty years digging around Egypt for ancient tombs. As one of the world's leading experts in the field, he often operated at the behest of the fabulously wealthy collector of antiquities, Lord Carnarvon, who had hired him to supervise his excavations in the Valley of the Kings along the Nile River.

Carter lived there in a modest mud-brick house as he roamed the area in search of an elusive tomb which he believed might still hold the remains of Tutankhamun, a mysterious Egyptian pharaoh of the eighteenth dynasty, who had ruled between 1332 and 1323 BC. "King Tut" had taken the throne at the age of nine or ten and died at about age eighteen, making his story all the more intriguing.

In 1922, however, Lord Carnarvon informed Carter that he would fund that quest for only one more year unless they struck pay dirt. That time was running out when, on November 4, 1922, Carter's water boy stumbled across steps in the sand that led to an important burial site. An ebullient Carter immediately wired his employer and the excited Lord Carnarvon soon arrived with his entourage to visit the site.

Carter's hands were trembling when he exposed the tomb in Carnarvon's presence. "At first I could see nothing, the hot air escaping from the chamber causing the candle flame to flicker," Carter later wrote, "but presently, as my eyes grew accustomed to the light, details of the room within emerged slowly from the mist, strange animals, statues, and gold—everywhere the glint of gold." Carter was dumbstruck with amazement, prompting the impatient Lord Carnarvon to ask, "Can you see anything?" The gaping archaeologist eventually composed himself enough to reply, "Yes, wonderful things!"

Together they had uncovered the best preserved and most intact pharaoh's tomb in the Valley of Kings. A year and a half later, Carter's team entered the burial chamber to find gold-covered shrines and jewel-studded chests. Raising the lid of Tutankhamun's sarcophagus revealed a coffin of pure gold that held the mummified remains of the boy, King Tut. Word of the discovery flashed across the globe, igniting the world's latest craze and turning Carter into a major celebrity.

Lord Carnarvon was not so lucky. While in Egypt he suffered a mosquito bite that became infected and he died three weeks later—an event that journalists famously ascribed to the "Mummy's Curse." The tale became a staple for Hollywood moviemakers. Carter's journal and subsequent public writings, photographs, and documentary film related details about the twentieth century's most exciting archaeological discovery.

BELOW: Howard Carter and one of his assistants examine the body of Tutankhamun. Historians nowadays take a more critical view of the looting of Egypt's antiquities by colonialist collectors such as Carnarvon and Carter.

(Nov. 26 Continued)

It was sometime before one could see, the hot air escaping caused the candle to flicker, but as soon as one's eyes became accustomed to the glimmer of light, the interior of the chamber gradually loomed before one, with its strange and wonderful medley of extraordinary and beautiful objects heaped upon one another. There was naturally short suspense for those present who could not see, when Lord Carnarvon said to me "Can you see anything?" I replied to him Yes, it is wonderful. I then with precaution made the hole sufficiently large for both of us to see. With the light of an electric torch as well as an additional candle we looked in. Our sensations and astonishment are difficult to describe as the better light revealed to us the marvellous collection of treasures: two strange ebony-black effigies of a King, gold sandalled, bearing staff and mace, loomed out from the cloak of darkness; Gilded couches in strange forms, lion-headed, Hathor-headed, and beast infernal; Exquisitely painted, inlaid, and ornamental caskets; flowers; alabaster vases, some beautifully executed of lotus and papyrus device; strange black shrines with a gilded monster appearing from within; Quite ordinary looking white chests; finely carved chairs; a golden inlaid throne; a heap of large curious white oviform boxes; beneath our very eyes, on the threshold, a lovely lotiform wishing-cup in translucent alabaster; stools of all shapes and design, of both common and rare materials; and, lastly a confusion of over turned parts of chariots glinting with gold, peering from amongst which was a marvellous—furniture—of a vanished civilization. The first impression of which suggests the property-room of an opera—house. Our sensations were bewildering and full of strange emotion. We questioned one another as to the meaning of it all. Was it a tomb or merely a cache? A sealed doorway between the two sentinel statues proved there was more beyond, and with the numerous cartouches bearing the name of Tut-Ankh-Amen on most of the objects before us, There was little doubt that there behind was the grave of that Pharoah.

We closed the hole, locked the wooden-grill which has been placed upon the first doorway, we mounted our donkeys and return home contemplating what we had seen.

ABOVE AND LEFT: *Howard Carter's diary and notes are part of the Griffith Institute collection at the University of Oxford.*

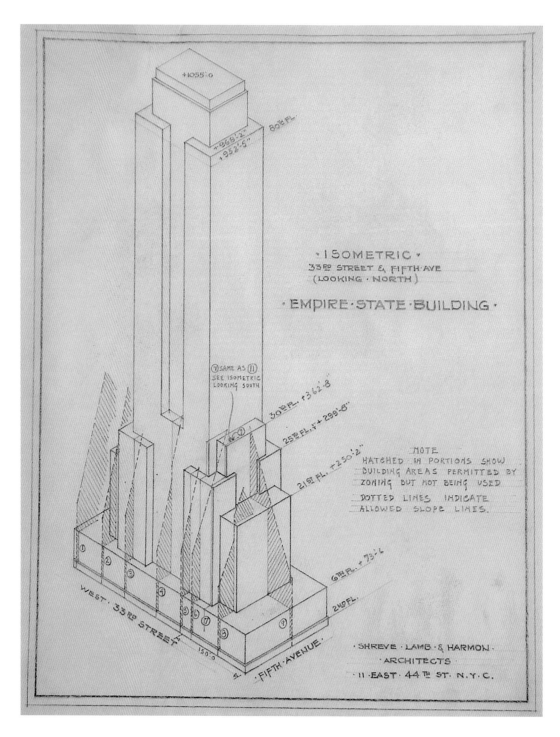

Empire State Building

(1929–31)

Conceived and built according to masterful plans, the tallest building of its day shoots up to become the world's most famous skyscraper—an architectural marvel and astonishing feat of engineering and construction that remains an American icon.

Oblivious to the impending Great Crash of the stock market, a group of industrialists connected to General Motors banded together in 1929 behind the idea of erecting the world's tallest building in Manhattan to eclipse the nearby Chrysler Building owned by their competitor. The site at Fifth Avenue between Thirty-third and Thirty-fourth Streets had previously been occupied by the exclusive Waldorf-Astoria Hotel, until they tore it down for their new symbol of sky-high American corporate power—the Empire State Building.

The architecture firm Shreve, Lamb, and Harmon Associates was chosen to design the colossus. William F. Lamb (1893–1952) produced the drawings in only two weeks, selecting an art deco style that looked like a pencil. Lamb used earlier designs for the Reynolds Building in Winston-Salem, North Carolina, and the Carew Tower in Cincinnati, Ohio as inspiration. His design later won several awards, including the gold medal from the Architectural League in 1931.

From a broad, five-story base covering two acres, the structure would tower 102 stories, rising 1,454 feet to the top of the antenna spire, making it the world's tallest skyscraper. Another distinctive feature would include windows that were flush instead of recessed, and the tone of the exterior would appear blonde.

The general contractor was Starrett Brothers & Eken, the recognized leader in skyscraper construction. Indeed, one of the brothers, William A. Starrett, had recently authored the book, *Skyscrapers and the Men Who Build Them*, in which he wrote: "Building skyscrapers is the nearest peacetime equivalent of war.… The analogy of war is the strife against the elements." In 1930–31 the firm compiled a notebook on the project, entitled *Notes on Construction of the Empire State Building*, consisting of seventy-seven pages of text typed on blue-lined graph paper and put in a three-ring binder. The presentation also included black-and-white photographs mounted with black corners on thirty-two sheets of brown pressboard. Both the text and the photos provided a detailed, step-by-step account of the building process for the historic skyscraper.

Commenced in the early years of the Great Depression, the project employed as many as 3,400 construction workers on any single day, many of them immigrants from Europe, as well as hundreds of fearless Mohawk Indian iron workers. At least five workers died during the frenetic building.

The whole project took an amazing twenty months from the signing of the first architectural contract in September 1929 to the formal opening on May 1, 1931; the construction was completed in an astonishing 410 days. The final cost was $40,948,900 (equivalent to $635,021,563 in 2015). As of 2007, it was still the second-largest single office complex in the US after the Pentagon. Immortalized in innumerable books and movies, it was most famously scaled by King Kong, who fended off attacking planes from its celestial spire, in 1933.

ABOVE: On April 24, 1930 the building was two stories high. A year later it would be complete.

Edward VIII's Instrument of Abdication

(1936)

After refusing to back out of the scandal over his intention to marry an American divorcé, England's bachelor king sits down at his desk to sign a historic document. With a few strokes of a pen he will announce his intent to become the first British monarch to voluntarily abdicate his throne.

Edward VIII (1894–1972) became King of England upon the death of his father, George V, on January 20, 1936, though he had not yet been crowned.

But when the forty-one-year-old bachelor revealed his wish to marry a divorced American woman named Wallis Warfield Simpson, whose second divorce was still pending, he faced staunch disapproval. Religious, legal, and political objections were raised. As nominal head of the Church of England, King Edward came up against the Church's longstanding policy barring any divorced person from remarriage if his or her ex-spouse was still alive. And there were other impediments as well.

Prime Minister Stanley Baldwin told him that Mrs. Simpson wasn't fit to be queen. Amid the many rumors swirling about her alleged adulterous affairs, J. Edgar Hoover's FBI secretly reported that the woman was romantically involved with Germany's then-Ambassador Joachim von Ribbentrop; and the American ambassador, Joseph Kennedy, described her as a "tart."

Nevertheless, Edward refused to break off the relationship, forcing the crisis to its climax.

On the morning of December 10, 1936, Edward assembled with his brothers in the drawing room of his country house in Surrey. Sitting at his desk, he signed seven copies of an Instrument of Abdication that lawyers had provided. The document stated: "I,

Edward the Eighth, of Great Britain, Ireland, and the British Dominions beyond the Seas, King, Emperor of India, do hereby declare My irrevocable determination to renounce the Throne for Myself and for My descendants, and My desire that effect should be given to this Instrument of Abdication immediately." As his brothers signed as witnesses, "the room was filled with a dignified dull murmur," he later recalled.

The following day, King Edward VIII publicly announced his decision to a worldwide radio audience and Parliament formally acted on the matter. By giving his royal assent to Parliament's abdication act, he relinquished the throne to his younger brother, George VI. George's first act as king was to give his brother the title of His Royal Highness the Duke of Windsor.

The Duke and Simpson were married in France on June 3, 1937 and lived in Paris. During World War II, Edward served as governor of the Bahamas. But the couple's pro-Nazi sympathies provided further embarrassment. Edward was heard to say, "After the war is over and Hitler will crush the Americans ... we'll take over." Thirty years after the abdication he told the New York *Daily News*, "it was in Britain's interest and in Europe's too, that Germany be encouraged to strike east and smash Communism forever."

Copies of the abdication instrument are kept in Britain's National Archives.

RIGHT: The Instrument of Abdication, signed by Edward VIII and his three brothers. The document was signed at Fort Belvedere, Edward's house in Windsor Great Park, Surrey.

INSTRUMENT OF ABDICATION

I, Edward the Eighth, of Great
Britain, Ireland, and the British Dominions
beyond the Seas, King, Emperor of India, do
hereby declare My irrevocable determination
to renounce the Throne for Myself and for
My descendants, and My desire that effect
should be given to this Instrument of
Abdication immediately.

In token whereof I have hereunto set
My hand this tenth day of December, nineteen
hundred and thirty six, in the presence of
the witnesses whose signatures are subscribed.

SIGNED AT
FORT BELVEDERE
IN THE PRESENCE
OF

Edward RI

Albert

Henry

George

The Radio Times, October 23, 1936   Vol. 53   No. 682   Registered at the G.P.O. as a Newspaper   Every Friday   TWOPENCE

THE RADIO TIMES

TELEVISION
N U M B E R
2d

ABOVE: The specially commissioned cover design by Eric Fraser featured the Alexandra Palace transmitter. The opening article explained how "engineers and programme builders have been busy for many months grappling with this fascinating new development by which sights as well as sounds can be broadcast."

Television Listings

(1936)

Once the BBC had introduced its audience to the "magic of television," the network began offering its potential viewers a brief weekly schedule of programs, which it published as a supplement to *The Radio Times*. The only catch was that you had to live within twenty-five miles of the sole transmitter to receive a signal.

After several years of faltering and flickering experiments with the new medium of television, the British Broadcasting Corporation in 1936 built the first television station at Alexandra Palace (nicknamed "Ally Pally"), and BBC program planners were ordered to develop the first TV programming in just nine days. The opening show, "Here's Looking at You," went on the air live on August 26, 1936, with announcer Leslie Mitchell saying, "Good afternoon, ladies and gentlemen. It is with great pleasure that I introduce you to the magic of television..."

After intermittent tests and broadcasts, the first regular high-definition television service was scheduled to begin on November 2. The initial service alternated on a weekly basis between Baird's 240-line intermediate film system and Marconi-EMI's 405-line all-electronic system. Two blocks of programs were broadcast every day except Sunday, between 3 or 4 PM and 9 or 10 PM.

After introducing the concept of TV broadcasts in its "Television Number" of October 23, 1936, the BBC quickly put together a supplement to its regular *Radio Times* magazine, starting October 30th, to reveal the opening lineup for the upcoming week. The weekly TV listings ran from Monday through Saturday as there was no Sunday broadcast.

The first advertised programs included such scintillating features as the weather, musical numbers, household demonstrations of interest to women, such as "Mrs. Daisy Pain will give some tips about ironing," and a Cabaret quarter of an hour in which Bubbles Stewart would do "impressions of film stars."

John Piper was slated to provide commentary about exhibitions currently on display at galleries in London, and there would also be a brief performance by "The Whistling Guard."

At 3 PM on November 2, 1936 the world's first regular high-definition service began transmitting as scheduled. There may have been only 100 to 500 television sets in Britain capable of receiving the broadcast, and all viewers had to reside within twenty-five miles of the Ally Pally transmitter. The huge and expensive TV machine made television viewing a novel luxury reserved for the rich, and the convention at that time was for viewers to dress up as if they were attending a stage play.

Three years later, the head of BBC Television, Gerald Cock, said he viewed television as "essentially a medium for topicalities." He added that, "Excerpts from plays during their normal runs, televised from the studio or direct from the stage, with perhaps a complete play at the end of its run would have attractive possibilities as part of a review of the nation's entertainment activities.

But, in my view television is from its very nature more suitable for the dissemination of all kinds of information than for entertainment."

Early issues of the first *Radio Times* television listings are now a hot collector's item.

THE RADIO TIMES
TELEVISION NUMBER

LEFT: The "Television Number" of The Radio Times *promised its readers that "the next few months will be full of interest ... You will be watching the beginnings of a new art."*

Munich Agreement

(1938)

After signing the Munich Agreement with Germany, Italy, and France, British Prime Minister Neville Chamberlain waves a copy of the document for all to see, claiming that it will ensure "peace for our time"— not knowing that Reich Chancellor Adolf Hitler remains bent on conquest.

Twenty years after the end of the Great War, Germany was again threatening to unleash the dogs of war. This time the disputed territory was the Sudetenland, a predominantly German-speaking area of Czechoslovakia, which the fascist ruler Hitler was threatening to seize by force if he didn't get his way.

Neville Chamberlain, the British Prime Minister, was determined to avert war, which he knew would be inevitable if Hitler invaded the sovereign nation that had been created in the aftermath of World War I. So he asked Hitler for a personal meeting and flew to meet the Führer at his Bavarian mountaintop retreat at Berchtesgaden outside Munich. The pair discussed the matter for three hours, then Chamberlain flew home to meet with his cabinet, then raced back to Germany for further negotiations in a desperate bid to avert war.

On September 29, 1938, Chamberlain met in Munich with Hitler, Italy's Benito Mussolini, and Edouard Daladier of France. Representatives of Czechoslovakia and the Soviet Union were excluded. The four powers agreed on the immediate cession of the Sudetenland to Germany if Hitler agreed not to make any further territorial demands. The meeting ended at 1:30 AM with the four heads of state signing the Munich Agreement.

Chamberlain believed he had won a great victory. As soon as he got off the plane from Germany, a jubilant Prime Minister was met by a cheering crowd at the Heston Aerodrome. Chamberlain waved a copy of the newly-signed Munich agreement in the air as proof of his diplomatic achievement, calling it the first step toward a lasting peace. "This morning I had another talk with the German Chancellor, Herr Hitler," he crowed, "and here is the paper which bears his name upon it as well as mine."

Chamberlain was feted at Buckingham Palace and the newspapers sang his praises. But Winston Churchill denounced the pact as "a total and unmitigated defeat," and elements of the German military, realizing what was in store, secretly plotted a possible coup to prevent Hitler's increasingly bellicose designs.

Sudetenland was of immense strategic importance to the Czechs and they regarded the agreement as a betrayal by the United Kingdom and France. However, Czechoslovakia was no match against Germany's military might, so its government reluctantly consented to abide by the terms of the pact.

Seven months later on March 15, to Chamberlain's horror, German tanks rolled into the rest of Czechoslovakia, signaling Hitler's first breach of the Munich Agreement. The Prime Minister's actions went down as the greatest example of failed "appeasement" in modern history.

An original copy of the Munich document, bearing the signatures of the four leaders, is held in Britain's National Archives.

We, the German Führer and Chancellor and the
British Prime Minister, have had a further
meeting today and are agreed in recognising that
the question of Anglo-German relations is of the
first importance for the two countries and for
Europe.

We regard the agreement signed last night
and the Anglo-German Naval Agreement as symbolic
of the desire of our two peoples never to go to
war with one another again.

We are resolved that the method of
consultation shall be the method adopted to deal
with any other questions that may concern our two
countries, and we are determined to continue our
efforts to remove possible sources of difference
and thus to contribute to assure the peace of
Europe.

September 30. 1938

Agreement

reached on the 29th of September 1938
between Germany, United Kingdom, France and Italy.

Germany, the United Kingdom, France and Italy, taking
into consideration the agreement, which has been already reached
in principle for the cession to Germany of the Sudeten German
territory, have agreed on the following terms and conditions
governing the said cession and the measures consequent thereon,
and by this agreement they each hold themselves responsible
for the steps necessary to secure its fulfilment.

1.) The evacuation will begin on October 1st.

2.) The United Kingdom, France and Italy agree that the evacuation
of the territory shall be completed by October 10th, without
any existing installations having been destroyed and that the
Czechoslovak Government will be held responsible for carrying
out the evacuation without damage to the said installations.

3.) The conditions governing the evacuation will be laid down in
detail by an international commission composed of representatives
of Germany, the United Kingdom, France, Italy and Czechoslovakia.

4.) The occupation by stages of the predominantly German territory
by German troops will begin on October 1st. The four territories
marked on the attached map will be occupied by German troops in
the following order: the territory marked number I on the 1st
and 2nd of October, the territory marked number II on the
2nd and 3rd of October, the territory marked number III on the
3rd, 4th and 5th of October, the territory marked number IV
on the 6th and 7th of October.

The

TOP: The Munich Agreement and the accompanying letter that were supposed
to "assure the peace of Europe." Only seven months later, German tanks rolled
into Czechoslovakia, signaling Hitler's first breach of the agreement. Winston
Churchill denounced the pact as "a total and unmitigated defeat."

ABOVE: Chamberlain jubilantly waves a copy of the signed Munich Agreement
on his arrival at Heston Aerodrome, on September 30, 1938.

100 Documents that Changed the World_____153

Geheimes Zusatzprotokoll.

Aus Anlass der Unterzeichnung des Nichtangriffs-
vertrages zwischen dem Deutschen Reich und der Union
der Sozialistischen Sowjetrepubliken haben die unter-
zeichneten Bevollmächtigten der beiden Teile in streng
vertraulicher Aussprache die Frage der Abgrenzung der
beiderseitigen Interessensphären in Osteuropa erörtert.
Diese Aussprache hat zu folgendem Ergebnis geführt:

1. Für den Fall einer territorial-politischen Umgestaltung in den zu den baltischen Staaten (Finnland,
Estland, Lettland, Litauen) gehörenden Gebieten bildet
die nördliche Grenze Litauens zugleich die Grenze der
Interessensphären Deutschlands und der UdSSR. Hierbei
wird das Interesse Litauens am Wilner Gebiet beider-
seits anerkannt.

2. Für den Fall einer territorial-politischen
Umgestaltung der zum polnischen Staate gehörenden Gebiete
werden die Interessensphären Deutschlands und der UdSSR
ungefähr durch die Linie der Flüsse Narew, Weichsel und
San abgegrenzt.

Die Frage, ob die beiderseitigen Interessen die
Erhaltung eines unabhängigen polnischen Staates erwünscht
erscheinen lassen und wie dieser Staat abzugrenzen wäre,
kann endgültig erst im Laufe der weiteren politischen

Entwicklung geklärt werden.

In jedem Falle werden beide Regierungen diese Frage
im Wege einer freundschaftlichen Verständigung lösen.

3) Hinsichtlich des Südostens Europas wird von
sowjetischer Seite das Interesse an Bessarabien betont.
Von deutscher Seite wird das völlige politische Desinter-
essement an diesen Gebieten erklärt.

4) Dieses Protokoll wird von beiden Seiten streng
geheim behandelt werden.

Moskau, den 23. August 1939.

Für die
Deutsche Reichsregierung
Ribbentrop

In Vollmacht
der Regierung
UdSSR:
W. Molotow

ABOVE: *The Nazi–Soviet Pact was signed by German Foreign
Minister Joachim von Ribbentrop and Soviet Foreign
Minister Vyacheslav Molotov on August 23, 1939. The non-
aggression treaty was meant to guarantee that neither side
would ally itself to, or aid, an enemy of the other side.*

RIGHT: *A cartoon by David Low from the* London Evening
Standard *(September 20, 1939), satirizing the Nazi–Soviet Pact.
Poland is represented by the prostrate figure.*

The Hitler–Stalin Non-Aggression Pact

(1939)

The world is shocked again by a non-aggression pact between two diametrically opposed tyrants, Adolf Hitler and Josef Stalin, who appear to have put aside their mutual hatred for the sake of their own immediate expansionist interests. Secret protocols of the document will later emerge that are even more damning.

On August 23, 1939, Nazis and communists publicly shook hands in Moscow as leaders of Germany and the Soviet Union signed a non-aggression treaty guaranteeing that neither side would ally itself to or aid an enemy of the other side. Hailed by its two principal negotiators, German Foreign Minister Joachim von Ribbentrop and Soviet Foreign Minister Vyacheslav Molotov, the document was also signed by Stalin, who even had himself photographed in smiling agreement with von Ribbentrop. The press also reported that Stalin had recently fired his Jewish foreign minister, Maksim Litvinov, to curry favor with Hitler.

Soviets and Nazis alike were flabbergasted by the rapprochement. But statesmen throughout Europe were even more alarmed because the treaty set in motion a chain of actions and reactions that quickly plunged them into another world war, for a week later Germany invaded Poland from the west, and sixteen days after that, Soviet troops stormed in from the east, dividing the country like two wolves sharing a carcass.

The concatenation of falling dominos swept all the way to England, where Chamberlain's Munich Agreement was suddenly obliterated. Germany invaded Western Poland, the Netherlands, Belgium, Luxembourg, France, Denmark, Yugoslavia, Greece, and Norway in rapid succession. The Soviets annexed Finland, Estonia, Latvia, Lithuania, and parts of Romania. More than a million people perished.

The Hitler–Stalin Pact evaporated when Nazi Germany invaded the Soviet Union at 3:15 AM on June 22, 1941 in Operation Barbarossa, setting in motion an even deadlier conflict that would ultimately cost tens of millions of lives.

Upon Germany's defeat, in May 1945 a captive German clerk handed over to the American military canisters containing a microfilm copy of the Nazi–Soviet Pact that von Ribbentrop had kept aside for safekeeping. It included a copy of a secret protocol related to the agreement—one that both powers had always concealed.

The secret text divided Romania, Poland, Lithuania, Latvia, Estonia, and Finland into German and Soviet "spheres of influence," that anticipated potential "territorial and political rearrangements" of those countries, thus indicating that both Stalin and Hitler were aware in advance of each other's expansionist intent. In other words, they had countenanced each other's future aggression.

In 1946 the treaty was published for the first time by the *St. Louis Post-Dispatch* and the *Manchester Guardian*. Copies were later reprinted in various scholarly works. The Soviet copy of the original document was finally declassified in 1992 and published in a Russian scientific journal in 1993.

Declaration of War Against Japan

(1941)

In the wake of Japan's surprise attack on Pearl Harbor, President Franklin D. Roosevelt crafts one of the most effective speeches in American history, declaring, "December 7, 1941—a date that will live in infamy... The facts of yesterday and today speak for themselves. The people of the United States have already formed their opinions and well understand the implications to the very life and safety of our nation."

On the afternoon of Sunday, December 7, 1941, President Roosevelt was interrupted by a telephone call from the Secretary of War, informing him that the Empire of Japan had attacked America's Pacific fleet at Pearl Harbor Naval Base in Hawaii.

Roosevelt immediately gathered the Vice President, members of his cabinet and other close advisers in the same room where Lincoln had convened his advisers after Fort Sumter. He also telephoned British Prime Minister Winston Churchill and began weighing his options. After assigning his speechwriters to work on a radio address he would give that night to the American people, FDR dictated a direct emotional appeal to Congress, which his secretary, Grace Tully, typed and copied. Although brief and direct, the approach carried echoes of Lincoln's Gettysburg Address.

The next day Roosevelt revised the draft with new military information and went over the remarks for style and content, making handwritten changes in pencil.

That afternoon the President addressed Congress to obtain a Declaration of War Against Japan. He began his address with the words: "Yesterday, December 7, 1941—a date that will live in infamy—the United States of America was suddenly and deliberately attacked by naval and air forces of the Empire of Japan." The solemn speech lasted only seven minutes.

As soon as it was over, the Senate voted, with all

eighty-eight members in favor. The House of Representatives approved the war declaration by 388 to 1, with the only exception being Rep. Jeannette Rankin (Republican–Montana), who had also voted against America's entry into World War I. Congress took only thirty-three minutes to pass the resolution and FDR signed it at 4:10 PM.

The domestic response was resoundingly positive. Three days later, on December 11, Japan's allies, Germany and Italy, declared war on the United States, bringing America into World War II.

Roosevelt's speech was a rallying cry. But after leaving the podium that day, his three-page typed speech with his handwritten changes was missing, prompting the President to ask his son, James, "Where is the speech?" His son replied, "I don't know." Efforts to find it proved futile for decades, until finally, in 1984 Dr. Susan Cooper, a curator for the National Archives in Washington, came across the document in papers of the Senate for 1941. Today it is held at the Franklin D. Roosevelt Presidential Library in Hyde Park, NY.

ABOVE: Roosevelt signs the Declaration of War Against Japan on December 8, 1941.

RIGHT: The draft speech, with handwritten changes in pencil.

DRAFT No. 1   December 7, 1941.

PROPOSED MESSAGE TO THE CONGRESS

Yesterday, December 7, 1941, a date which will live in ~~world history~~ *infamy*

the United States of America was ~~simultaneously~~ *suddenly* and deliberately attacked

by naval and air forces of the Empire of Japan.

The United States was at the moment at peace with that nation and was

~~continuing the~~ *still in* conversations with its Government and its Emperor looking

toward the maintenance of peace in the Pacific. Indeed, one hour after

Japanese air squadrons had commenced bombing in ~~Hawaii and the Philippines~~ *Oahu*

the Japanese Ambassador to the United States and his colleague delivered

to the Secretary of State a formal reply to a ~~former~~ *recent American* message. ~~from the~~

~~Secretary.~~ *While* This reply ~~contained a statement~~ *stated* that diplomatic negotiations *it seemed useless*

~~must be considered at an end,~~ *it* ~~But~~ contained no threat ~~and no~~ hint of ~~an~~ *or war or*

armed attack.

It will be recorded that the distance ~~of Manila, and especially~~ of

Hawaii, from Japan makes it obvious that the attacks ~~were~~ *was* deliberately

planned many days *or years weeks* ago. During the intervening time the Japanese Govern-

ment has deliberately sought to deceive the United States by false

statements and expressions of hope for continued peace.

12/2/42

γ Chamber	Time	# 3	# 1	# 6
.925	12¹²PM	.95	—	—
.93	12¹³	.965	.73	.78
#2(10¹⁰)		# 3(10¹⁰)	#1(10¹⁰)	#6 (10⁹)
—	2²⁴ PM	.97	.92	.99
—	2²³	.96	.905	.985
.945	2³⁴	.91	.82	.975
.94	2⁴⁰	.83	.67	.97
.94	2⁴⁸	.81	.62	.975
.935	2⁵⁷	.67	.38	.96
.92	3⁰²	.51	.14	.95
.885	3⁰⁵	.20	0	.905
.875	3²⁶	.14	0	.895
.860	3²⁸	.09	0	.88
.850	3²⁹	.06	0	.87
3³⁰ rod in				
.96	3³¹	.95	.9	.99
.96	3³³	.97	.95	.995
.96	3³⁷	.955	.90	.99
.96	3³⁷	.935	.86	.99
.955	3³⁸	.91	.8	.99
.95	3³⁸½	.87	.72	.98
.94	3³⁹	.82	.61	.975
.94	3³⁹½	.74	.46	.97
.93	3⁴⁰	.64	.18	.96
.926	3⁴⁰½	.55	.16	.95
.92	3⁴¹½	.48	.10	.94
.90	3⁴²½	.35	.02	.93

※ We're cookin!

ABOVE: *"We're cookin!"* The notebook that recorded the dawning of the atomic age. Physicists at the University of Chicago performed the world's first controlled, self-sustaining nuclear chain reaction capable of harnessing the vast energy released by atomic fission.

158_____100 Documents that Changed the World

Manhattan Project Notebook

(1942)

Columns of penciled mathematical notations along with a cryptic comment—jotted at an underground squash court beneath an old football stadium at the University of Chicago—provide graphic eyewitness testimony to World War II's most secretive project and the dawn of the nuclear age.

On December 2, 1942, less than a year after Pearl Harbor, a group of men with clipboards and notebooks gathered around a strange-looking brick-like structure about 24 square feet that towered from floor to ceiling in a corner of the concrete womb beneath Stagg Field. Their leader, Enrico Fermi (1901–54), a Nobel Prize-winning physicist, had carefully constructed the stacked rows, known as Chicago Pile-1, with 40,000 blocks of graphite and 19,000 pieces of uranium metal and uranium oxide fuel uranium set within cadmium-covered wooden timbers.

Fermi conducted his experiment at 3:25 PM, hoping to start and stop the world's first nuclear chain reaction, harnessing the power of the atom. Consistent with his calculations, the cadmium-covered boards served as the reactor control rods, regulating the nuclear reaction to keep it from burning out of control and wreaking havoc in the middle of densely populated Chicago.

Upon checking all of the readings, and duly recording the data, Fermi and his colleagues pronounced the experiment a success, with one of the engineers writing in his spiral notebook, "We're cookin!"

Afterwards the team celebrated with a glass of Chianti and each one signed his name on the bottle's straw wrapper as a memento of their historic achievement—the world's first controlled, self-sustaining nuclear chain reaction capable of harnessing the vast energy released by atomic fission. Although the reaction they had created that day was too weak (only 0.5 watts) to power even a single light bulb, everyone present knew that the world would never be the same again. But none of them could breathe a word of it to anyone for years, because this was a crucial element of America's super-secret Manhattan Project, the massive enterprise to build an atomic bomb.

The prospect of making bigger and more dangerous nuclear reactions prompted Fermi to move his experimental station from Chicago to a more remote site in Argonne Woods. Other project activities were also carried out at Los Alamos, New Mexico; Hanford, Washington; Oak Ridge, Tennessee; and other locations.

With the dropping of the first two atomic bombs on Japan in August 1945, Fermi became known as one of the "fathers of the atomic age." The spot where he conducted his famous experiment is now marked by Henry Moore's "Nuclear Energy" sculpture and a historical plaque.

The Manhattan Project notebook is part of the Records of the Atomic Energy Commission, Record Group 326, kept in the National Archives.

BELOW: Workers in the Y-12 plant at Oak Ridge, Tennessee. As part of the Manhattan Project, the Y-12 plant developed "Little Boy," the atomic bomb that was dropped on Hiroshima on August 6, 1945.

Wannsee Protocol

(1942)

A select group of Hitler's henchmen meet at a mansion outside Berlin to coordinate plans for the implementation of the "Final Solution of the Jewish Question," taking special security measures to cover their tracks. But an incriminating document survives.

On January 20, 1942, fifteen high-ranking Nazi Party and German government officials conferred at a lavish villa in Wannsee. The attendees included high-ranking representatives from the Foreign Office, the justice, interior, and state ministries, and officers from the Schutzstaffel (SS).

Tasked by Hitler himself, and acting on the written authorization of Hermann Göring, SS-Obergruppenführer Reinhard Heydrich, the Chief of the Reich Main Security Office, had convened the group to ensure that all of the necessary departments would be carrying out plans for most of the remaining Jews of German-occupied Europe to be deported to Poland and exterminated. It was to be the greatest organized and systematic campaign of mass murder in world history.

Using statistics prepared by SS-Lieutenant Colonel Adolf Eichmann, chief of the RSHA Department IV B4 (Jewish Affairs), Heydrich reported that there were approximately eleven million Jews in Europe, half of them in countries not yet under German control. The Wannsee Protocol set forth the detailed and sequential plan for their annihilation.

The policy decision had already been made at the highest level. Heydrich outlined how European Jews would be rounded up from west to east and sent to killing centers in occupied Poland, where they would be systematically killed. He also defined in precise terms who would be liquidated. The protocol called for millions of other persons in occupied territories to be removed by "natural causes"

(mass starvation, exposure, and disease), and their property and food transferred to Germans.

Although the 90-minute conference involved meticulous planning and records, the officers in charge later tried to couch the minutes in vague bureaucratic jargon to conceal what was planned. Despite their euphemisms—such as the use of the term "the Final Solution"—the message was clear to all participants: they were ordered to carry out the genocide of European Jewry.

In the end, nobody balked, and cognac and cigars were enjoyed before the attendees saluted each other and went about their business.

The report of the meeting was carefully sanitized to disguise its murderous nature, and each copy of the Top Secret protocol was strictly controlled. After Heydrich was assassinated in June 1942, the Nazis thought they had destroyed all of the incriminating Wannsee files. But in 1947 a prosecutor at the International Military

Tribunal at Nuremberg obtained from the German Foreign Office number sixteen [Martin Luther's copy] of the thirty copies that had been prepared, and it provided a smoking gun.

The Wannsee House, site of the conference, is now a Holocaust Memorial.

LEFT: *Heydrich's letter to Martin Luther following the Wannsee conference.* RIGHT: *Page six of the fifteen-page document lists the number of European Jews to be annihilated in the Final Solution: 330,000 in England alone; eleven million in total.*

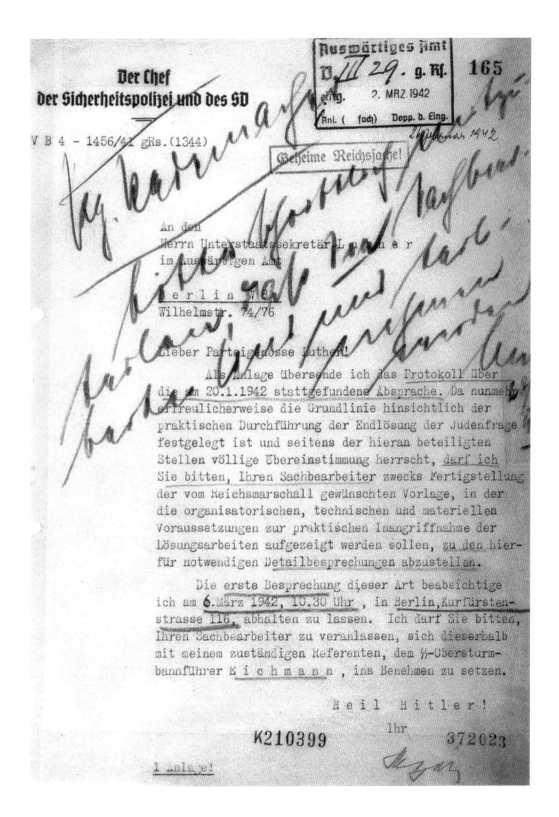

Der Chef
der Sicherheitspolizei und des SD

Ausmärtiges Amt
D.II 29. g.Rf. 165
eing. 2. MRZ. 1942
Anl. (fach) Dopp. d. Eing.

V B 4 - 1456/41 gRs. (1344)

Geheime Reichssache!

An den
Herrn Unterstaatssekretär L u t h e r
im Auswärtigen Amt

B e r l i n W 8.
Wilhelmstr. 74/76

Lieber Parteigenosse Luther!

Als Anlage übersende ich das Protokoll über
die am 20.1.1942 stattgefundene Absprache. Da nunmehr
erfreulicherweise die Grundlinie hinsichtlich der
praktischen Durchführung der Endlösung der Judenfrage
festgelegt ist und seitens der hieran beteiligten
Stellen völlige Übereinstimmung herrscht, darf ich
Sie bitten, Ihren Sachbearbeiter zwecks Fertigstellung
der vom Reichsmarschall gewünschten Vorlage, in der
die organisatorischen, technischen und materiellen
Voraussetzungen zur praktischen Inangriffnahme der
Lösungsarbeiten aufgezeigt werden sollen, zu den hier-
für notwendigen Detailbesprechungen abzustellen.

Die erste Besprechung dieser Art beabsichtige
ich am 6.März 1942, 10.30 Uhr , in Berlin,Kurfürsten-
strasse 116, abhalten zu lassen. Ich darf Sie bitten,
Ihren Sachbearbeiter zu veranlassen, sich dieserhalb
mit meinem zuständigen Referenten, dem ﬀ-Obersturm-
bannführer E i c h m a n n , ins Benehmen zu setzen.

H e i l H i t l e r !

Ihr

K210399   372023

1 Anlage!

Anne Frank's Diary

(1942–44)

A young Jewish girl hiding with her family in an attic reveals her most intimate thoughts in a diary that goes on to become probably the most famous account of life during the Holocaust, read by tens of millions of people.

Anne Frank (1929–44) was a German-Jewish teenager who was forced to go into hiding in Nazi-occupied Amsterdam, Holland during the Holocaust. Shortly after receiving a diary for her thirteenth birthday, the girl started recording entries on June 14, 1942, and she continued writing down her impressions while confined with her family and four other fugitives as they hid behind a bookcase in a concealed attic space in her father's office building.

The young girl's entries were made in the form of letters to several imaginary friends and she also employed pseudonyms to conceal the identities of her fellow fugitives and accomplices. Like many other normal teenagers, Anne agonized over her conflicted feelings about her family and a possible romantic interest, as well as her evolving thoughts about life. But her extraordinary depth and fine literary ability, combined with her optimism in the face of such adversity made her account a literary and historical treasure.

"It's a wonder I haven't abandoned all my ideals," she wrote shortly before her arrest,

> they seem so absurd and impractical. Yet I cling to them because I still believe, in spite of everything, that people are truly good at heart… I see the world being slowly transformed into a wilderness, I hear the approaching thunder that, one day, will destroy us too, I feel the suffering of millions. And yet, when I look up at the sky, I somehow feel that everything will change for the better that this cruelty too shall end, that peace and tranquility will return once more.

Anne would end up spending two years and one month closeted in the hideaway, before the group was betrayed and sent off to concentration camps. Of the eight persons in hiding in the attic, only her father would survive. Anne succumbed to typhus in Belsen-Belsen in March 1945. She was just fifteen.

A family friend later retrieved the diary from the attic and presented it to Anne's father after the war. Upon reading it, Otto Frank persevered to get it published.

The diary first appeared in Amsterdam in 1947 and was subsequently published in the US and the United Kingdom as *Anne Frank: The Diary of a Young Girl* in 1952. Its immense popularity inspired award-winning stage and movie versions. To date the book has sold more than thirty million copies in sixty-seven languages.

The original manuscript was bequeathed to the Netherlands Institute for War Documentation.

LEFT: The red and white checkered diary that Anne was given on her thirteenth birthday—June 12, 1942. Anne wrote the diary as a series of letters to imaginary friends, her favorite being "Kitty." "The nicest part is being able to write down all my thoughts and feelings, otherwise I'd absolutely suffocate."

Germany's
Instrument of Surrender

(1945)

Solemn-faced generals from the victors and the vanquished convene at a table in Gen. Dwight D. Eisenhower's headquarters in northeastern France for Germany's unconditional surrender. But after the document signing, the Soviets demand a more formal surrender in Berlin the next day.

On May 7, 1945, a former high school in Reims, France provided the setting for the abrupt surrender of the Third Reich. Converted to serve as the Supreme Headquarters of the Allied Expeditionary Force (SHAEF), the area swarmed with armed sentries, Jeeps, and a small caravan of grim-faced Nazi officers. Across a plain conference table, alongside map-covered walls, a phalanx of warriors from the opposing armies regarded each other with cold contempt. Despite the season, the Germans wore gloves.

Those seated included representatives of the four Allied Powers—France, Great Britain, the Soviet Union, and the United States—along with a German contingent headed by Generaloberst Alfred Jodl, who had been authorized to sign on behalf of the German Army. Eisenhower had sent as his delegate Lt. Gen. Walter Bedell Smith. Beneath Smith's calm demeanor there was chaos because at the last minute the Soviets made clear that they wanted a second, more formal, surrender to be held in Berlin the next day.

Also in the room were a corps of other officers, orderlies, and guards, as well as sixteen journalists who had been flown to the location on the condition that they not release any report until the SHAEF gave its green light.

Copies of the English-language version of the surrender instrument had been hurriedly typed by one of the command's British secretaries, Susan Hibbert, and she was among the onlookers for the formal signing.

Asked if they understood the terms of surrender, Jodl said "yes." The surrender document called for German forces to surrender unconditionally to the Supreme Commander of the Allied Expeditionary Forces and simultaneously to the Soviet High Command "all forces on land, sea and in the air" who were under German control. Any German forces that failed to abide by the terms of surrender would be subject to appropriate punishment.

Jodl signed the first Instrument of Surrender at 2:41 AM local time and continued until he had signed the copies in other languages. Then he asked for leave to speak and when it was granted he said:

> With this signature the German people and armed forces are for better or for worse delivered into the victor's hands. In this war, which has lasted more than five years, both have achieved and suffered perhaps more than any other people in the world.

As soon as the ceremony was over, the reporter for the Associated Press rushed to a telephone and called in his story, in violation of the news embargo. After the Soviets orchestrated a second, more public surrender in Berlin the following day, May 8, was officially celebrated as Victory in Europe Day.

Jodl was later tried, convicted, and hanged at Nuremberg for war crimes.

RIGHT: The Instrument of Surrender, which ordered Germany to cease all military, naval and air operations on May 8, 1945 at 11:31 PM Central European time. The photograph shows Jodl signing the document in Reims in the early hours of May 7th.

Only this text in English is authoritative

ACT OF MILITARY SURRENDER

1. We the undersigned, acting by authority of the German High Command, hereby surrender unconditionally to the Supreme Commander, Allied Expeditionary Force and simultaneously to the Soviet High Command all forces on land, sea, and in the air who are at this date under German control.

2. The German High Command will at once issue orders to all German military, naval and air authorities and to all forces under German control to cease active operations at 2301 hours Central European time on 8 May and to remain in the positions occupied at that time. No ship, vessel, or aircraft is to be scuttled, or any damage done to their hull, machinery or equipment.

3. The German High Command will at once issue to the appropriate commanders, and ensure the carrying out of any further orders issued by the Supreme Commander, Allied Expeditionary Force and by the Soviet High Command.

4. This act of military surrender is without prejudice to, and will be superseded by any general instrument of surrender imposed by, or on behalf of the United Nations and applicable to GERMANY and the German armed forces as a whole.

- 1 -

5. In the event of the German High Command or any of the forces under their control failing to act in accordance with this Act of Surrender, the Supreme Commander, Allied Expeditionary Force and the Soviet High Command will take such punitive or other action as they deem appropriate.

Signed at Rheims at 0241 on the 7th day of May, 1945.
France

On behalf of the German High Command.

Jodl

IN THE PRESENCE OF

On behalf of the Supreme Commander,
Allied Expeditionary Force.

W. B. Smith

On behalf of the Soviet
High Command.

Sousloparov

Major General, French Army
("Witness)

CHARTER OF THE UNITED NATIONS

AND

STATUTE OF THE
INTERNATIONAL COURT OF JUSTICE

SAN FRANCISCO · 1945

LEFT AND BELOW: The first page of the Charter and the signing ceremony, held at the Veterans' War Memorial Building, San Francisco, on June 26, 1945.

United Nations Charter

(1945)

In the closing weeks of World War II, representatives of forty-six governments gather in San Francisco to draft the charter for an effective replacement for the League of Nations—an international body that will help to maintain peace and security in the world.

Notwithstanding the failure of the League of Nations to prevent a second global conflict, the victorious powers emerging from World War II were determined to create an effective international government to keep the peace. President Franklin D. Roosevelt had coined the term "United Nations" in 1942 when marshaling nations to fight against the Axis Powers.

Shortly after Germany's surrender and FDR's death, in June 1945 representatives of forty-six nations attended the UN's founding conference in San Francisco. With the war in the Pacific nearing its end, the delegates were determined to craft a mechanism that would prevent another violent global conflagration.

Many of the challenges they faced were the same as those addressed by the League of Nations in 1918–19. But this time they also needed to find a way to resolve the problems that had doomed the earlier effort. The nations on the losing side of World War II were not present at the conference. But those on the winners' side faced their own challenges.

One mechanism the drafters devised was to create a permanent Security Council consisting of five major powers—the Republic of China, France, Great Britain, the US, and USSR—each of whom would hold a unique veto power, allowing them to block any action they wished. That way, it was thought that the major powers would have more of a stake to continue in the organization. Designated as the lead apparatus responsible for ensuring world peace, the Security Council's decisions were also made binding on all member states.

The UN Charter called for a main body, composed of all the member nations, to be called the General Assembly. The document defined international security in broader terms than the League had done, hoping to assist smaller nations as well. This time security was expanded to include military protection, economic and social development, and the upholding of human rights and international justice.

The Charter of the United Nations consists of a preamble and a series of articles grouped into chapters. It was publicly signed with great fanfare on June 26, 1945, with President Truman telling those assembled, "The time for action is now!"

Truman signed the ratified treaty on August 8, the same day the Soviet Union declared war on Japan and the US dropped the second atomic bomb on Nagasaki. The Charter came into force on October 24, 1945 and the UN is still operating.

LEFT: A United Nations poster from 1945, promoting the Charter's call "for understanding—for peace."

George Orwell's 1984

(1946–49)

A determined author—sick, impoverished, and pursued by demons—struggles in a remote Scottish farmhouse to complete his bleak dystopian novel about life in a totalitarian state. "BIG BROTHER IS WATCHING YOU," he warns. The future has arrived.

Eric Blair (1903–50) was an English essayist, journalist, critic, and novelist, who used the pen name George Orwell to write lucid prose with a social conscience. He had served as an imperial policeman in Burma and a fighter against fascism in the Spanish Civil War, but chronic lung problems kept him out of the military service in World War II; however he kept up with his pen, writing his anti-Stalinist allegorical novella, *Animal Farm*, in 1945.

Orwell's life turned grimmer when he lost his home to a German rocket bomb, and his wife died during a routine medical procedure. In order to survive and support his son, he labored over another novel, which he tentatively called *The Last Man in Europe*. A friend provided a vacant house on a rocky tip of the island of Jura in Scotland's Inner Hebrides wherein he could complete the work. Although suffering from tuberculosis, Orwell battled illness and deadline pressures to pound out the letters on a battered Remington portable typewriter.

"I am just struggling with the last stages of this bloody book [which is] about the possible state of affairs if the atomic war isn't conclusive," Orwell wrote to a friend. By November 30, 1948 he was done.

"It was a bright cold day in April, and the clocks were striking thirteen," the novel began. "On each landing, the poster with the enormous face gazed from the wall. It was one of those pictures which are so contrived that the eyes follow you about when you move. BIG BROTHER IS WATCHING YOU, the caption beneath it ran."

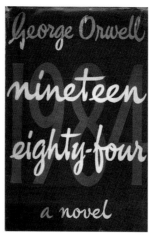

Orwell's novel was published in June 1949 and quickly hailed as a masterpiece, but its completion had taken its toll. Orwell died of tuberculosis on January 21, 1950. Over time his chilling futuristic vision has become widely regarded as probably the "definitive novel of the twentieth century." Translated into more than sixty-five languages, it has sold millions of copies and introduced many prophetic concepts into postmodern discourse. "WAR IS PEACE. FREEDOM IS SLAVERY. IGNORANCE IS STRENGTH." As much about language as politics, such terms as "doublethink," "newspeak," and "Big Brother" are now part of everyone's political vocabulary along with the term "Orwellian," signifying diametrically opposed meanings cast in ideological and euphemistic language.

A facsimile of *1984* was published in 1984 showing images of Orwell's frenzied original drafts alongside the final published version. The surviving manuscript of the novel is at the Brown University Library. Orwell's distinctive title remains a mystery. Were the two final digits reversed to reflect the torturous year of its completion—a scary future that is really rooted in the present?

ABOVE: The original hardback edition, published by Secker & Warburg in June 1949.

RIGHT: Orwell's typescript gives a fascinating insight into his extensive rewrites. The opening lines might not have been so memorable without his judicious edits.

1.

~~//~~ It was a /cold, ~~blowy~~ day in early April, and ~~a million radios~~
~~were striking~~ thirteen. Winston Smith, pushed open the glass door of
Victory Mansions, turned to the right down the passage-way and pressed the button of the lift. Nothing happened. He had just pressed a
second time when a door at the end of the passage opened, letting out
a smell of boiled greens and old rag mats, and the aged prole who
acted as porter and caretaker thrust out a grey, seamed face and stood
for a moment sucking his teeth and watching Winston malignantly.

"Lift ain't working," he announced at last.

"Why isn't it working?"

"No lifts ain't working. The currents is cut orf at the main.
The 'eat ain't working neither. All currents to be cut orf during
daylight hours. Orders!" he barked in military-style, and slammed the
door again, leaving it uncertain whether the grievance he evidently
felt was against Winston, or against the authorities who had cut-off
the current.

Winston remembered now. It was part of the economy drive in
preparation for Hate Week. The flat was seven flights up,, and winston,
conscious of his thirty-nine years and of the varicose ulcer above
his right ankle, rested at each landing to avoid putting himself out
of breath. On every landing the same poster was gummed to the wall -
a huge coloured poster, too large for indoor display. It depicted
simply an enormous face, the face of a man of about forty-five, with
ruggedly handsome features, thick black hair, a heavy moustache and

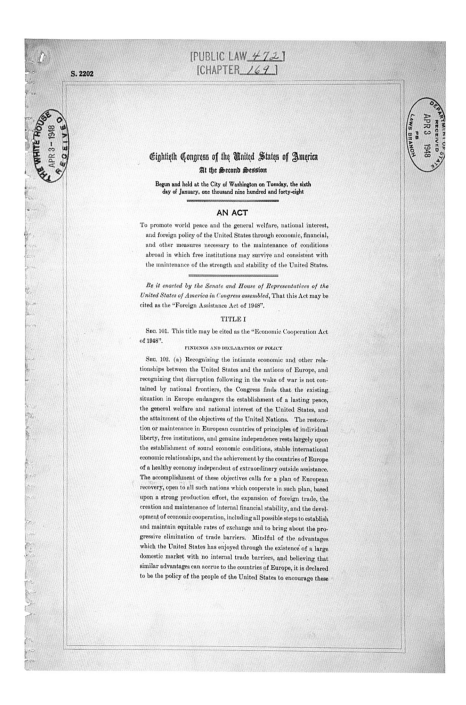

[PUBLIC LAW *472*]
[CHAPTER *169*]

S. 2202

Eightieth Congress of the United States of America
At the Second Session

Begun and held at the City of Washington on Tuesday, the sixth
day of January, one thousand nine hundred and forty-eight

AN ACT

To promote world peace and the general welfare, national interest,
and foreign policy of the United States through economic, financial,
and other measures necessary to the maintenance of conditions
abroad in which free institutions may survive and consistent with
the maintenance of the strength and stability of the United States.

Be it enacted by the Senate and House of Representatives of the
United States of America in Congress assembled, That this Act may be
cited as the "Foreign Assistance Act of 1948".

TITLE I

SEC. 101. This title may be cited as the "Economic Cooperation Act
of 1948".

FINDINGS AND DECLARATION OF POLICY

SEC. 102. (a) Recognizing the intimate economic and other relationships between the United States and the nations of Europe, and
recognizing that disruption following in the wake of war is not contained by national frontiers, the Congress finds that the existing
situation in Europe endangers the establishment of a lasting peace,
the general welfare and national interest of the United States, and
the attainment of the objectives of the United Nations. The restoration or maintenance in European countries of principles of individual
liberty, free institutions, and genuine independence rests largely upon
the establishment of sound economic conditions, stable international
economic relationships, and the achievement by the countries of Europe
of a healthy economy independent of extraordinary outside assistance.
The accomplishment of these objectives calls for a plan of European
recovery, open to all such nations which cooperate in such plan, based
upon a strong production effort, the expansion of foreign trade, the
creation and maintenance of internal financial stability, and the development of economic cooperation, including all possible steps to establish
and maintain equitable rates of exchange and to bring about the progressive elimination of trade barriers. Mindful of the advantages
which the United States has enjoyed through the existence of a large
domestic market with no internal trade barriers, and believing that
similar advantages can accrue to the countries of Europe, it is declared
to be the policy of the people of the United States to encourage these

ABOVE: The Marshall Plan was signed into law as the Economic Cooperation Act on April 3, 1948.

OPPOSITE: Marshall arrives at Harvard on June 5, 1947 to deliver his speech on European economic recovery.

Marshall Plan

(1947)

Addressing Europe's utter devastation from World War II, a former US Army military commander turned Secretary of State proposes an ambitious blueprint for European recovery that entails unprecedented financial aid from the United States.

In his role as Army Chief of Staff from 1939 to 1945, General George Marshall (1880–1959) had helped lead the Allied Powers to victory and earned the reputation as the greatest military organizer of his time. He was one of America's most admired and trusted figures.

Shortly after the war, as US Secretary of State under President Harry S. Truman, Marshall was tasked to advance America's position on the urgent need for Europe's rehabilitation. On June 5, 1947 he delivered an address proposing a program of massive aid to the war-ravaged nations. Although Marshall was speaking to a large commencement audience at Harvard University, President Truman's political advisers had avoided seeking any press coverage at home in the belief that American taxpayers might not favor such a plan. So instead, they arranged for the BBC to carry the speech via radio to audiences in Europe as a means of generating needed foreign support.

The 1,200-word speech was straight and to the point, and delivered without oratorical flourishes; its content was of enormous economic and political import. Marshall said the war's destruction of Europe's infrastructure was hampering any recovery efforts to such an extent it could slow the region's health and stability for many years to come.

He suggested it was in America's enlightened self-interest to do whatever it could "to assist in the return of normal economic health in the world, without which there can be no political stability and no assured peace. Our policy is directed not against any country or doctrine but against hunger, poverty, desperation, and chaos. Its purpose should be the revival of a working economy in the world so as to permit the emergence of political and social conditions in which free institutions can exist."

Marshall called for a comprehensive program of massive US foreign aid, aimed at rebuilding devastated regions, removing trade barriers, modernizing industry, and achieving renewed prosperity.

Most nations of Western Europe readily accepted the offer. But the Soviet Union declined, believing that it would give the US too much say in the affairs of communist bloc countries. President Truman adopted the Marshall Plan and sent it to Congress where it was passed and signed into law as the Economic Cooperation Act on April 3, 1948.

The program offered financial aid, mostly for the purchase of American goods. Over the next four years, the US contributed $17 billion (more than $160 billion in current dollar value) in economic support to help rebuild Western European economies, including West Germany's.

For being its architect and advocate, Marshall was awarded the Nobel Peace Prize in 1953, and the term "Marshall Plan" came to stand for a large-scale rehabilitation program.

Universal Declaration of Human Rights

(1948)

Activists from different nationalities and backgrounds work together for two years to devise an unprecedented universal declaration of human rights that will transcend parochial political, religious, cultural, and ideological beliefs in order to clearly define the basic rights of all humankind.

In 1946 an International Commission of Human Rights consisting of eighteen members from various backgrounds was formed within the United Nations under the chairmanship of Eleanor Roosevelt, the former First Lady. Mrs. Roosevelt gave a Canadian law professor, John Peters Humphrey, the daunting task of serving as principal drafter of an international bill of human rights that would prove acceptable to the diverse world body.

Humphrey and his staff pored over previous rights documents created throughout history in order to produce a 408-page report that could guide their work. The French member, René Cassin, then used Humphrey's materials to write the first draft, which he structured after the Code Napoléon.

The subcommittee's final draft was later discussed by the Commission and presented to the UN General Assembly for its consideration. The vote was held on December 10, 1948 in Paris, where forty-eight voted in favor, none were opposed, two were absent, and eight abstained.

A member of the drafting subcommittee, Hernán Santa Cruz of Chile, later recalled: "I perceived clearly that I was participating in a truly significant historic event…there was an atmosphere of genuine solidarity and brotherhood among men and women from all latitudes, the like of which I have not seen again in any international setting."

The Universal Declaration of Human Rights proclaims: "Everyone is entitled to all the rights and freedoms set forth in this Declaration, without distinction of any kind, such as race, colour, sex, language, religion, political or other opinion, national or social origin, property, birth or other status." Its thirty articles grant an assortment of basic individual freedoms, such as the right to life, liberty, and security of person, to all persons in the world. The Declaration forbids slavery and torture, and calls for equal justice under law. Everyone is entitled to education and allowed to freely participate in cultural activities. Specific remedies are provided to combat violations.

Considered the first global expression of human rights, the UN's Declaration is a milestone document in history, yet one which is never fully adhered to.

The original text is now available from the UN website in 439 different translations. The anniversary of its adoption is commemorated as International Human Rights Day.

RIGHT: Eleanor Roosevelt, Chair of the International Commission of Human Rights, reviews a printed poster of the English-language edition (opposite).

THE UNIVERSAL DECLARATION
OF Human Rights

WHEREAS recognition of the inherent dignity and of the equal and inalienable rights of all members of the human family is the foundation of freedom, justice and peace in the world,

WHEREAS disregard and contempt for human rights have resulted in barbarous acts which have outraged the conscience of mankind, and the advent of a world in which human beings shall enjoy freedom of speech and belief and freedom from fear and want has been proclaimed as the highest aspiration of the common people,

WHEREAS it is essential, if man is not to be compelled to have recourse, as a last resort, to rebellion against tyranny and oppression, that human rights should be protected by the rule of law,

WHEREAS it is essential to promote the development of friendly relations among nations,

WHEREAS the peoples of the United Nations have in the Charter reaffirmed their faith in fundamental human rights, in the dignity and worth of the human person and in the equal rights of men and women and have

determined to promote social progress and better standards of life in larger freedom,

WHEREAS Member States have pledged themselves to achieve, in co-operation with the United Nations, the promotion of universal respect for and observance of human rights and fundamental freedoms,

WHEREAS a common understanding of these rights and freedoms is of the greatest importance for the full realisation of this pledge,

NOW THEREFORE THE GENERAL ASSEMBLY

PROCLAIMS this Universal Declaration of Human Rights as a common standard of achievement for all peoples and all nations, to the end that every individual and every organ of society, keeping this Declaration constantly in mind, shall strive by teaching and education to promote respect for these rights and freedoms and by progressive measures, national and international, to secure their universal and effective recognition and observance, both among the peoples of Member States themselves and among the peoples of territories under their jurisdiction.

ARTICLE 1 —All human beings are born free and equal in dignity and rights. They are endowed with reason and conscience and should act towards one another in a spirit of brotherhood.

ARTICLE 2 —1. Everyone is entitled to all the rights and freedoms set forth in this Declaration, without distinction of any kind, such as race, colour, sex, language, religion, political or other opinion, national or social origin, property, birth or other status.

2. Furthermore, no distinction shall be made on the basis of the political, jurisdictional or international status of the country or territory to which a person belongs, whether this territory be an independent, Trust or Non-Self-Governing territory, or under any other limitation of sovereignty.

ARTICLE 3 —Everyone has the right to life, liberty and the security of person.

ARTICLE 4 —No one shall be held in slavery or servitude; slavery and the slave trade shall be prohibited in all their forms.

ARTICLE 5 —No one shall be subjected to torture or to cruel, inhuman or degrading treatment or punishment.

ARTICLE 6 —Everyone has the right to recognition everywhere as a person before the law.

ARTICLE 7 —All are equal before the law and are entitled without any discrimination to equal protection of the law. All are entitled to equal protection against any discrimination in violation of this Declaration and against any incitement to such discrimination.

ARTICLE 8 —Everyone has the right to an effective remedy by the competent national tribunals for acts violating the fundamental rights granted him by the constitution or by law.

ARTICLE 9 —No one shall be subjected to arbitrary arrest, detention or exile.

ARTICLE 10 —Everyone is entitled in full equality to a fair and public hearing by an independent and impartial tribunal, in the determination of his rights and obligations and of any criminal charge against him.

ARTICLE 11 —1. Everyone charged with a penal offence has the right to be presumed innocent until proved guilty according to law in a public trial at which he has had all the guarantees necessary for his defence.

2. No one shall be held guilty of any penal offence on account of any act or omission which did not constitute a penal offence, under national or international law, at the time when it was committed. Nor shall a heavier penalty be imposed than the one that was applicable at the time the penal offence was committed.

ARTICLE 12 —No one shall be subjected to arbitrary interference with his privacy, family, home or correspondence, nor to attacks upon his honour and reputation. Everyone has the right to the protection of the law against such interference or attacks.

ARTICLE 13 —1. Everyone has the right to freedom of movement and residence within the borders of each state.

2. Everyone has the right to leave any country, including his own, and to return to his country.

ARTICLE 14 —1. Everyone has the right to seek and to enjoy in other countries asylum from persecution.

2. This right may not be invoked in the case of prosecutions genuinely arising from non-political crimes or from acts contrary to the purposes and principles of the United Nations.

ARTICLE 15 —1. Everyone has the right to a nationality.

2. No one shall be arbitrarily deprived of his nationality nor denied the right to change his nationality.

ARTICLE 16 —1. Men and women of full age, without any limitation due to race, nationality or religion, have the right to marry and to found a family. They are entitled to equal rights as to marriage, during marriage and at its dissolution.

2. Marriage shall be entered into only with the free and full consent of the intending spouses.

3. The family is the natural and fundamental group unit of society and is entitled to protection by society and the State.

ARTICLE 17 —1. Everyone has the right to own property alone as well as in association with others.

2. No one shall be arbitrarily deprived of his property.

ARTICLE 18 —Everyone has the right to freedom of thought, conscience and religion; this right includes freedom to change his religion or belief, and freedom, either alone or in community with others and in public or private, to manifest his religion or belief in teaching, practice, worship and observance.

ARTICLE 19 —Everyone has the right to freedom of opinion and expression; this right includes freedom to hold opinions without interference and to seek, receive and impart information and ideas through any media and regardless of frontiers.

ARTICLE 20 —1. Everyone has the right to freedom of peaceful assembly and association.

2. No one may be compelled to belong to an association.

ARTICLE 21 —1. Everyone has the right to take part in the government of his country, directly or through freely chosen representatives.

2. Everyone has the right of equal access to public service in his country.

3. The will of the people shall be the basis of the authority of government; this will shall be expressed in periodic and genuine elections which shall be by universal and equal suffrage and shall be held by secret vote or by equivalent free voting procedures.

ARTICLE 22 —Everyone, as a member of society, has the right to social security and is entitled to realisation, through national effort and international co-operation and in accordance with the organisation and resources of each State, of the economic, social and cultural rights indispensable for his dignity and the free development of his personality.

ARTICLE 23 —1. Everyone has the right to work, to free choice of employment, to just and favourable conditions of work and to protection against unemployment.

2. Everyone, without any discrimination, has the right to equal pay for equal work.

3. Everyone who works has the right to just and favourable remuner-

ation insuring for himself and his family an existence worthy of human dignity, and supplemented, if necessary, by other means of social protection.

4. Everyone has the right to form and to join trade unions for the protection of his interests.

ARTICLE 24 —Everyone has the right to rest and leisure, including reasonable limitation of working hours and periodic holidays with pay.

ARTICLE 25 —1. Everyone has the right to a standard of living adequate for the health and well-being of himself and of his family, including food, clothing, housing and medical care and necessary social services, and the right to security in the event of unemployment, sickness, disability, widowhood, old age or other lack of livelihood in circumstances beyond his control.

2. Motherhood and childhood are entitled to special care and assistance. All children, whether born in or out of wedlock, shall enjoy the same social protection.

ARTICLE 26 —1. Everyone has the right to education. Education shall be free, at least in the elementary and fundamental stages. Elementary education shall be compulsory. Technical and professional education shall be made generally available and higher education shall be equally accessible to all on the basis of merit.

2. Education shall be directed to the full development of the human personality and to the strengthening of respect for human rights and fundamental freedoms. It shall promote understanding, tolerance and friendship among all nations, racial or religious groups, and shall further the activities of the United Nations for the maintenance of peace.

3. Parents have a prior right to choose the kind of education that shall be given to their children.

ARTICLE 27 —1. Everyone has the right freely to participate in the cultural life of the community, to enjoy the arts and to share in scientific advancement and its benefits.

2. Everyone has the right to the protection of the moral and material interests resulting from any scientific, literary or artistic production of which he is the author.

ARTICLE 28 —Everyone is entitled to a social and international order in which the rights and freedoms set forth in this Declaration can be fully realized.

ARTICLE 29 —1. Everyone has duties to the community in which alone the free and full development of his personality is possible.

2. In the exercise of his rights and freedoms, everyone shall be subject only to such limitations as are determined by law solely for the purpose of securing due recognition and respect for the rights and freedoms of others and of meeting the just requirements of morality, public order and the general welfare in a democratic society.

3. These rights and freedoms may in no case be exercised contrary to the purposes and principles of the United Nations.

ARTICLE 30 —Nothing in this Declaration may be interpreted as implying for any State, group or person any right to engage in any activity or to perform any act aimed at the destruction of any of the rights and freedoms set forth herein.

UNITED NATIONS

Adopted by the United Nations General Assembly at its 183rd meeting, held in Paris on 10 December, 1948

Issued by U.N. Department of Public Information

THE GENEVA CONVENTIONS OF AUGUST 12 1949

ICRC

IV

GENEVA CONVENTION
THE PROTECTION OF CIVILIAN
ME OF WAR OF 12 AUGUST 1949

PART I

ERAL PROVISIONS

Contracting Parties undertake to respect
for the present Convention in all

*Respect
for the
Convention[1]*

to the provisions which shall be
he present Convention shall apply to all
y other armed conflict which may arise
High Contracting Parties, even if the
by one of them.

*Application
of the
Convention*

apply to all cases of partial or total
a High Contracting Party, even if the
armed resistance.

in conflict may not be a party to the
s who are parties thereto shall remain
lations. They shall furthermore be
lation to the said Power, if the latter
ns thereof.

ed conflict not of an international
ry of one of the High Contracting
ct shall be bound to apply, as a
s:

*Conflicts
not of an
international
character*

part in the hostilities, including
who have laid down their arms and
or any other cause, shall in all circumstances be treated

placed *hors de combat* by sickness, wounds, detention,

[1] The marginal notes or titles of articles have been drafted by the Swiss Federal
Department of Foreign Affairs.

*ABOVE: Although the treaties are officially called the Geneva Conventions, the 1949 agreements, which updated the
previous treaties of 1864, 1906, and 1929, are usually referred to as the Geneva Convention (singular).*

Geneva Convention

(1949)

In the wake of World War II's unparalleled atrocities against non-combatants, existing treaties were updated to cover the treatment of non-combatant civilians in occupied areas. The result was ratified by 196 countries.

Prior to World War II, three international treaties (adopted in 1864, 1906, and 1929) established protections for wounded and sick soldiers and sailors, and extensively defined the basic wartime rights of prisoners-of-war. Owing to their sponsorship by the International Committee of the Red Cross based in Geneva, the agreements were known as the Geneva Conventions.

Shocked by the rampant abuses against civilians that had been committed in World War II, plenipotentiaries from almost every country in the world worked together for four months and then approved the text of the Fourth Geneva Conventions, which reaffirmed, expanded, and updated the three previous Geneva agreements and added another class of protected parties. The Fourth Geneva Convention sets forth the basic principles of international law for the Protection of Civilian Persons in Time of War, covering all individuals "who do not belong to the armed forces, take no part in the hostilities and find themselves in the hands of the Enemy or an Occupying Power."

The 1949 treaty provides that such protected civilians "shall in all circumstances be treated humanely, without any adverse distinction founded on race, colour, religion or faith, sex, birth or wealth, or any other similar criteria." They must be shielded from acts or threats of violence, "outrages upon personal dignity, in particular humiliating and degrading treatment," and cared for if they are wounded or sick. "Protected persons are entitled to respect for their persons, their honour, their family rights, their religious convictions and practices, and their manners and customs."

Protected civilians must be allowed to exchange family news of a personal kind and aided to secure news about other family members who may have been displaced by the conflict. They must be allowed to practice their religion with spiritual leaders of their own faith. Interned civilians possess the same rights as POWs. Wherever possible families should be housed together and provided with the facilities that can enable them to live as a family. Wounded or sick civilians, civilian hospitals and staff, and hospital transport by land, sea, or air must be specially respected and may be placed under protection of the Red Cross or Red Crescent. Protected civilians cannot be used as human shields or discriminated against because of race, religion or political opinion. Nor can they be subjected to collective punishment, torture, mutilation, rape or other indecent treatment.

The United Nations Security Council is the final international tribunal for all issues related to the Geneva Conventions. The most serious violations, known as "grave breaches," are eligible to be treated as war crimes.

Although the application of the laws remains a source of constant controversy, as evidenced by many recent debates and waves of inhumane treatment across the globe, the documents are still considered a cornerstone of contemporary international law.

ABOVE: Signing of the Geneva Convention.

Population Registration Act

(1950)

The ruling party of white-dominated South Africa establishes a new "pillar" of apartheid, even more stringent than America's Jim Crow racial segregation laws. It requires the creation of a racial register for the nation's entire population, represented in a unique document for each individual.

S lavery of blacks in South Africa began under Dutch rule and continued until the British abolished it in 1834. With the removal of the last vestiges of British rule and the establishment of the Union of South Africa in the 1930s, however, racial segregation intensified under the banner of apartheid (meaning "the state of being apart")—a movement of white supremacy that was championed by the Afrikaners (white South Africans of Dutch, German, Belgian, or French ancestry).

Following the general election of 1948, the new ruling National Party went about establishing apartheid as South Africa's governing policy. After enacting a series of laws regarding marriage, the lawmakers passed the Population Registration Act Number Thirty of 1950, which required that each inhabitant of South Africa be classified and registered in accordance with his or her "racial characteristics" in keeping with the apartheid system.

The law required everyone to be identified and registered from birth as one of four distinct racial groups: White, Colored, Bantu (Black African), and

Indian (workers from India having been imported under British colonial rule). Every person over eighteen was required to obtain an identity card specifying his or her racial group. Official Boards were established to resolve any disputes over the racial designation, so that every person could be classified by "race."

A "White Person" was defined as one who "in appearance is obviously a white person who is generally not accepted as a coloured person; or is generally accepted as a white person and is not in appearance obviously a white person." A "Bantu" was "a person who is, or is generally accepted as, a member of any aboriginal race or tribe of Africa," and a "Coloured" was "a person who is not a White Person or a Bantu..."

Apartheid law determined rights, privileges, and economic status based on race. But administration of the apartheid system was impossible. As Nelson Mandela later noted, "Where one was allowed to live and work could rest on such absurd distinctions as the curl of one's hair or the size of one's lips." World opinion turned against the regime. Apartheid was eventually abandoned before it would have been overthrown.

Although the South African Parliament repealed the act on June 17, 1991, its effects will be felt for generations to come. The surviving racial identity documents serve as a tangible and official reminder of racist repression.

LEFT: An exhibition of South African identity cards in the Apartheid Museum, Johannesburg. RIGHT: The first page of the Act defines its use of the terms "coloured," "ethnic," "native" and "white."

Act No. 30
of 1950.

ACT

To make provision for the compilation of a Register of the Population of the Union; for the issue of Identity Cards to persons whose names are included in the Register; and for matters incidental thereto.

(Afrikaans Text signed by the Officer Administering the Government.)
(Assented to 22nd June, 1950.) *

BE IT ENACTED by the King's Most Excellent Majesty, the Senate and the House of Assembly of the Union of South Africa, as follows :—

1. In this Act, unless the context otherwise indicates— *Definitions.*

   (i) "alien" means an alien as defined in section *one* of the Aliens Act, 1937 (Act No. 1 of 1937); (xv)

   (ii) "board" means a board constituted in terms of section *eleven*; (x)

   (iii) "coloured person" means a person who is not a white person or a native; (iv)

   (iv) "Director" means the Director of Census appointed under section *four* of the Census Act, 1910 (Act No. 2 of 1910), and includes the Assistant Director of Census and any officer acting under a delegation from or under the control or direction of the Director; (ii)

   (v) "ethnic or other group" means a group prescribed and defined by the Governor-General in terms of sub-section (2) of section *five*; (iii) .

   (vi) "fixed date" means the date upon which the census is taken in the year 1951 in terms of section *three* of the Census Act, 1910 (Act No. 2 of 1910); (xiii)

   (vii) "identity card" means the identity card referred to in section *thirteen* but does not include an identity card which has lapsed in terms of any regulation; (viii)

   (viii) "identity number" means the identity number assigned to a person in terms of section *six*; (ix)

   (ix) "Minister" means the Minister of the Interior; (vi)

   (x) "native" means a person who in fact is or is generally accepted as a member of any aboriginal race or tribe of Africa; (vii)

   (xi) "prescribed" means prescribed by regulation; (xiv)

   (xii) "register" means the register referred to in section *two*; (xi)

   (xiii) "regulation" means a regulation made under section *tw.nty*; (xii)

   (xiv) "this Act" includes the regulations; (v)

   (xv) "white person" means a person who in appearance obviously is, or who is generally accepted as a white person, but does not include a person who, although in appearance obviously a white person, is generally accepted as a coloured person. (i)

Act No. 30 of 1950.

2. There shall, as soon as practicable after the fixed date, be compiled by the Director and thereafter maintained by him, a register of the population of the Union. *Compilation and maintenance of population register.*

3. The particulars required for the compilation of the register in respect of the population of the Union as at the fixed date shall be extracted by the Director from the forms and returns received by him under the Census Act, 1910 (Act No. 2 of 1910), in connection with the census taken on the fixed date and from such other records as may be available to the Director. *Data from which register to be compiled.*

4. There shall be included in the register, in three separate parts thereof, the names of— *What persons to be included in the register.*

   (a) (i) all South African citizens within the Union on the fixed date;

     (ii) all South African citizens who enter or are born in the Union after the fixed date; and

     (iii) all persons who become South African citizens in the Union after the fixed date;

19 Portugal Place
Cambridge.
19 March '53

My Dear Michael,

Jim Watson and I have probably made a most important discovery. We have built a model for the structure of des-oxy-ribose-nucleic-acid (read it carefully) called D.N.A. for short. You may remember that the genes of the chromosomes — which carry the hereditary factors — are made up of protein and D.N.A.

Our structure is very beautiful. D.N.A. can be thought of roughly as a very long chain with flat bits sticking out. The flat bits are called the "bases". The formula is rather

...this... ...much nicer than this.

...exciting thing is that while there ...bases, we find we can only ...pairs of them together. The... ...They are Adenine, Guanine... ...I will call them A, G, & ...find that the two pairs

ABOVE: Pages one and three of Crick's seven-page letter to his son.

OPPOSITE: Crick's rough sketch of DNA structure was later drawn up by his wife, Odile, and published in the April 25, 1953 edition of Nature.

DNA

(1953)

A father-to-son letter by one of the discoverers of the most important scientific breakthroughs of the twentieth century reveals the first known written description of "the secret of life." Before closing his note, he advises: "Read this carefully so that you understand it. When you come home we will show you the model."

In early 1953 the molecular biologists Francis Crick (1916–2004) and James Watson (1928–) were research scientists at the Medical Research Council unit of the Cavendish Laboratory at Cambridge University. The pair had been pursuing their overwhelming desire to figure out the true structure of Deoxyribonucleic acid (DNA), a molecule thought to contain the "blueprint of life" of all known living organisms and many viruses.

On March 19, 1953 Crick penned a handwritten letter to his twelve-year-old scientifically inclined son, Michael, who was sick with the flu at his boarding school in England. In it Crick shared some exciting news. "Jim Watson and I have probably made a most important discovery," he wrote. The pair had just figured out the double-helix structure of DNA.

"We have built a model for the structure of des-oxy-ribose-nucleic-acid (read it carefully) called DNA for short," the elder Crick wrote. He described DNA as being "like a code" and explained how its bases— guanine, adenine, thymine, and cytosine—pair up to hold together two twisting strands of molecules. He also spelled out how DNA replicates itself and sketched some drawings of its structure to illustrate what he meant. "Read this carefully so that you understand it. When you come home we will show you the model," he told the boy. "Lots of love, Daddy."

Scientists had been aware of DNA since 1869 when a Swiss researcher discovered a mysterious substance in pus. By 1927 the Russian biologist Nikolai Koltsov was suggesting that traits could be inherited via a "giant hereditary molecule" made up of "two mirror strands that would replicate in a semi-conservative fashion using each strand as a template." But Watson and Crick revolutionized science's understanding of DNA.

Crick's seven-page letter was written more than a month before the publication of his famous article with Watson in *Nature*, which announced DNA's structure and genetic implications. Watson and Crick formally announced their discovery at a Solvay conference on proteins that was held in Belgium on April 8, 1953, but the announcement didn't receive any media coverage. Although Watson had written a letter to fellow biologist Max Delbrück five days earlier, that document dealt mostly with DNA's structure and it did not contain as much information about how DNA might reproduce itself. So Michael Crick later described his father's note as "the first written description of what my father calls 'how life comes from life.'"

In 2013 the document was sold for $5.3 million—a record-breaking price for a letter sold at auction.

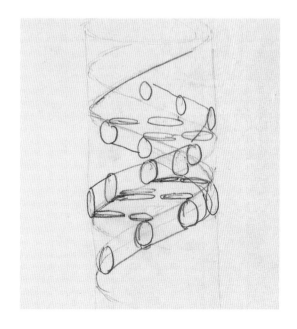

Treaty of Rome

(1957)

Nations from a continent divided by language, culture, and history attempt to come together to form a common economic union. But right from the start, problems behind the scenes indicate that doing even the most basic tasks together may sometimes prove difficult.

Centuries of conflict culminating in two world wars had made Europe's leaders worried about their future. Recovery from the catastrophes was slow, painful, and uneven, leading several nations to favor the establishment of a common economic community.

Following a series of international meetings and agreements on the subject, an Intergovernmental Conference on the Common Market and Euratom (European Atomic Energy Community) was slated to begin in Belgium in June 1956. Representatives of six nations (France, Germany, Italy, Belgium, the Netherlands, and Luxembourg) gathered at a magnificent castle estate, the Château de Val-Duchesse, outside Brussels to draft an agreement. The United Kingdom had also been invited but the British prime minister, Harold Macmillan, quipped that he did not want to join a club of "six nations, four of whom we had to rescue from the other two."

The participants shared some common concerns—their nations had suffered invasion, defeat, and foreign occupation during the war, resulting in long-term distress—and they wanted to protect their democratic institutions from future takeover. Economic collaboration was seen as key.

The drafters worked in secrecy for nine months before coming up with the final version. Then they hurried to have it ratified, knowing that France's imminent election of the fierce nationalist Gen. Charles de Gaulle would doom its approval. The formal signing ceremony was set for a few days later at the historic Hall of the Horatii and Curiatii in the Palazzo dei Conservatori in Rome.

RIGHT AND OPPOSITE: The document and the signing ceremony, at the magnificent Hall of the Horatii and Curiatii in the Palazzo dei Conservatori.

But then disaster struck. All of the necessary equipment and supplies needed for the conference—the typewriters, mimeograph machines, and embossed official paper—were delayed at the Swiss and Italian borders, for lack of the required certificates, and upon their arrival at the hall the designated space was blocked by huge Rubens paintings. So the vital materials had to be put in the basement until other arrangements could be made. But janitors had mistakenly tossed the paper and crucial stencils into the garbage.

With time running out, the panicked organizers quickly devised the only solution they could: in place of the treaty document, they prepared a blank sheet of paper for the heads of state to sign, and barred members of the press from viewing the agreement's text.

On March 25, 1957, amid considerable pomp and splendor, the heads of state officially signed the Treaty of Rome, establishing the European Economic Community (EEC)—an agreement that would ultimately form the basis for the European Common Market and the European Union, but a document which had actually consisted of only a signature page.

The story of the famous "blank page" was finally revealed in 2007.

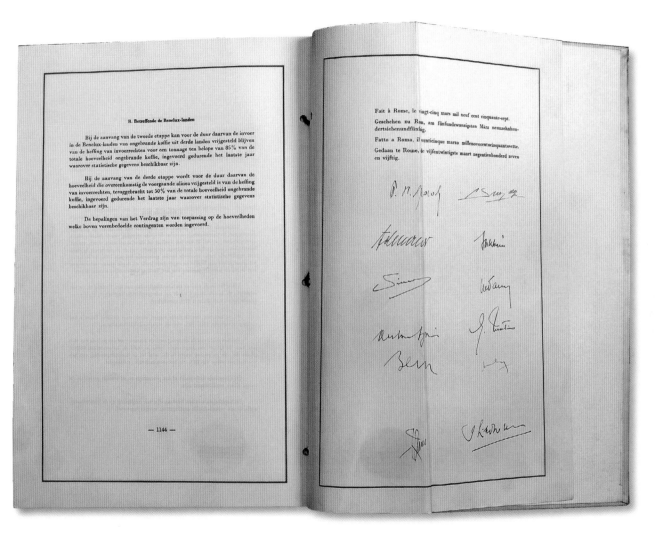

B. Betreffende de Benelux-landen

Bij de aanvang van de tweede etappe kan voor de duur daarvan de invoer in de Benelux-landen van ongebrande koffie uit derde landen vrijgesteld blijven van de heffing van invoerrechten voor een tonnage ten belope van 85% van de totale hoeveelheid ongebrande koffie, ingevoerd gedurende het laatste jaar waarover statistische gegevens beschikbaar zijn.

Bij de aanvang van de derde etappe wordt voor de duur daarvan de hoeveelheid die overeenkomstig de voorgaande alinea vrijgesteld is van de heffing van invoerrechten, teruggebracht tot 50% van de totale hoeveelheid ongebrande koffie, ingevoerd gedurende het laatste jaar waarover statistische gegevens beschikbaar zijn.

De bepalingen van het Verdrag zijn van toepassing op de hoeveelheden welke boven vorenbedoelde contingenten worden ingevoerd.

— 1144 —

Fait à Rome, le vingt-cinq mars mil neuf cent cinquante-sept.

Geschehen zu Rom, am fünfundzwanzigsten März neunzehnhundertsiebenundfünfzig.

Fatto a Roma, il venticinque marzo millenovecentocinquantasette.

Gedaan te Rome, de vijfentwintigste maart negentienhonderd zeven en vijftig.

January 17, 1961

The inauguration is a ~~beginning~~ an end
as well as a beginning — Today we are
~~in~~ ... ...
here ... on the all ...
...
the three ... are ... today and
all those others men who stood in
this same place, took the same
oath, made the same commitment
to the preservation of the American constitution and
its promise. ...
that we have made today.
~~world~~ ...

We are a young people — but
an old Republic. ... though we
are old — at least as ... ...
I believe ... are ...
we must not forget that we
are ... that this we are descended
from ... ...

John F. Kennedy's Inaugural Address

(1961)

A glamorous new President takes up the torch for a new generation and delivers one of the greatest speeches in American history. Adopting the cadences of Lincoln and language drawn from the Bible, his address exudes youthful idealism, a sense of history, strong ideas, and soaring rhetoric.

On a bright but frigid January day, John F. Kennedy was inaugurated as the thirty-fifth President of the United States in an event that 80 million Americans watched live on television.

The youthful Kennedy had worked on his inaugural address for two months, scribbling notes on yellow notepads and exchanging messages and drafts with his chief speechwriter, Ted Sorenson, who collected bushels of striking ideas and eloquent expressions from JFK's circle of top advisors. Together the pair honed each sentence to strike the perfect image and tone.

The result was a masterpiece of memorable phrases that had been adapted from others, such as Kennedy's line "Let us never negotiate out of fear. But let us never fear to negotiate," which resembled a suggestion from Harvard economist John Kenneth Galbraith. Or Kennedy's "If a free society cannot help the many who are poor, it cannot save the few who are rich," which had slightly altered a phrase from former Democratic presidential candidate Adlai Stevenson II.

It also utilized an assortment of skilled rhetorical devices and striking sentence structure to craft a speech that would deliver Kennedy's messages in a distinctive classical form. Using elevated language that stirred emotions for national traditions and ideals, JFK called for

ABOVE AND OPPOSITE: A handwritten draft of Kennedy's inaugural address, written three days before he delivered his speech at the United States Capitol in Washington, DC on January 20, 1961.

citizens to work together for the common good. "Let every nation know," he wrote,

whether it wishes us well or ill, that we shall pay any price, bear any burden, meet any hardship, support any friend, oppose any foe to assure the survival and the success of liberty....All this will not be finished in the first one hundred days. Nor will it be finished in the first one thousand days; nor in the life of this Administration; nor even perhaps in our lifetime on this planet. But let us begin....Now the trumpet summons us again—not as a call to bear arms, though arms we need—not as a call to battle, though embattled we are—but a call to bear the burden of a long twilight struggle, year in and year out, 'rejoicing in hope; patient in tribulation,' a struggle against the common enemies of man: tyranny, poverty, disease, and war itself. And so, my fellow Americans, ask not what your country can do for you; ask what you can do for your country.

Although the address was only 1,364 words long, making it one of the shortest inaugural addresses ever delivered, its abundance of bold concepts, sharp juxtaposition, and strong phrasing made it one of the most powerful speeches Americans had heard in many years.

Best known for its televised version, John F. Kennedy's Inaugural Address is also preserved in its original document form, with drafts and supporting office files kept in the John F. Kennedy Library and National Archives and Records Administration.

Beatles' Recording Contract with EMI

(1962)

As four fresh-faced, working-class, pop musicians from Liverpool sign a recording contract with EMI, two of them requiring a parent's signature because they are so young, nobody could ever imagine what it will mean for all concerned—and the music world.

On October 1, 1962, the record producer George Martin of EMI (Electric and Musical Industries Ltd) reached for his pen to sign a new recording contract with the pop group known as—what were they called? Oh, yes, that's right, "the Beatles"—not realizing that the paper under his nose would later become regarded as "one of the most important documents in music history," and that he would ultimately be called "the fifth Beatle."

As a top manager for the well-established and highly successful multinational music recording and publishing company, headquartered at 3 Abbey Road, St John's Wood, London, Martin had put the group through a rigorous audition process since June.

Back then the boys' manager, Brian Epstein, had negotiated the deal for his clients—John Winston Lennon, James Paul McCartney, George Harrison, and Richard Starkey (aka Ringo Starr)—to perform on EMI's Parlophone label after three other EMI labels had all rejected them. At the time, nobody could have known that the contract would launch what many critics now think of as the most successful commercial partnership in music history. But it did.

The October contract bears the signatures of the four Beatles, plus the fathers of George Harrison and Paul McCartney who had to consent because their sons were under twenty-one. In it the Beatles agreed to pay Epstein (NEMS Enterprises) 15, 20, or 25 percent of their revenues, based on how much the band earned. The Beatles would then share any income among themselves after various expenses had been deducted.

Curiously, the Beatles had already signed a managerial contract with Epstein on January 24, but Epstein had held back from signing because he didn't have enough faith in himself to help them. "In other words," he later said, "I wanted to free them of their obligations if I felt they would be better off."

The band's rise was meteoric. Four days after signing the October deal, EMI released their first single, "Love Me Do," which reached number seventeen on the UK charts. The follow-up, "Please, Please Me," hit number two, and by year's end, three more releases—"From Me to You," "She Loves You," and "I Want to Hold Your Hand"—all shot to number one, later to be followed by fourteen more UK number-one hits. And EMI's other success was also meteoric. In 1963, fifteen out of the nineteen number-one singles in the UK were EMI's and the following year eight EMI artists held the number-one position for forty-one weeks. The British invasion was underway.

The eight-page mimeographed typescript of the October contract was auctioned in London in 2008 for £250,000 ($480,000). In 2014 the document was acquired by a reality show actor, Yossi Dina, of *Beverly Hills Pawn*.

RIGHT: The signed contract—bearing the signatures of the four Beatles, plus the fathers of two who had to consent because their sons were under twenty-one—and a photograph of the directors of EMI with the band.

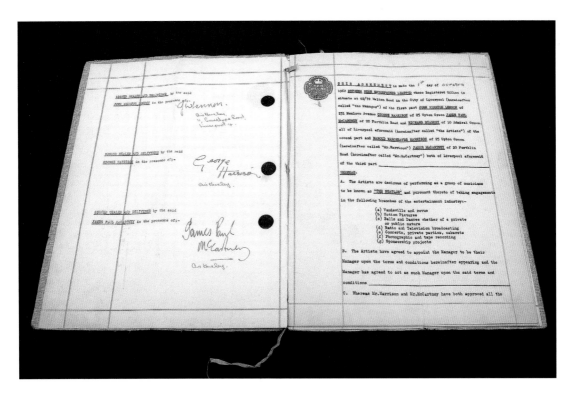

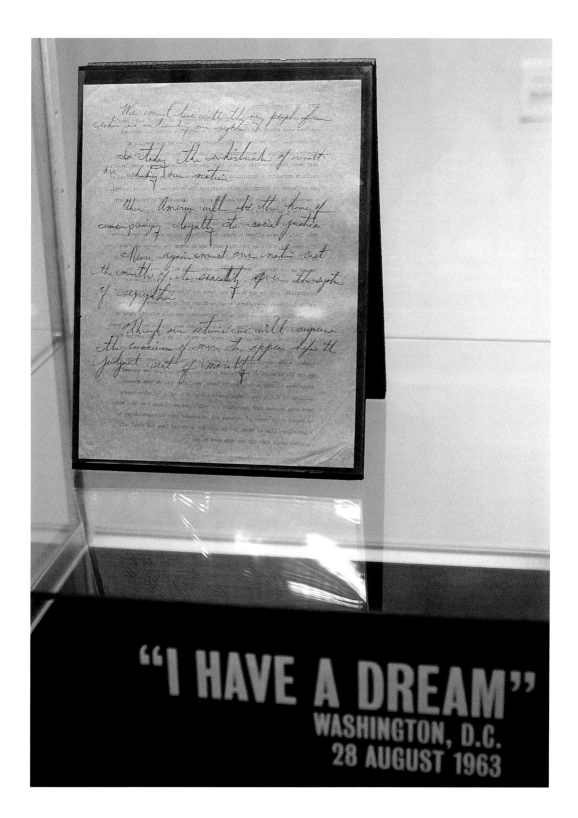

"I HAVE A DREAM"
WASHINGTON, D.C.
28 AUGUST 1963

Martin Luther King, Jr., "I Have a Dream"

(1963)

As leader of the biggest peaceful protest in American history, the country's top African-American civil rights champion implores the nation to make good on its claims of freedom and justice for all people. And what becomes of the original document bearing his rhetorical masterpiece?

Standing on the steps of the Lincoln Memorial on August 28, 1963, Rev. Martin Luther King, Jr. took the microphone to voice the case of America's growing civil rights movement. The crowd of more than 250,000 participants of the March on Washington for Jobs and Freedom and dozens of reporters and broadcasters from all of the major news media followed his every word.

Nobody in the audience could see the three-page typewritten document from which he was reading; everyone was transfixed by what they were hearing.

King began with a fitting reference to the Emancipation Proclamation which had freed millions of slaves a hundred years before, then added: "So we have come here today to dramatize a shameful condition." Using flourishes from Lincoln, the Bible, the Declaration of the Independence, the Pledge of Allegiance, and other classic works, the preacher also employed a bevy of skillful rhetorical devices.

But sensing that the words lacked power, the impassioned gospel singer Mahalia Jackson cried out, "Tell 'em about the dream, Martin!" referring to moving passages she had heard King deliver in a recent speech. In fact, the previous night King's speechwriter Clarence Jones had included the "dream" motif in a draft, but King had apparently cut it out at the urging of another advisor, who thought it would sound trite.

When the moment was right, King departed from his prepared text to deliver a partly improvised ending built on repetition, which began, "So even though we face the difficulties of today and tomorrow, I still have a dream."

"I have a dream," he continued, "that my four little children will one day live in a nation where they will not be judged by the color of their skin, but by the content of their character. I have a dream today!"

The ad-libbed portion turned out to be the most memorable part of his address, receiving strong applause.

When he was through, King folded the document and was about to put it into his pocket when one of his young security guards, a basketball player named George Raveling, asked if he could have it. King gave it to him and then was engulfed by well-wishers.

Later that year, *Time* magazine named King "Man of the Year," and a few months later he became the youngest person to win the Nobel Peace Prize. Yet his full speech did not appear in writing until August 1983. A few months after its appearance in print, Raveling fully realized the document's importance, and he retrieved the historic artifact from his basement. Today he keeps it in a vault for his heirs.

Surveys have rated the "I Have a Dream" speech as the greatest American oration of the twentieth century. But the most famous part is missing from the document.

LEFT: A handwritten draft of King's famous speech on display at Sotheby's, New York. This draft was part of a Martin Luther King collection of papers bought by Morehouse College, Atlanta, for $32 million in 2006.

Quotations from Chairman Mao Tse-tung

(1964)

The aging Chairman of China's Communist Party issues a small primer of selected inspirational quotations for soldiers that helps to fuel the Cultural Revolution and quickly becomes the best-selling book in the world—Mao's "Little Red Book."

As father of the People's Republic of China and leader of its ongoing revolution, Mao Tse-tung (Mao Zedong) (1893–1976) wasn't pleased when the other leaders of his party sought to push him aside over economic policies. In order to assert himself, in January 1964 Mao had a little booklet prepared containing excerpts from his selected speeches and writings. It offered 200 of his most revolutionary quotations on various topics, ostensibly intended as a motivational primer for soldiers of the People's Liberation Army.

Copies were given to delegates of a party conference, asking them to comment on it. Based on their response, the work was expanded and printed as *Quotations from Chairman Mao Tse-tung*. The revised version was promptly distributed to units of the PLA, who also were asked for their input. The PLA's chief political organ gave it their enthusiastic approval, issuing a new revised edition that was buttressed with the slogan, "Workers of the World, Unite!"

After still more discussions, in May 1965 another version with 427 quotations was published. Some of the sayings included: "We should support whatever the enemy opposes and oppose whatever the enemy supports." "All wars that are progressive are just, and all wars that impede progress are unjust." "Political power grows out of the barrel of a gun."

Pocket-sized, with a durable waterproof cover, the book created such a sensation that the Ministry of Culture set the goal of having 99 percent of the country's population read the document. Copies were everywhere. As the catechism of the growing Cultural Revolution, it elevated Mao to godlike status. Citizens were expected to memorize and recite passages and were severely punished if they failed; anyone who allowed the book to be damaged or destroyed could expect harsh imprisonment or worse. The quotations were held up as the standard against which all true revolutionaries were judged.

The response was so great that in 1966 the party's Propaganda Department ordered the document printed for foreign consumption and it was translated and distributed worldwide, in a red vinyl cover, gaining the nickname "The Little Red Book." At its peak of popularity, radicals from Havana to Berkeley carried a copy in their back pocket. Estimates of the number of copies printed range from 2 to 6.5 billion, making it the "most popular book of the twentieth century."

In 2002 the earliest available 1965 copy sold at Sotheby's, New York, for $13,000.

RIGHT: A market stall selling copies of the vinyl-covered "Little Red Book" and a poster promoting it. Mao's face was usually depicted above the masses, emerging from sunshine and leading the people to a bright future.

88th CONGRESS
2nd SESSION

S. J. RES. *189*

(NOTE.—Fill in all blank lines except those provided for the date and number of resolution.)

IN THE SENATE OF THE UNITED STATES

AUG 5 - 1964

Mr. _____ introduced the following joint resolution; which was read twice and referred to the Committee on FOREIGN RELATIONS AND ARMED SERVICES JOINTLY.

JOINT RESOLUTION

To promote the maintenance of international peace

(Insert title of joint resolution here)

and security in Southeast Asia.

1   *Resolved by the Senate and House of Representatives of the United*

2   *States of America in Congress assembled,*

WHEREAS naval units of the Communist regime in Vietnam, in violation of the principles of the Charter of the United Nations and of international law, have deliberately and repeatedly attacked United States naval vessels lawfully present in international waters, and have thereby created a serious threat to international peace; and

WHEREAS these attacks are part of a deliberate and systematic campaign of aggression that the Communist regime in North Vietnam has been waging against its neighbors and the nations joined with them in the collective defense of their freedom; and

WHEREAS the United States is assisting the peoples of Southeast Asia to protect their freedom and has no territorial, military, or political ambitions in that area, but desires only that these peoples should be left in peace to work out their own destinies in their own way;

Now therefore, BE IT

Gulf of Tonkin Resolution

(1964)

A joint resolution of Congress authorizes President Lyndon B. Johnson to use conventional military force in Southeast Asia, thereby providing legal cover for the US to wage war in Vietnam—but the document is based on distortions and lies, showing that Congress and the American people were misled.

According to the US Defense Department, on August 2, 1964 the USS *Maddox*, a US destroyer on patrol in the Gulf of Tonkin off Vietnam, exchanged fire with three North Vietnamese Navy torpedo boats. Two days later the *Maddox* and the destroyer *Turner Joy* both reported they had been attacked by North Vietnamese torpedo boats in another act of aggression.

Although the communist North Vietnamese government in Hanoi disputed the allegations, US officials cited the incident as an act of military aggression. On August 4, President Lyndon B. Johnson announced in a televised national address that due to North Vietnam's attacks on US ships in the Gulf of Tonkin, he would ask Congress to authorize a necessary military response.

Johnson was facing an election in three months and it seemed likely that many Americans would support such an action; maybe it would even help his campaign against the hawkish Republican nominee, Barry Goldwater.

The Tonkin Gulf Resolution stated that "Congress approves and supports the determination of the President, as Commander in Chief, to take all necessary measures to repeal any armed attack against the forces of the United States and to prevent any further aggression."

The measure was passed by a unanimous vote of all 416 members in the House and the Senate approved it by eighty-eight to two, with only Democratic Senators Wayne Morse of Oregon and Ernest Gruening of Alaska casting the nay votes. (Morse warned, "I believe this resolution to be a historic mistake.")

On August 10, President Johnson signed the joint resolution that authorized him to use whatever conventional military force he deemed necessary—the equivalent of a declaration of war. Then he began using the resolution to support escalation of US military involvement in South Vietnam.

Seven years later, the release of a secret Defense Department study would expose that, contrary to the official line, the North Vietnamese had not carried out an "unequivocal, unprovoked" attack on US vessels in Tonkin. By 2005 the release of more previously classified documents and tapes from the National Security Agency plus other new disclosures would reveal that high government officials had distorted facts and deceived Congress and the public about what had actually happened. The crucial information that had served as the pretext for America's decade-long war in Southeast Asia would become deeply discredited.

The original draft of the Gulf of Tonkin Resolution is in the National Archives.

LEFT: The original draft of the Resolution, which claimed that "naval units of the Communist regime in Vietnam ... have deliberately and repeatedly attacked United States naval vessels."

Apollo 11 Flight Plan

(1969)

In preparation for the first manned moon landing, NASA produces a detailed Flight Plan featuring a minute-by-minute timeline of activities by the spaceship and its three-member crew, from the launch from Cape Kennedy until the capsule's scheduled splashdown in the Pacific four days later—a meticulous astronautical manual for one of the greatest technological achievements in history.

Eight years after President Kennedy's pledge to put a man on the moon before the Soviets, America's state-of-the-art space program was poised to make history as the whole world watched in awe.

The Apollo program had involved 400,000 engineers, technicians, and scientists from 20,000 companies and the military in cutting-edge research and logistic activities at a cost of $24 billion. But in July 1969 all of that complex preparation and expense would boil down to a simple question: would the mission succeed or would it fail? Three astronauts' lives would hang in the balance. And the operation would be broadcast live to a worldwide television audience.

On July 1, 1969, the Manned Spacecraft Center in Houston issued a 363-page Final Flight Plan for NASA's scheduled launch of the Apollo 11 on July 16. It spelled out the mission in complete and precise technical detail.

The spacecraft was to carry its three-man crew—Mission Commander Neil Armstrong, Command Module Pilot Michael Collins, and Lunar Module Pilot Edwin E. "Buzz" Aldrin Jr.—on a history-making journey.

The five-part plan provided a minute-by-minute timeline of activities for each member of the mission crew, starting with the launch and lift-off from Kennedy Space Center Launch Complex 39A at 9:32 AM. The detailed instructions and data tracking continued through the flight, lunar orbit, moon exploration, return flight and reentry and splashdown.

Apollo 11 was programmed to travel 240,000 miles in seventy-six hours before entering into a lunar orbit on July 19. The next day, Armstrong and Aldrin were trained to man the lunar module *Eagle* while Collins remained behind in the command module. Two hours later, the *Eagle* would begin its descent to the lunar surface and land on the southwestern edge of the Sea of Tranquility.

During their 21 hours and 36 minutes on the moon, the astronauts were scheduled to carry out a wide assortment of duties including taking photographs and samples of the terrain, planting a US flag, running various scientific tests, and speaking by telephone with President Nixon. Aldrin and Armstrong would sleep that night on the surface of the moon, then return to the command module.

The Apollo 11 mission proceeded exactly according to plan. Black and white video from the voyage was transmitted to Earth with amazing clarity as 600 million people, one-fifth of the world's population, watched on television.

The flight plans, officially known as "flight data files," for Apollo 8 to Apollo 17, and other records related to the Apollo program, are in the custody of the National Archives in Fort Worth, Texas.

RIGHT: Edwin E. "Buzz" Aldrin Jr.'s copy of the Apollo 11 flight plan, dated July 1, 1969. The 365-page plan provided a minute-by-minute timeline of activities for each member of the mission crew.

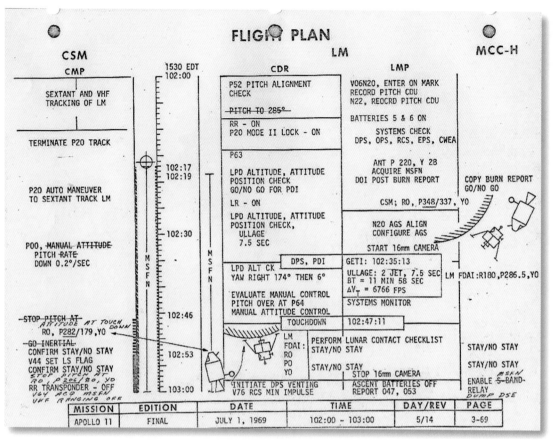

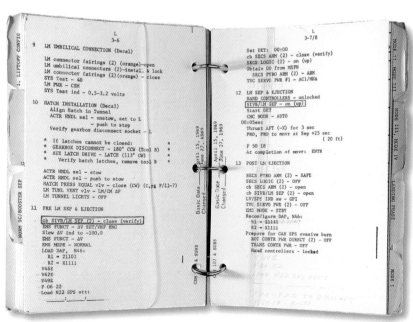

APPLE COMPUTER COMPANY
PARTNERSHIP AGREEMENT

TO WHOM IT MAY CONCERN: **AMENDMENT**

By virtue of a re-assessment of understandings by and between all parties
to the Agreement of April 1, 1976, WOZNIAK, JOBS, and WAYNE, the
following modifications and amendments are herewith appended to the said
Agreement, and made a part thereof. These modifications and amendments,
having been concluded on this 12th day of April, 1976, hereby supercede, and
render void, all contrary understandings given in the Agreement of April 1, 1976.

ARTICLE A:
As of the date of this amendment, WAYNE shall hereinafter cease to function in
the status of "Partner" to the aforementioned Agreement, and all obligations,
responsibilities, agreements, and understandings of the Agreement of April 1,
1976, are herewith terminated. It is specifically understood, and agreed to,
by all of the parties to the original agreement, and the amendments hereto
appended, WOZNIAK, JOBS, and WAYNE, that that portion of all financial
obligations incurred by WAYNE, on the part of the COMPANY, prior to the
date of this amendment, is herewith terminated, and that WAYNE's portion
of obligations (10%) to the creditors of the COMPANY are herewith assumed,
jointly and equally, by the remaining partners to the original agreement,
namely, WOZNIAK and JOBS. It is further mutually understood, and agreed,
that WAYNE shall incur no obligations or responsibilities in, or for, the
COMPANY, nor shall WAYNE be held liable in any litigation, initiated by or
instituted against, the COMPANY, with regard to the conduct of the COMPANY's
business with any creditor, vendor, customer, or any other party, nor with
reference to or arising from any product of the COMPANY, as of the first day
of April, 1976.

ARTICLE B:
In consideration of the relinquishment of WAYNE's former percentage of
ownership, and for all efforts thusfar conducted in honor of the aforementioned
agreement during its term of activity, the remaining parties to the partnership,
WOZNIAK, and JOBS, agree to pay and deliver to WAYNE, as their sole obligations
under the terms of this amendment, the sum of eight hundred dollars ($800.00).

IN WITNESS WHEREOF: These amendments have been appended to the original
Agreement and made a part thereof, and have been executed by each of the parties
hereto, on this 12th day of April, 1976.

Mr. Stephen G. Wozniak (WOZNIAK)

Mr. Steven P. Jobs (JOBS)

Mr. Ronald G. Wayne (WAYNE)

Apple Computer Company

(1976)

Starting from a makeshift workshop in a family garage, two young college dropouts in Silicon Valley, California form their own company to market a do-it-yourself kit for hobbyists to make their own moderately priced microcomputer. Their original partnership agreement and incorporation papers establish a venture that will change the world.

In 1976 Steve Jobs (1955–2011) was a self-taught computer geek working out of his parents' garage in Los Altos, California, with a couple of nerdish buddies, "Woz" and "Wayne." Ronald Wayne sold his share to the other two for $800, but Steve Wozniak (1950–) and Jobs mutually agreed to hold all rights, title, and interest in and to their fledgling company "for the manufacture and marketing of computer devices, components, and related material."

They called it the Apple Computer Company.

Their first product was a kit that computer hobbyists could purchase for $666 to assemble their own microcomputer, which they called the Apple I. Sold as an assembled circuit board, it lacked even such basic features as a keyboard, monitor, and case. But the machine had some novel features, including its use of a TV screen as the display system. The Apple I was also easier to start up than other machines on the market and faster than the teleprinters used on contemporary machines of that era. Computer freaks marveled at its masterful design.

Although they were operating on a shoestring, Jobs and Wozniak were able to make and sell 200 of the machines at a good profit, which got their venture off on the right foot.

The Apple Computer Company was legally incorporated in California on January 3, 1977.

Apple, Inc. went on to help spur the world's personal computer revolution. It grew to become a leading multinational corporation that manufactures consumer electronics, personal computers, computer software, and commercial servers; it is also a digital distributor of popular media content. Apple's core product lines include the iPhone smart phone, iPad tablet computer,

iPod portable media player, and Macintosh computer line. Since its founding it has remained one of the world's most innovative companies.

Woznick left the company in 1981 and Jobs passed away in 2011. Yet as of March 2013 Apple was the largest publicly traded company in the world by market capitalization, with over 72,800 full-time employees and a value of more than $415 billion.

In 2010 the company's original founding legal documents from 1976, signed by Jobs, Wozniak and Wayne, were sold at auction for $1.4 million.

ABOVE: An original Apple I, including operating instructions and a photo signed by Steve Wozniak, sold at Christie's in 2014 for $360,000.

OPPOSITE: A couple of weeks after Apple Computer Company was founded, Ronald Wayne sold his 10 percent share for $800. In 2015 Apple became the first US company to be valued at over $700 billion.

Internet Protocol

(1981)

A bushy-bearded and laid-back computer engineer from Los Angeles writes a forty-five-page technical document establishing how the Internet will work and what its culture will be—based on cooperation, openness, tolerance, simplicity, and integrity. His fellow Internet pioneers call him "God of the Internet."

Although he was barely known outside computer circles, Jon Postel (1943–98) was a world shaker. In 1969 he helped set up the first node on the ARPANET, which was the precursor to the modern Internet, and over the next twenty years he was as responsible as anyone for establishing both the technical protocols that make the Internet work and for founding the Internet community to which billions of users belong.

In 1981 Postel wrote a forty-five-page technical document titled "RFC: 791"—the Internet Protocol for short—which built on the work of his fellow computer scientists Robert Kahn and Vinton Cerf, and it was approved by the Internet Engineering Task Force as the Transfer Control Protocol (TCP/IP).

There already existed a means of sending messages from one computer to another via a small network of linked computers, however that activity was originally intended to carry out only a limited set of activities. All of the network's members were involved in government work. Under Postel's TCP/IP, the "Internet" was transformed into a network connecting networks that freely moved data around, unchanged, and unexamined, according to basic standards that gave it structure and made it function efficiently. The TCP/IP determines the way data is moved through a network. The new Internet

was simpler to implement, subscribe to, and maintain. "In general," he wrote, "an implementation must be conservative in its sending behavior, and liberal in its receiving behavior."

After the new network was tested, in November 1981 Postel published a transition plan whereby the 400 ARPANET hosts were to be migrated from the older NCP protocol to TCP/IP by January 1, 1983, after which point all hosts not switched would be cut off. The transition went smoothly.

After Postel's untimely death in 1998, Tim Berners-Lee, the computer scientist who is credited as the inventor of the World Wide Web, said:

> Those of us who came into the Internet after its beginning inherited not only a wonderful idea and technology, but also a wonderful society, sets of values and ways of working which are only too rare elsewhere. Jon Postel stood at the centre of this, not only in his work—the service he performed as a public trust, but also for the things which, in doing that, he stood for. The concept that some things belong to everybody. Doing things because they are the right thing to do. Tolerance of different opinions—and so on—now known as the Internet culture. His death leaves us with a heavy responsibility to continue that tradition.

RIGHT: Two pages from the 1981 document and a photograph from 1994 showing Jon Postel, "God of the Internet," pointing to a hand-drawn map of the Internet's top-level domains.

2. OVERVIEW

2.1. Relation to Other Protocols

The following diagram illustrates the place of the internet protocol in the protocol hierarchy:

```
+------+ +------+ +------+    +------+
|Telnet| | FTP  | | TFTP | ...| ...  |
+------+ +------+ +------+    +------+
   |        |        |          |
   +-----+  +-----+  +-----+    +-----+
   | TCP |  |     | UDP | ... | ... |
   +-----+  +-----+  +-----+    +-----+
      |        |        |          |
   +--------------------------------+----+
   |    Internet Protocol & ICMP         |
   +-------------------------------------+
                     |
   +--------------------------------+
   |    Local Network Protocol      |
   +--------------------------------+
```

Protocol Relationships

Figure 1.

Internet protocol interfaces on one side to the higher level host-to-host protocols and on the other side to the local network protocol. In this context a "local network" may be a small network in a building or a large network such as the ARPANET.

2.2. Model of Operation

The model of operation for transmitting a datagram from one application program to another is illustrated by the following scenario:

We suppose that this transmission will involve one intermediate gateway.

The sending application program prepares its data and calls on its local internet module to send that data as a datagram and passes the destination address and other parameters as arguments of the call.

The internet module prepares a datagram header and attaches the data to it. The internet module determines a local network address for this internet address, in this case it is the address of a gateway.

[Page 5]

It sends this datagram and the local network address to the local network interface.

The local network interface creates a local network header, and attaches the datagram to it, then sends the result via the local network.

The datagram arrives at a gateway host wrapped in the local network header, the local network interface strips off this header, and turns the datagram over to the internet module. The internet module determines from the internet address that the datagram is to be forwarded to another host in a second network. The internet module determines a local net address for the destination host. It calls on the local network interface for that network to send the datagram.

This local network interface creates a local network header and attaches the datagram sending the result to the destination host.

At this destination host the datagram is stripped of the local net header by the local network interface and handed to the internet module.

The internet module determines that the datagram is for an application program in this host. It passes the data to the application program in response to a system call, passing the source address and other parameters as results of the call.

```
Application                                      Application
Program                                            Program
   \                                                 /
Internet Module    Internet Module    Internet Module
   \                /      \                /
   LNI-1          LNI-1    LNI-2          LNI-2
     \             /         \             /
     Local Network 1         Local Network 2
```

Transmission Path

Figure 2

[Page 6]

– 48 –

Geschehen zu Berlin am 31. August 1990

in zwei Urschriften in deutscher Sprache.

Für die
Bundesrepublik Deutschland

Für die
Deutsche Demokratische Republik

*ABOVE AND RIGHT: The German Reunification agreement (above) culminated in the
Two Plus Four Treaty, which was signed in Moscow on September 12, 1990 (right).*

Two Plus Four Treaty

(1990)

Forty-five years after the end of a world war started by Germany's aggression, and the division of the country by occupying powers, will the two Germanys and the four victors agree that Germany should once again become united? And if so, on what basis?

Upon its defeat in 1945, Germany was split into two separate areas with the East controlled by the communist Soviet Bloc and the West aligned with the capitalist European Community. Berlin was divided into two sectors that later became separated by the Berlin Wall. West Germany rose to become an "economic miracle" while East Germany's Soviet-style police state made less economic progress but still performed relatively well compared to other communist countries.

In 1989, however, amid a period of loosening grip by the Soviet Union, a rebellion of East Germans known as the "Peaceful Revolution" suddenly brought a spontaneous dismantling of the Wall on November 9, followed by rapid transitions to democratic rule. During the tumult, West German Chancellor Helmut Kohl called for the unification of East (German Democratic Republic, GDR) and West Germany (Federal Republic of Germany, FRG)—a move carrying great potential implications for the world, given a united Germany's two previous wars.

On May 18, 1990, the two German states agreed to a monetary, economic, and social union, which amounted to West Germany annexing East Germany, thereby

assuming responsibility for the final transition from communist rule. This "Treaty Establishing a Monetary, Economic and Social Union between the German Democratic Republic and the Federal Republic of Germany," took effect on July 1, 1990.

Discussions had been going on for months in the four nations that had occupied Germany, debating whether German reunification was a good idea. After forty-five years, and the apparent easing of the Cold War, some of the fears and anger had subsided. But although public opinion in some countries remained sharply divided, official opposition was quickly overcome.

The result was a formal agreement involving the two German states and the four occupying powers (the Soviet Union, France, United Kingdom, and the United States). The Treaty on the Final Settlement with Respect to Germany (*Vertrag über die abschließende Regelung in bezug auf Deutschland*), best known as the "Two Plus Four Treaty," was signed in Moscow on September 12, 1990.

Under the new agreement, the four powers renounced all rights they held in Germany under the Potsdam Agreement, thereby allowing a united Germany to become a fully sovereign state. Germany also renounced any foreign claims to additional territory or other expansion. All Soviet forces were ordered to leave Germany by the end of 1994. The size of Germany's armed forces was capped at no more than 370,000 personnel along with other restrictions. Germany also agreed to abide by the terms of the United Nations Charter.

The treaty took effect March 15, 1991.

Afterwards, an account of the unification by the German government concluded: "When the last allied troops left Berlin in August and September 1994, it was clear the postwar era was well and truly over."

First Website

(1991)

A young English computer software consultant and some of his colleagues employed at the headquarters of a major European particle physics research laboratory in Switzerland establish the world's first "website" to try to convince skeptics to buy into their newfangled concept of the World Wide Web—but can their early digital documents be recovered for posterity?

In 1989 a young English computer software consultant employed at the headquarters of the European Organization for Nuclear Research (CERN) outside Geneva received permission from his supervisor to develop his idea for a project called ENQUIRE, which was designed to facilitate large-scale automatic data sharing among research scientists scattered across the globe, based on the futuristic concepts known as "hypertext" and "hyperlinks." Although CERN's stated purpose was to operate the world's largest particle physics laboratory for its twenty-one European member states and Israel, the world-class research organization also carried out some groundbreaking activities in data sharing technology.

Berners-Lee called his new idea "The World Wide Web," or W3, defined as "a wide-area hypermedia information retrieval initiative aiming to give universal access." He and his Belgian colleague, Robert Cailliau, used CERN equipment including a NeXT computer and router to create through the Internet what they called a "website." The CERN website went online in 1991. It described the basic features of the web, informed its users how to access other members' documents and how a new member could set up their own server. The original NeXT machine—the world's first web server—is still at CERN, and the World Wide Web with zillions of websites is everywhere.

One might say that the rest is history. Except Berners-Lee and his colleagues did not keep track of their early web pages, so those interesting pieces of history were lost. But a team at CERN is trying to restore the original webpage and other pieces of memorabilia from the earliest days, in an effort to preserve some of the digital assets that are associated with the birth of the web. "For a start," the project explains:

> we would like to restore the first URL—put back the files that were there at their earliest possible iterations. Then we will look at the first web servers at CERN and see what assets from them we can preserve and share. We will also sift through documentation and try to restore machine names and IP addresses to their original state. Beyond this we want to make http://info.cern.ch—the first web address—a destination that reflects the story of the beginnings of the web for the benefit of future generations.

In 1993 CERN delighted computer users everywhere when it decided to relinquish all intellectual property to its invention of the World Wide Web, thereby putting the software in the public domain for everyone to use for free.

RIGHT: Tim Berners-Lee at CERN in 1994, with an early version of the World Wide Web software.
OPPOSITE: The homepage of the first website described itself as an "information retrieval initiative aiming to give universal access to a large universe of documents."

World Wide Web

The WorldWideWeb (W3) is a wide-area hypermedia information retrieval initiative aiming to give universal access to a large universe of documents.

Everything there is online about W3 is linked directly or indirectly to this document, including an executive summary of the project, Mailing lists , Policy , November's W3 news , Frequently Asked Questions .

What's out there?
    Pointers to the world's online information, subjects , W3 servers, etc.
Help
    on the browser you are using
Software Products
    A list of W3 project components and their current state. (e.g. Line Mode ,X11 Viola , NeXTStep , Servers , Tools , Mail robot , Library)
Technical
    Details of protocols, formats, program internals etc
Bibliography
    Paper documentation on W3 and references.
People
    A list of some people involved in the project.
History
    A summary of the history of the project.
How can I help ?
    If you would like to support the web..
Getting code
    Getting the code by anonymous FTP , etc.

Bin Ladin Determined To Strike in US

Clandestine, foreign government, and media reports indicate Bin Ladin since 1997 has wanted to conduct terrorist attacks in the US. Bin Ladin implied in US television interviews in 1997 and 1998 that his followers would follow the example of World Trade Center bomber Ramzi Yousef and "bring the fighting to America."

> After US missile strikes on his base in Afghanistan in 1998, Bin Ladin told followers he wanted to retaliate in Washington, according to a ███████████ service.

> An Egyptian Islamic Jihad (EIJ) operative told an██████ service at the same time that Bin Ladin was planning to exploit the operative's access to the US to mount a terrorist strike.

The millennium plotting in Canada in 1999 may have been part of Bin Ladin's first serious attempt to implement a terrorist strike in the US. Convicted plotter Ahmed Ressam has told the FBI that he conceived the idea to attack Los Angeles International Airport himself, but that Bin Ladin lieutenant Abu Zubaydah encouraged him and helped facilitate the operation. Ressam also said that in 1998 Abu Zubaydah was planning his own US attack.

> Ressam says Bin Ladin was aware of the Los Angeles operation.

Although Bin Ladin has not succeeded, his attacks against the US Embassies in Kenya and Tanzania in 1998 demonstrate that he prepares operations years in advance and is not deterred by setbacks. Bin Ladin associates surveilled our Embassies in Nairobi and Dar es Salaam as early as 1993, and some members of the Nairobi cell planning the bombings were arrested and deported in 1997.

Al-Qa'ida members—including some who are US citizens—have resided in or traveled to the US for years, and the group apparently maintains a support structure that could aid attacks. Two al-Qa'ida members found guilty in the conspiracy to bomb our Embassies in East Africa were US citizens, and a senior EIJ member lived in California in the mid-1990s.

> A clandestine source said in 1998 that a Bin Ladin cell in New York was recruiting Muslim-American youth for attacks.

We have not been able to corroborate some of the more sensational threat reporting, such as that from a ███████████ *service in 1998 saying that Bin Ladin wanted to hijack a US aircraft to gain the release of "Blind Shaykh" 'Umar 'Abd al-Rahman and other US-held extremists.*

— Nevertheless, FBI information since that time indicates patterns of suspicious activity in this country consistent with preparations for hijackings or other types of attacks, including recent surveillance of federal buildings in New York.

The FBI is conducting approximately 70 full field investigations throughout the US that it considers Bin Ladin–related. CIA and the FBI are investigating a call to our Embassy in the UAE in May saying that a group of Bin Ladin supporters was in the US planning attacks with explosives.

"Bin Laden Determined to Strike in US"

(2001)

On August 6, 2001, the Central Intelligence Agency delivers the President's Daily Brief to George W. Bush at his Texas ranch, warning that Osama bin Laden is preparing a major attack against the United States. Disclosure of the document will fuel speculation about possible negligence by the Bush administration.

Eight months after America suffered the deadliest attack in its history, *CBS Evening News* revealed the existence of a secret memo dated thirty-six days before 9/11, which had warned President George Bush that Osama bin Laden and al-Qaeda were plotting an imminent terrorist assault against the United States.

The President's Daily Brief in question, dated August 6, 2001, was later declassified and released to the 9/11 Commission in April 2004 and published in redacted form in the *9/11 Commission Report* on July 22, 2004. The report showed that the top-secret document, presented to Bush that day by the Central Intelligence Agency, had also carried an ominous heading: "Bin Laden Determined to Strike in US." The two-page cryptic warning, written by CIA Senior Analyst Barbara Sude, mentioned the World Trade Center and Washington as targets and cited bin Laden's desire to hijack a US aircraft. It also stated that bin Laden had implied in interviews since 1998 that his followers would follow the example of 1992 World Trade Center bomber Ramzi Yousef and "bring the fighting to America."

The memo was later described as "perhaps the most famous presidential briefing in history." It was also the only PDB which the Bush administration released to the public. Today it is considered one of the most historically significant documents associated with 9/11.

Many Bush defenders later attempted to downplay criticism that the administration had ignored CIA warnings, claiming that the PDB of August 6 did not specify when or where the attack would occur.

Further investigation by Kurt Eichenwald, a former *New York Times* reporter who gained access to additional PDBs of that period, concluded that Bush had previously received more than forty other direct warnings about al-Qaeda attacks going back to the spring of 2001, yet he had not ordered any preventive action. Bush's intelligence briefings were usually given in person by CIA Director George Tenet and usually attended by Vice President Dick Cheney and National Security Advisor Condoleezza Rice. Neither of them appeared to have taken any precautions either.

"Could the 9/11 attack have been stopped," Eichenwald asked, "had the Bush team reacted with urgency to the warnings contained in all of those daily briefs? We can't ever know. And that may be the most agonizing reality of all."

LEFT: The August 6, 2001 memo is one of the most historically significant documents associated with 9/11.

RIGHT: A poster in New York inspired by Bush's comment following the attacks: "I want justice. And there's an old poster out west that says, 'Wanted: Dead or Alive.'"

Iraq War Resolution

(2002)

In the frenzied aftermath of the 9/11 attacks, the Bush administration wins a joint resolution from Congress which spells out the authorization for military action against Iraq. Viewed in hindsight, the document's case for war may not appear as strong as it did then.

A year after the attacks on the World Trade Center and Washington, the administration of President George W. Bush sought a joint resolution from Congress, just as President Johnson had done with the Tonkin Gulf Resolution to justify US military action in Vietnam, and just as Bush's father, President George H.W. Bush, had done before commencing the first Gulf War.

Following his September 12 statement before the UN General Assembly asking for quick action by the Security Council in enforcing the resolutions against Iraq, Bush issued the document titled, "Authorization for Use of Military Force against Iraq Resolution of 2002," setting forth the basis for the United States to wage war against Saddam Hussein's Iraq.

In response to the President's proposals, HJ Resolution 114 sponsored by Rep. Dennis Hastert (R-Illinois), the House Speaker, and Rep. Dick Gephardt (D-Missouri), the House Minority Leader, was approved on October 10, by a vote of 296–133. The following morning, SJ Resolution 46 sponsored by Sen. Joe Lieberman (D-Connecticut), passed the Senate by a vote of 77 to 23, and it was signed into law on October 16.

The sweeping resolution authorized President Bush

ABOVE: In his United Nations address of September 12, 2002, Bush referred to Iraq as a "grave and gathering danger." OPPOSITE: A memo following Resolution 114, which authorized the president to "defend the national security of the United States against the continuing threat posed by Iraq."

to use the Armed Forces "as he determines to be necessary and appropriate" in order to "defend the national security of the United States against the continuing threat posed by Iraq; and enforce all relevant United Nations Security Council Resolutions regarding Iraq."

The resolution cited several factors as justifying the use of military force against Iraq, among them that Iraq was "continuing to possess and develop a significant chemical and biological weapons capability" and "actively seeking a nuclear weapons capability" that posed a "threat to the national security of the United States and international peace and security in the Persian Gulf region." It also pointed to Iraq's "capability and willingness to use weapons of mass destruction against other nations and its own people." The document claimed that members of al-Qaeda were "known to be in Iraq," that Iraq was continuing to "aid and harbor other terrorist organizations," and to "pay bounties to families of suicide bombers." It also said that the governments of Turkey, Kuwait, and Saudi Arabia wanted Saddam Hussein removed from power.

On March 16, 2003, the US government advised UN weapons inspectors to immediately leave Iraq, and on March 20 the US commenced a surprise military invasion of Iraq without declaring war.

Historians continue to debate whether the authorization for war was justified, particularly given the failure of US forces to find weapons of mass destruction. Like the Tonkin Gulf resolution, the Iraq resolution remains one of the most controversial documents in American history.

107TH CONGRESS
2D SESSION

H. J. RES. 114

Union Calendar No. 451

[Report No. 107–721]

To authorize the use of United States Armed Forces against Iraq.

IN THE HOUSE OF REPRESENTATIVES

Mr. HASTERT (for himself and Mr. ~~~
resolution: which ~~~

OCTOBER 2, 2002

~~~uced the following joint
~~~ternational Relations

~~~e of the Whole House
~~~ printed

~~~rinted in italic]
~~~n italic]

~~~esolution as introduced

U.S. Department of Jus~~~

Office of Legal Counsel

Office of the Deputy Assistant Attorney General

Washington, D.C. 20530

October 21, 2002

MEMORANDUM FOR DANIEL J. BRYANT
ASSISTANT ATTORNEY GENERAL
OFFICE OF LEGISLATIVE AFFAIRS

From: John C. Yoo
       Deputy Assistant Attorney General

Re: <u>Authorization for Use of Military Force Against Iraq Resolution of 2002</u>

This memorandum confirms the views of the Office of Legal Counsel, expressed to you last week, on H. J. Res. 114, the Authorization for Use of Military Force Against Iraq Resolution of 2002. This resolution authorizes the President to use the United States Armed Forces, "as he determines to be necessary and appropriate," either to "defend the national security of the United States against the continuing threat posed by Iraq," or to "enforce all relevant United Nations Security Council resolutions regarding Iraq." H. J. Res. 114, § 3(a).

We have no constitutional objection to Congress expressing its support for the use of military force against Iraq.[1] Indeed, the Office of Legal Counsel was an active participant in the drafting of and negotiations over H. J. Res. 114. We have long maintained, however, that resolutions such as H. J. Res. 114 are legally unnecessary. *See, e.g., Deployment of United States Armed Forces into Haiti*, 18 Op. O.L.C. 173, 175-76 (1994) ("the President may introduce troops into hostilities or potential hostilities without prior authorization by the Congress"); *Proposed Deployment of United States Armed Forces into Bosnia*, 19 Op. O.L.C. 327, 335 (1995) ("the President has authority, without specific statutory authorization, to introduce troops into hostilities in a substantial range of circumstances"). As Chief Executive and Commander in Chief of the Armed Forces of the United States, the President possesses ample authority under the Constitution to direct the use of military force in defense of the national security of the United States, as we explain in Section I of this memorandum, and as H. J. Res. 114 itself acknowledges when it states that "the President has authority under the Constitution to take

---

[1] Congress has expressed its support for the use of military force on a number of occasions throughout U.S. history, including, most recently, in response to the attacks of September 11, 2001. *See* Authorization for Use of Military Force, Pub. L. No. 107-40, 115 Stat. 224 (2001); *see also* Act of May 28, 1798, 1 Stat. 561 (Quasi War with France); Act of Feb. 6, 1802, 2 Stat. 129 (First Barbary War); Act of Jan. 15, 1811, 3 Stat. 471 (East Florida); Act of Feb. 12, 1813, 3 Stat. 472 (West Florida); Act of Mar. 3, 1815, 3 Stat. 230 (Second Barbary War); Act of Mar. 3, 1819, 3 Stat. 510 (African Slave Trade); Joint Resolution of June 2, 1858, 11 Stat. 370 (Paraguay); Joint Resolution of Apr. 20, 1898, 30 Stat. 738 (Spanish-American War); Joint Resolution of Apr. 22, 1914, 38 Stat. 770 (Mexico); Joint Resolution of Jan. 29, 1955, 69 Stat. 7 (Formosa); Joint Resolution of Mar. 9, 1957, 71 Stat. 5 (codified at 22 U.S.C. § 1962) (Middle East); Joint Resolution of Aug. 10, 1964, 78 Stat. 384 (Gulf of Tonkin); Authorization for Use of Military Force Against Iraq Resolution, Pub. L. No. 102-1, 105 Stat. 3 (1991).

ON

~~~ces against

~~~ aggression
~~~he United
~~~wait and
~~~ty of the

First Tweet

(2006)

A shy young entrepreneur has an idea for an instant messaging system that will enable any user to communicate brief text messages to the world via a cellphone. Then he sends out his first communiqué—never dreaming that it will make him a billionaire.

In early 2006, exactly two years after the launch of Facebook, the phenomenally successful social networking service, a thirty-year-old digital age innovator in San Francisco had the idea for a new kind of free social networking and microblogging service. Jack Dorsey and some of his friends (Evan Williams, Biz Stone, and Noah Glass) received financial backing and proceeded to develop the project, which they called Twitter.

Dorsey thought the name seemed especially apt because it signified "a short burst of inconsequential information," like the chirps of birds, and Twitter was envisioned as an online social networking service that would enable its registered users to send and receive short bursts of messages up to 140-characters, called tweets, which would be posted through a website interface. Unregistered users could only read them, but not send any tweets.

On March 21, 2006 at 9:50 PM, Dorsey posted his first tweet, which said: "just setting up my twttr," and four months later the site was launched. Twitter quickly caught on, gaining more than 100 million users in 2012. In July 2014 the number had grown to 500 million, of which 271 million were classified as active users. The advertising revenue rapidly made Dorsey a billionaire.

Exceeding Dorsey's initial expectation, some of the tweets proved to be both useful and even consequential. Millions of sports fans used Twitter to communicate instant news about athletic contests, concerts, and other social events. After its use by protesters in Moldova was dubbed the "Twitter Revolution" in 2009, the social networking service was credited as a vital tool for political activists. Tweets and other social media became recognized as an effective source of breaking news, especially during natural emergencies and terror attacks. Twitter was the first to report that a plane had landed in the Hudson River on January 15, 2009, and that a helicopter was hovering above Abbottabad, Pakistan at 1:00 AM on May 2, 2011 (the mission that killed Osama bin Laden). In 2010 NASA astronaut T.J. Creamer became the first person to tweet from outer space, sending messages that were followed by millions of readers. Tweets were used to warn about school shootings and traffic delays.

Twitter also became the Achilles heel of scores of errant politicians and celebrities, whose impulsive postings of inappropriate images and comments resulted in their twittering fall from grace.

But Twitter and other forms of social media are not without their critics. Malcolm Gladwell, for example, has called Twitter "a way of following (or being followed by) people you may never have met," and questioned whether it can ever engender strong motivation. Others deride the simplistic mentality of pronouncements that reduce commentary to 140 characters.

LEFT: The first tweet was originally posted by Jack Dorsey on March 21, 2006: "just setting up my twttr." Barack Obama composes the first presidential tweet under the watchful eye of Dorsey in July 2011.

WikiLeaks

(2007)

Prompted by the failure of the mainstream news media to report important, in-depth information to the public, a shadowy shoestring alliance of brazen computer experts takes matters into their own hands and revolutionizes the nature of investigative journalism in the digital age.

When several major American newspapers published excerpts from leaked defense documents known as the Pentagon Papers, thereby revealing many of the hidden antecedents of the Vietnam War, the boldness and scope of the disclosures seemed immense. But that was before the digital age, before millions of documents could be retrieved, copied and shared almost instantaneously.

Similar in spirit to Daniel Ellsberg's release of the Pentagon Papers in 1971, top-secret digital documents began to be leaked in 2007. This time the mastermind was not the leaker, but the one who directly disseminated the leaked information. An Australian computer hacker named Julian Assange, working with other renegades, began posting large numbers of leaked classified documents on the Internet, along with companion news stories, through a website conduit called WikiLeaks.

In its first three years of existence, WikiLeaks was responsible for bringing to light some of the world's biggest stories: it exposed chilling military gun-sight footage from a deadly Baghdad airstrike in which journalists and civilians were murdered by a US Army gunship; shocking details about secret drone strikes in Yemen and elsewhere; prison abuses at Guantánamo Bay; embarrassing reports of the US spying on diplomats overseas; old State Department cables involving Henry Kissinger; and many other revelations, all of which were documented by millions of official reports that had been kept secret. WikiLeaks also prepared major exposés against the Chinese Public Security Bureau, the former president of Kenya, the Premier of Bermuda, Scientology, the Catholic and Mormon Churches, the largest Swiss private bank, and Russian companies.

Some of the stories were simultaneously accompanied by major news reports by *The Guardian*, *The New York Times*, and *Der Spiegel*. The WikiLeaks team reportedly consisted of only five full-time staffers and 800 part-time volunteers, all of whom worked for free. The Europe-based group described itself as "an uncensorable system for untraceable mass document leaking."

Although Assange and his associates refused to identify the sources of their information, one alleged leaker, US Army Private Bradley Manning (now known as Chelsea Manning) was prosecuted and convicted by the US government. In 2013 Manning was sentenced to thirty-five years in prison for violating the Espionage Act and other offenses. Assange and WikiLeaks, however, have remained at large.

WikiLeaks was both honored and vilified; the organization and its media partners won several journalistic awards, and its leaders and contributors were pursued and threatened by several governments around the world. Assange was forced to seek sanctuary from prosecution. As of early 2015 he was still fighting extradition.

ABOVE: The WikiLeaks homepage explains how it aims to defend freedom of speech in accordance with the principles of the Universal Declaration of Human Rights: "One of our most important activities is to publish original source material alongside our news stories so readers and historians alike can see evidence of the truth."

LEFT: Julian Assange, editor-in-chief of WikiLeaks, clutches court papers after fighting extradition and being released on bail in December 2010.

3-D Map of the Universe

(2011)

Plotted on a scale that defies the imagination, the most complete map of outer space documents the known universe in 3-D. The 2MASS Redshift Survey (2MRS) probably ranks as the greatest and most complex data map yet devised.

In May of 2011, scientists at the Harvard-Smithsonian Center for Astrophysics announced that they had compiled the most complete three-dimensional map of the nearby universe ever created. By employing the principle that near-infrared light penetrates intervening dust better than visible light, astronomers were able to see and scan more of the cosmos than anyone had previously envisioned, capturing 91 percent of the world's entire night sky in three near-infrared wavelength bands.

Even with 300 researchers using space-age telescopes, super-computers and other advanced technology, the 2MASS Redshift Survey (2MRS) took ten years of complex and painstaking work to achieve.

Astronomers from the University of Massachusetts utilized twin 1.3-meter-wide super telescopes and auxiliary instruments at two world-class observatories—the Fred Lawrence Whipple Observatory atop the 8,500-foot-high peak of Mt. Hopkins in Arizona, and the Cerro Tololo Inter-American Observatory located on a 7,200-foot-high summit in Chile's Andes. Their scanning catalogued all detected stars and galaxies, formed an extensive survey of low-mass stars, and detected the first "brown dwarfs." But because the survey had compiled only a two-dimensional image, scientists had to work out a way to account for distances.

To do this, the project incorporated knowledge that a galaxy's light is "redshifted," or stretched to longer wavelengths, by the ongoing expansion of the universe. The farther the galaxy, the greater its redshift, so redshift measurements helped identify galaxy distances.

Researchers then measured each cosmic object's redshift, which denotes how much its light has been shifted toward the red end of the color spectrum. This movement happens because of the so-called Doppler Effect, which causes the wavelength of light to be

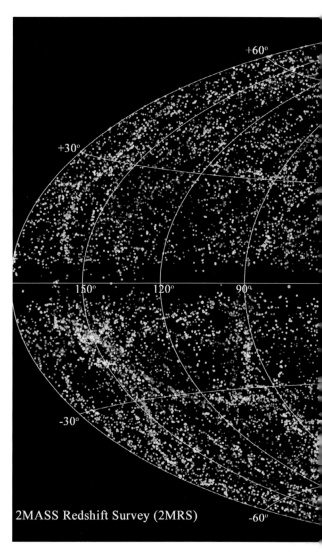

BELOW: The 2MRS map shows galaxies and dark matter up to 380 million light-years from Earth. Purple dots are galaxies closest to Earth, red dots are furthest away.

stretched when the light's source is moving away from us. (This was no easy task as it entailed one-and-a-half million redshifts.)

The project gathered a monumental volume of data. Software packages allowed the researchers to observe the sky from a range of dates, print off data based on the observations and (in some versions) control a telescope. The complicated process assembled data from a collection of star catalogues, 3-D models, and computing platforms. This massive undertaking required a vast databank and scores of analysts working in unison at many locations across the globe. The effort produced innumerable scientific papers, data sets, and data visualizations on their cosmic cartography.

2MASS Redshift was not the first or the last 3-D map of the universe. But it may be the greatest thus far.

The data can be downloaded from the Smithsonian Astrophysical Observatory.

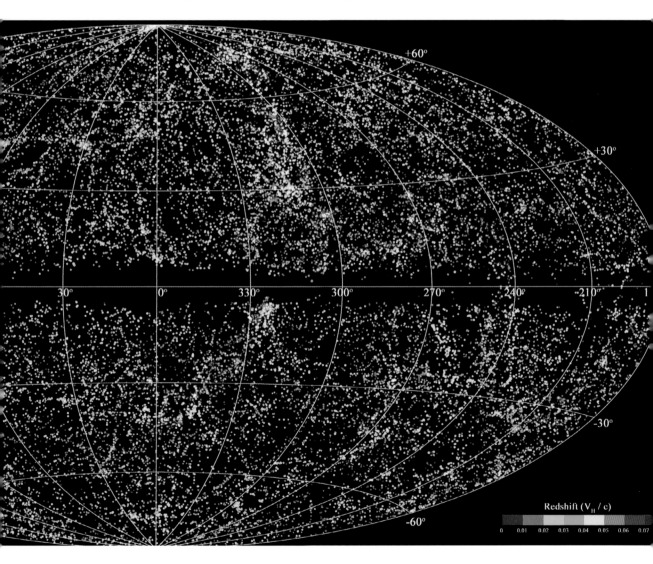

To whom it may concern,

I have been invited to write to you regarding your investigation of mass surveillance.

I am Edward Joseph Snowden, formerly employed through contracts or direct hire as a technical expert for the United States National Security Agency, Central Intelligence Agency, and Defense Intelligence Agency.

In the course of my service to these organizations, I believe I witnessed systemic violations of law by my government that created a moral duty to act. As a result of reporting these concerns, I have faced a severe and sustained campaign of persecution that forced me from my family and home. I am currently living in exile under a grant of temporary asylum in the Russian Federation in accordance with international law.

I am heartened by the response to my act of political expression, in both the United States and beyond. Citizens around the world as well as high officials - including in the United States - have judged the revelation of an unaccountable system of pervasive surveillance to be a public service. These spying revelations have resulted in the proposal of many new laws and policies to address formerly concealed abuses of the public trust. The benefits to society of this growing knowledge are becoming increasingly clear at the same time claimed risks are being shown to have been mitigated.

Though the outcome of my efforts has been demonstrably positive, my government continues to treat dissent as defection, and seeks to criminalize political speech with felony charges that provide no defense. However, speaking the truth is not a crime. I am confident that with the support of the international community, the government of the United States will abandon this harmful behavior. I hope that when the difficulties of this humanitarian situation have been resolved, I will be able to cooperate in the responsible finding of fact regarding reports in the media, particularly in regard to the truth and authenticity of documents, as appropriate and in accordance with the law.

I look forward to speaking with you in your country when the situation is resolved, and thank you for your efforts in upholding the international laws that protect us all.

With my best regards,

Edward Snowden
31 October 2013

SIGNED

WITNESSED

Edward Snowden Files

(2013)

A 29-year-old computer wizard working for America's super-secret spy agency becomes the biggest whistleblower in US history, leaking huge caches of classified documents that expose his nation's "unconstitutional" and "illegal" cyber surveillance. Foreign leaders protest, but reaction in the US is polarized.

In 2006, a young American computer expert named Edward Snowden (1983–) went to work for the Central Intelligence Agency as a technician/IT specialist with top-secret clearance. Over the next six years he moved on to other positions in cyber intelligence, employed by Dell and Booz Allen Hamilton as cover for his high-level administrative work for the National Security Agency.

As Snowden became more aware of the nature and scope of US cyber spying, he expressed concerns to multiple coworkers and two supervisors about the program's apparent violations of US and international law. However his superiors ignored his complaints and told him to simply continue doing his job, which increased his crisis of conscience.

In 2012 and early 2013 he began downloading classified documents that exemplified his concerns. As a Hawaii-based "system administrator" with special security clearance, Snowden enjoyed direct access to the NSA central computer in Ft. Meade, Maryland, with the ability to look at any file he wished as a "ghost user," making his actions hard to trace. He was able to use simple thumb drives, "web crawler" software and other relatively unsophisticated technology to "scrape

ABOVE: The temporary passport that gave Snowden exile in Russia from 2013 to 2014.

LEFT: Snowden's letter of October 31, 2013 claims that he "witnessed systemic violations of law" by his government that "created a moral duty to act."

data" from the NSA systems, downloading many large and extremely sensitive files.

Some of the agency's secret surveillance included programs which harvested millions of emails, contact lists, cell phone locations and other data from hundreds of millions of Americans' Google and Yahoo accounts. The NSA was spying on top corporate executives, foreign heads of state, the chief of the European Union, and other important figures, monitoring their personal and official communications. In some instances, it was seeking sexual information in order to discredit certain individuals.

In 2012–13 Snowden furnished copies of selected classified documents to top reporters in the US, United Kingdom, Germany, France, Brazil, Sweden, Canada, Italy, the Netherlands, Norway, Spain, and Australia. He also insisted that his identity be publicly revealed. The disclosures generated considerable controversy and caused Snowden to be charged with two counts of violating the Espionage Act and theft of government property. His US passport was revoked in 2013 and since then he has been living in exile in Russia. As of 2015 attempts are still being made to extradite him so that he can stand trial back in the United States.

The full extent of Snowden's disclosure is unknown, but US intelligence sources have estimated the number of files at 1.7 million. Several news organizations and reporters have won major prizes for their reports based on some of the documents. At the same time, Snowden remains a controversial figure and public opinion about him has been divided. The impact of his whistleblowing on government spying remains to be seen.

Acknowledgments

As always, this book benefited from the sage advice of Professor Tamar Gordon
and the kindness of other family and friends. I also wish to thank Frank Hopkinson
and David Salmo at Pavilion Books for their expert assistance.

The publisher wishes to thank the following for kindly supplying the images that appear in this book:
Alamy: 122, 212. Anne Frank Zentrum, Berlin: 13, 162. AP: 128, 183. AP/Christie's: 195. Apartheid
Museum: 176, 177. Arxiu Municipal de Girona: 46. Beinecke Rare Book & Manuscript Library: 57.
Berlin State Library: 53. Biblioteca Ambrosiana: 45 (top). Biblioteca Nazionale Marciana: 18 (right).
Bodleian Library: 28. Bridgeman Images: 26. British Cartoon Archive: 155. British Library: 2–3, 30, 35,
36. Cambridge University Library: 74, 104, 105, 220, 222. Central Intelligence Agency: 202. CERN: 200,
201. Cheongju Early Printing Museum: 43. Chester Beatty Library: 45 (bottom). Congress.gov: 205 (right).
Corbis: 70–71, 81, 89, 206–207. Cour de Cassation: 97. Echo – Cultural Heritage Online: 61. Ed Westcott/
American Museum of Science and Energy: 159. EMI: 185 (bottom). European Commission Audiovisual
Library: 180. Executive Office of the President of the United States: 204. Folger Shakespeare Library:
62. Franklin D. Roosevelt Presidential Library and Museum: 165 (bottom). German Museum of Books
and Writing: 55. Getty Images: 37, 49 (top), 181, 185 (top), 199. Griffith Institute: 144, 145. Harold Rider
Collection, ArchiTech Gallery, Chicago: 146. Harvard-Smithsonian Center for Astrophysics: 210–211.
Hereford Cathedral: 40–41. Historisches Museum der Pfalz Speyer: 96. Imaging Papyri Project, University
of Oxford: 29, 224. International Committee of the Red Cross: 174, 175. International Institute of Social
History: 108. Israeli Antiquities Authority: 22. John F. Kennedy Presidential Library and Museum: 182.
Karpeles Manuscript Library: 110 (right). Lebendiges Museum Online: 198. Library of Congress: 58, 64,
84, 100, 106–107, 124, 136, 139. Louvre Museum: 17. Maggs Bros Ltd: 103. Mary Evans Picture Library: 54,
77, 141 (top), 154. Metropolitan Museum of Art: 18 (left), 33. Mitchell Archives: 76. Mullock's: 102. Musée
Champollion: 98. Museo del Prado: 47. Museo Naval de Madrid: 49 (bottom). National Air and Space
Museum, Smithsonian Institution: 193 (bottom). National Archives (UK): 78, 130, 149, 153 (top). National
Archives and Records Administration (USA): 34, 86, 93, 94, 117, 118, 120, 121, 134, 138, 141 (bottom), 156,
157, 158, 165 (top), 166 (top), 167, 170, 172, 173, 190, 193 (top). National Gallery: 39. National Portrait
Gallery: 79. Newberry Library: 90. OECD PHOTO OCDE: 171. Oriental Institute, University of Chicago:
23. Parliamentary Archives: 114. Penguin Books: 223. Radio Times: 150, 151. Reuters Pictures: 203, 208,
213. Secker & Warburg: 168, 169. Sotheby's, New York: 186, 194, 219. Spink/BNPS: 153 (bottom). Stanford
University: 32. Thomas Fisher Rare Book Library: 69. Tokyo National Museum: 31. Twitter, Inc: 206 (top).
United States White House: 206 (bottom). University of California, Riverside: 21. University of Minnesota:
101 (top). USC News Service/Irene Fertik: 197 (bottom). US Department of Justice: 205 (left). ViaLibri:
85. WikiLeaks: 209. Washington National Cathedral: 63. UN Photo Library/McLain: 166 (bottom). United
States Holocaust Memorial Museum: 142. University of Southern California: 197 (top). US Patent and
Trademark Office: 125. Wannsee Conference House Memorial: 160, 161. Wellcome Library: 178, 179.
Yinqueshan Han Tombs Bamboo Slips Museum: 20.

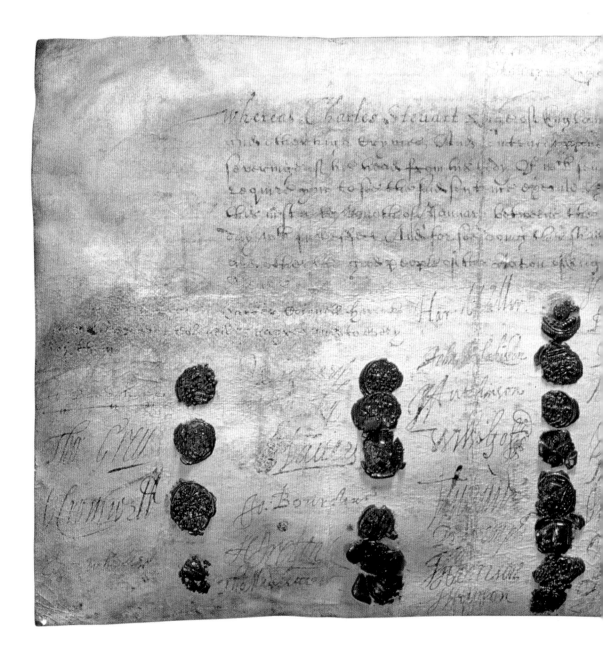

ABOVE: The most dramatic document in Britain's Parliamentary Archives—the death warrant of Charles I. Oliver Cromwell's signature can be seen far left. As a member of the Rump Parliament (1649–53), Cromwell dominated the short-lived Commonwealth of England (see page 70).

100 Documents that Changed the World_____217

Index

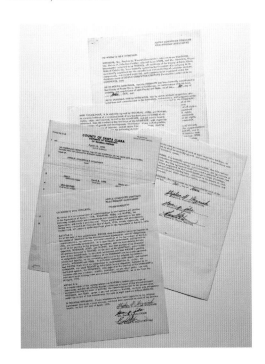

ABOVE: Apple Computer Company's founding legal documents, signed by Jobs, Wozniak and Wayne, were sold at auction for $1.4 million in 2010 (see page 194).

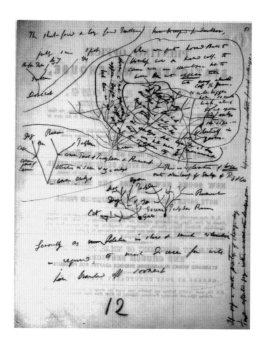

*ABOVE: A page from Charles Darwin's notebooks on his
theory of natural selection. His findings transformed the
way that scientists viewed the natural world (see page 104).*

ABOVE: A Penguin paperback edition of George Orwell's dystopian novel that coined the terms "doublethink," "newspeak," and "Big Brother" (see page 168).

ABOVE: Third-century AD papyrus fragments from Plato's Republic—one of the most influential works of philosophy and moral/political theory ever written (see page 28).